Paul's New SAT
Math 800
2nd Edition

Paul Kim

PaulAcademy

Paul's New SAT
Math 800
2nd Edition

Paul Academy

The Tiger Mom's Secret Weapon

How Asian Students really achieve SAT success

While teaching the SAT, I hungered to find the same quality of SAT test questions as the real College Board test, because the practice questions of leading test prep companies were slightly different from the real thing. They didn't match the real content or they were just too easy. The difference was so big that I had a hard time accurately predicting my students' scores. I decided to make new SAT books with new principles for success.

1. Fully Comprehensive

I have created comprehensive vocabulary lists based on how frequently each word has appeared in previous tests. I didn't want students to be forced to purchase three or four vocabulary books in order to get all the information they needed, and I didn't want them to have to study words they would never need. My grammar book provides concise, efficient coverage of every grammar rule that has been tested, and contains 4 top-quality practice tests. My essay book has a full list of released questions and a strategy that quickly allows any student to reach their highest possible score. My math book focuses more on the advanced tactics for students wanting to perfect their scores to 800.

2. Question Difficulty Level: CollegeBoard

Previously, there were only a few prep books on the market aimed at Advanced Learners (scoring over 700 in each section), but even though the questions in the book were difficult, the skills they taught were irrelevant to success in the SAT. My book strictly adheres to the topics, skills, and reasoning that CollegeBoard actually tests.

3. Linking Concepts to Real CollegeBoard examples

When I explain a concept in my books, I find example questions in both the Official SAT guide and my own practice tests to drive the concept home. Students always know exactly what to expect and how to use what they are learning.

Using these three principles, my students' scores skyrocketed. I received many requests to make my strategies public, and so here now they are finally being printed. It has become the number one choice for reliable, comprehensive SAT success in the Asian market, and it will no doubt work for you, too.

Paul Kim

CONTENTS

What's Inside

This book contains fundamental math concepts that you will need in both high school and beyond. Each concept is followed by SAT-style practice questions that help you apply the concept to take the test. This book also contains three full-length (Math only) practice tests for the SAT, which we at Paul Academy have created based off the tests released by the College Board. These tests will simulate a real test and help you prepare for the actual exam.

How to Use This Book

If you have only a limited amount of time to prepare for the SAT, you should start with the practice tests immediately. When you get a question wrong, label it incorrect but do not write down the answer. Try to solve the question again. If you simply made a mistake, you should be able to correct your error. If you still have trouble, you may want to review the relevant concepts in the book. Review the concept and take notes, then try the practice questions at the end of the chapter.

If you have plenty of time to prepare for the exam, start with the diagnostic test to gauge your strengths and weaknesses. Focus on the questions you got incorrect. Try to solve them again without looking at the answer. If you still have trouble, you may want to review the relevant concepts. Each question in the test is categorized, so you can find the chapter concepts quickly. Review the concept and take notes, then try the practice questions at the end of the chapter. When you're ready, take a full-length practice test.

And Lastly

Do not worry! The SAT may seem daunting at first, but you can prepare yourself to be ready on test day. Also, if you are in 11th grade or lower, you can always take the test again before you apply to college. In fact, studies have shown that most students score higher on their second try, so it is recommended that you take the test at least twice.

Introduction to the SAT

What You Need to Know About the Test

What is the SAT?

The SAT is an entrance exam used by most colleges and universities to make admissions decisions. It is a multiple choice, pencil-and-paper test administered by the College Board.

What's on the SAT?
The redesigned SAT is 3 hours long, or 3 hours and 50 minutes long if you choose to take the optional essay. It includes 4 timed sections (plus the essay).

Redesigned SAT			
Section	Exam length	Number of questions	Exam method
Reading	65min	52	4 LP 1 DP
Writing & Language	35min	44	4 Passages
Essay	50min	1	1 EP 1 RP
Math	80min	58	Calculator / 38 questions NO Calculator / 20 questions
Total	180min (230 min with essay)	154 (155 with essay)	

※LP: Long Passages, DP: Dual Passages, EP: Essay Prompt, RP: Reading Passage

Reading Section
The Reading Section is 65 minutes long and consists of 52 multiple-choice questions, all of which are passage-based.
There are a total of 5 passages and 2-3 charts or graphs in the Reading Section. The passages are excerpts from literature, science and social science articles and journals, and historical documents.

Writing & Language Section
The Writing & Language Section is 35 minutes long and consists of 44 multiple-choice questions. There are a total of 4 passages in the Writing & Language Section. The passages cover a range of topics including history/social science, science, and career information.

Math Test

Range	Number of questions	Percentage of total questions
Heart of Algebra (Creating, Solving, Interpreting Linear Expressions)	21	36%
Problem Solving and Data Analysis	16	27%
Passport to Advanced Math (Quadratic/Exponential Functions)	15	26%
Additional Topics (Area/Volume Calculation, Investigation of Lines, Angles, Triangles and Circles Using Theorem, Working with Trigonometric Functions	6	11%
Total	**58**	**100%**

The Math Test (which is the focus of this book) is 80 minutes long and is divided into 2 sections: the Calculator Section and the NO Calculator Section. The NO Calculator Section is 25 minutes long and consists of 20 questions, including 5 student response questions, which are also known as gridin questions. In them, you will be asked to write your answer and bubble in the appropriate numbers in the answer key. The Calculator Section is 55 minutes long and consists of 38 questions, including 8 grid-ins questions.

Classification	Question type	Exam length
Calculator	30 multiple choice 8 grid-ins	55minutes
NO calculator	15 multiple choice 5 grid-ins	25minutes
Total	**58 questions**	**80minutes**

Optional Essay

In the Essay Section of the exam, you will be asked to read a short passage and explain how the author effectively builds his or her argument. The key is to analyze the writer's rhetorical strategy, logic, and argument, and then put it into your own words.

Scoring Your Test

The redesigned SAT is scored on a scale of 400~1600. Each section of the SAT is graded separately, based on your raw score for each section. The optional essay is graded separately on a scale of 0 to 24.

1) Total Score (400~1600) = Evidence-Based Reading and Writing (200~800) + Math (200~800)

2) Essay (0~24) = Reading (0~8) + Writing (0~8) + Analysis (0~8)

Scoring Tips

Unlike previous versions of the SAT, there is no penalty for wrong answers. This means that you should always guess, even if you are unsure about the right answer. Also, there are only 4 answer choices in the current version of the SAT. Learning how to eliminate wrong answer choices quickly will be extremely beneficial. For more information, watch our video guides on multiple choice strategy and process of elimination (POE) at paulprep.com.

How can I take the SAT?

The SAT schedule is available on the College Board website at www.collegeboard.org. You can sign up online or through mail using an SAT registration booklet.

It is important to register early for the exam as there may not be any spots available if you wait until the last minute.

Paul's SAT Math 800

Diagnostic Test

Q1

Which of the following numbers is NOT a solution to the inequality $2r-6 \geq 3r-4$?

A) 0

B) -2

C) -5

D) -6

Q2

$$x-3y=17$$
$$-6y-4x=22$$

What is the solution (x, y) to the system of equations above?

A) $(-1, -6)$

B) $(5, -2)$

C) $(2, -5)$

D) $(-4, -3)$

Q3

Nikolai leased a car at $890.99 per month. There is a one−time commission fee of $55.49 and a tax of 5% on his monthly lease price. Which of the following represents Nikolai's total payment, in dollars, for leasing the car for x months?

A) $1.05(890.99x)+55.49$

B) $1.05(890.99x+55.49)$

C) $1.05x(890.99+55.49)$

D) $1.05(890.99x)+55.49x$

Q4

If $(px+1)(qx-4)=6x^2+rx-4$ for all values of x, and $p+q=5$, what are the two possible values of r?

A) 2 and 3

B) -5 and 3

C) -5 and -10

D) 3 and 4

Q5

If $2a-b=5$, what is the value of $\dfrac{16^a}{2^{2b}}$?

A) 4^4

B) 2^{10}

C) 512

D) Cannot be determined from the given information

Q6

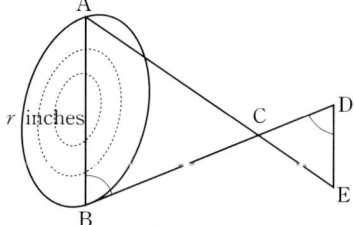

A geologist wants to determine the length r, in inches, of a tree stump in the forest as represented in the sketch above. The lengths represented by AC, CB, CD, and DE on the sketch were determined to be 40 inches, 30 inches, 15 inches, and 10 inches, respectively. Segments AE and BD intersect at C, and $\angle ABC$ and $\angle CDE$ have the same measure. What is the value of r?

Q7

A line in the $xy-$plane meets the $x-$axis at $(1,0)$ and has a slope of -2. Which of the following points lies on the line?

A) $(0, -1)$
B) $(3, 0)$
C) $(0, 2)$
D) $(1, -2)$

Q8

In a right triangle, one angle measures $r°$, where $\cos r° = \dfrac{2}{5}$. What is $\sin(90°-r°)$?

Calculator

Q9

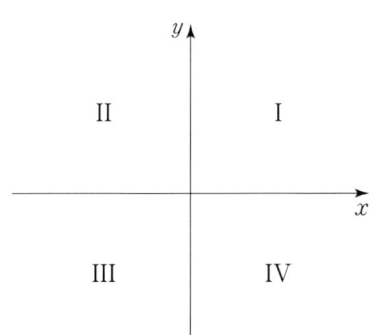

If the system of inequalities $y < -2x-1$ and $y \le \dfrac{1}{2}-x+1$ is graphed on the $xy-$plane above, which quadrant contains no solutions to the system?

A) Quadrant I
B) Quadrant II
C) Quadrant III
D) There are solutions in all four quadrants.

Q10

Height of Trees (in feet)				
1	8	8	8	8
9	10	10	10	10
11	11	11	12	12

The table above lists the height, to the nearest foot, of a random sample of 15 black willow trees. The outlier measurement of 1 foot is an error. Of the mean, median, and range of the values listed, which will change the most if the 1$-$foot measurement is removed from the data?

A) Mean
B) Median
C) Range
D) They will all change by the same amount.

Q11

	None	1 to 12	13 or more	Total
Group A	23	50	77	150
Group B	11	87	52	150
Total	34	137	129	300

The data in the table above were collected at a shooting range where people fired 20 shots on a fixed target. Group A consisted of 150 people who personally owned a gun, and Group B consisted of 150 people who did not personally own a gun. If a person is chosen at random from those who hit none to 12 shots on target, what is the probability that the person belonged in Group A?

A) $\dfrac{73}{100}$

B) $\dfrac{98}{100}$

C) $\dfrac{73}{171}$

D) $\dfrac{171}{300}$

Q12

If $y = x^2 + x + 1$, which of the following best shows this equation on a $xy-$coordinate plane?

A)

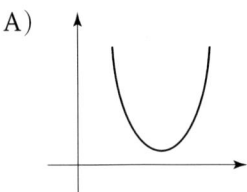

B)

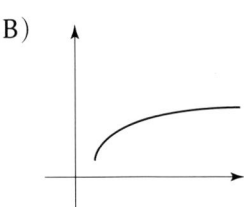

C)

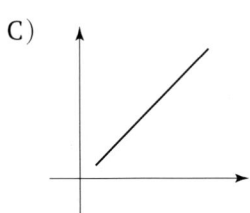

D)

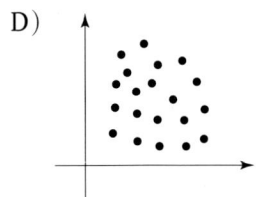

Q13

		Teams			
		Rockets	Mavericks	Spurs	Total
Texans	Male	38	35	57	130
	Female	47	54	39	140
	Total	85	89	96	270

Texan basketball fans responded to a survey that asked to choose one team they support out of the three basketball teams in Texas. The survey data were broken down as shown in the table above. Which of the following categories accounts for approximately 33 percent of all the survey respondents?

A) Male fans of the Rockets

B) Female fans of the Spurs

C) Male and female fans of the Mavericks

D) Male and female fans of the Spurs

Q14

On Friday, 4500 men and women attended a basketball game. The ratio of men to women was 2 to 3. How many men attended the basketball game?

A) 450

B) 900

C) 1800

D) 2700

Q15

In May, Sunny called s people every day for 10 days, and Khalim called k people every day for 5 days. Which of the following represents the total number of people called by Sunny and Khalim in May?

A) $10s + 5k$

B) $10k + 5s$

C) $50sk$

D) $15sk$

Q16

$$1 \text{ yard} = 3 \text{ feet}$$
$$12 \text{ inches} = 1 \text{ foot}$$

5 yardsticks in a straight line. However, all he has are 6−inch rulers. How many 6−inch rulers does Tim need to glue together to reach the same length as 5 yardsticks?

A) 15
B) 30
C) 36
D) 180

Q17

Viktor owns a poultry farm with two types of hens. He noticed that Breed A hens lay 30 percent less eggs than Breed B hens do. Based on Viktor's observation, if Breed A hens laid 140 eggs, how many eggs did the Breed B hens lay?

A) 98
B) 140
C) 200
D) 245

Q18

$$f(x) = \frac{1}{(x-1)^2 + 6(x-1) + 9}$$

For what value of x is the function f above undefined?

A) −2
B) −1
C) 0
D) 1

Q19

For what value of a is $|a-2|+3$ equal to 0?

A) −5
B) −1
C) 2
D) There is no such value of a.

Q20

For a polynomial $f(a)$, the value of $f(4)$ is 1. Which of the following must be true about $f(a)$?

A) The remainder when $f(A^0$ is divided by $a-1$ is 4.

B) $a-1$ is a factor of $f(a)$.

C) $a+1$ is a factor of $f(a)$.

D) The remainder when $f(a)$ is divided by $a-4$ is 1.

Q21

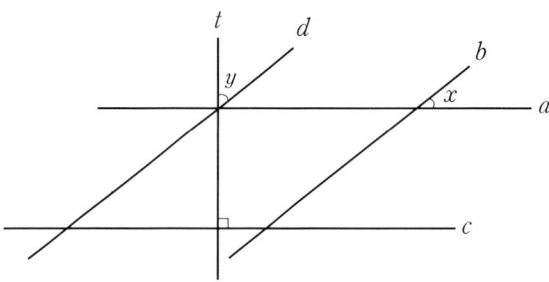

In the figure above, lines a and c are parallel, and lines b and d are parallel. If lines t and c are perpendicular and $\angle x$ is 43°, what is the measure of $\angle y$?

A) 43°
B) 47°
C) 86°
D) 90°

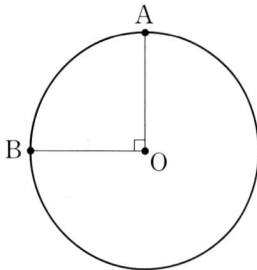

In the circle above, O is the center of the circle and Points A and B lie on the circumference of the circle.

If $\angle AOB$ is $90°$ and length of arc $\overarc{AB}$ is 3π, what is the area of the circle above?

A) 36π

B) 12π

C) 6π

D) 3π

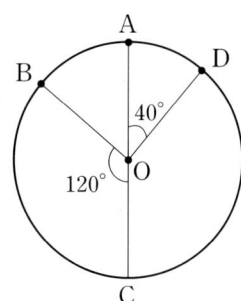

In the circle above, $\angle AOD$ is $40°$ and $\angle BOC$ is $120°$. If the length of arc $\overarc{BC}$ is 6π, what is the length of arc $\overarc{AD}$?

A) 2π

B) 3π

C) 18π

D) 81π

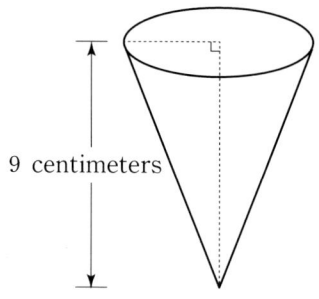

9 centimeters

The Jen and Berrie's ice cream store uses waffle cones in the shape of the cone above. If the volume of the waffle cone is 12π cubic centimeters, what is the circumference of the base of the cone, in centimeters?

A) 4π

B) 6π

C) $\dfrac{4}{\sqrt{3}}\pi$

D) Cannot be determined from the given information

Which of the following is the equation of a circle in the $xy-$plane with center $(1,\ 3)$ and a radius with endpoint $\left(\dfrac{7}{4},\ 4\right)$?

A) $(x-1)^2+(y-3)^2=\dfrac{25}{16}$

B) $(x+1)^2+(y+3)^2=\dfrac{25}{16}$

C) $(x-1)^2+(y-3)^2=\dfrac{5}{4}$

D) $(x+1)^2+(y+3)^2=\dfrac{5}{4}$

Diagnostic Test Answers

No Calculator

Q1. A
1-1. Linear Equations/Inequalities

Q2. C
1-2. Systems of Equations/Inequalities

Q3. A
1-3. Equations & Inequalities in Context

Q4. C
3-1. Factoring

Q5. B
3-5. Powers & Roots

Q6. 20
4-1. Triangles

Q7. C
1-4. Equations/Inequalities in the Coordinate Plane

Q8. 2/5
4-8. Trigonometry

Calculator

Q9. A
1-4. Relationships among Equations/Inequalities-in the Coordinate Plane

Q10. C
2-1. Statistics

Q11. C
2-2. Probability

Q12. A
3-4. Functions

Q13. C
2-6. Percentages

Q14. C
2-4. Ratio

Q15. A
2-5. Rate

Q16. B
2-4. Ratio

Q17. C
2-6 Percentages

Q18. A
3-2. Equations

Q19. D
3-3. Absolute Value

Q20. D
3-2. Equations

Q21. B
4-2. Polygons

Q22. A
4-4. Circles

Q23. A
4-4.Circles

Q24. A
4-5. Solids

Q25. A
4-7. Circle Equation

Chapter 1

Heart of Algebra

A. Single Variable Equation

$ax=b$

If $a\neq0$, the solution is $x=\dfrac{b}{a}$

If $a=0$, $b=0$, the solution for x is every number.

If $a=0$, $b\neq0$, there is no solution for x.

a and b may not be integers.

They may be expressions:

ie. $(2y-1)x=0$

For possible values of x to be all real numbers, $2y-1$ needs to equal 0.

$$2y-1=0$$
$$2y=1$$
$$y=\dfrac{1}{2}$$

Collecting the term means adding, subtracting, multiplying, or dividing both sides of the equation with the same number in order to cancel out constants so that the variable stands alone on one side of the equation.

$$3x-9=4x+2$$

"Collecting the term" means to put all the terms containing a variable on the left side, and all the constants on the right side

VARIABLE SIDE		CONSTANT SIDE
$3x-4x$	$=$	$2+9$

Now just do the math.

$$-x=11$$
$$x=-11$$

Now you can solve equations!

B. Basic Principles of Linear Equations/Inequalities

Steps to Solve

1) If there are fractions, eliminate the denominators and expand.
2) Collect the terms.
3) Divide by the coefficient of x to isolate x.
   *Be careful with inequalities - negative numbers flip the sign.

Eliminating Denominators

$$\frac{2}{x} = \frac{3}{x+1}$$

1) Multiply both sides by the denominators.

$$\frac{2}{x}(x)(x+1) = \frac{3}{x+1}(x)(x+1)$$

2) Cancel out.

$$\frac{2}{\cancel{x}}(\cancel{x})(x+1) = \frac{3}{\cancel{x+1}}(x)(\cancel{x+1})$$

$$2(x+1) = 3x$$

3) Expand.

$$\overbrace{2(x+1)} = 3x$$

$$2x+2 = 3x$$

◢ Exercise

Let's solve the next equation:

$2x - 9 = 5$

First, collect the terms.

$2x = 5 + 9$

$\quad = 14$

Divide both sides of the equation by 2 in order to get the value of x.

$x = 7$

Let's try another, this time with fractions.

$$\frac{2}{x} = \frac{1}{2x+3}$$

$$\frac{2}{\cancel{x}} \times \cancel{x} \times (2x+3) = \frac{1}{\cancel{2x+3}} \times x \times \cancel{(2x+3)}$$

Do the math and cancel out the denominators, and get the next equation.

$2(2x+3)=x$

$4x+6=x$

Now, collect the terms.

$3x=-6$

$x=-2$

... And there you have it. Good Job!

Example Questions

1. If $4a+8=24$, what is the value of $8a-9$?

A) 4

B) 16

C) 23

D) 32

2. If $\dfrac{3}{a}=\dfrac{6}{a+15}$, what is the value of $\dfrac{a}{3}$?

A) 3

B) 5

C) 15

D) 45

3. If $\dfrac{5}{6}a-\dfrac{1}{6}a=\dfrac{1}{2}+\dfrac{1}{6}$, what is the value of a?

C. Inequalities

1) Properties

(i) $a > b$

$a + c > b + c$ You can add the same number to both sides

(ii) $a > b$

$ac > bc$ You can multiply both sides by a positive number.

(iii) $a > b$

$ac < bc$, if $c < 0$ BUT you must flip the sign's direction when multiplying by a negative number.

(iv) If $a < b$ and $b < c$, then $a < c$

(v) If $a < b$ and $x < y$, then $a + x < b + y$

2) Solving Multiple Inequalities

Be sure to do the same thing to these three sides.

$c \leq ax + b \leq d$

$c - b \leq ax \leq d - b$

If $a > 0$, $\dfrac{c-b}{a} \leq x \leq \dfrac{d-b}{a}$

If $a < 0$, $\dfrac{d-b}{a} \leq x \leq \dfrac{c-b}{a}$

◢ Exercise

Let's solve an inequality.

$3x + 9 \leq 6$

Collect the terms.

$3x \leq -3$

Divide both sides of the inequality by 3.

$x \leq -1$

Pretty straight forward, right?

But here's a tricky one.

$3x + 9 \leq 4x + 6$

Both sides don't have a common denominator so let's just collect the terms.

$-x \leq -3$

Now the tricky part is here.

When multiplying by a negative number to both sides of an inequality, the inequality sign ALWAYS TURNS THE OTHER WAY.

$x \geq 3$

Example Questions

1. If $4x-2 \geq 6$ what is the minimum possible value for $2x+3$?

A) 2

B) 4

C) 7

D) 8

2. If $2x+7+5(x-2) \geq 6x+7$, what is the minimum possible value of x?

A) 3

B) 7

C) 10

D) 11

3. If $3a-5 \leq 2$, what is the maximum possible value for $6a-9$?

A) 3

B) 5

C) 7

D) 9

1. If $\dfrac{2x-y}{2y}=\dfrac{2}{5}$, which of the following must also be true?

A) $\dfrac{y}{x}=\dfrac{9}{10}$

B) $\dfrac{x}{y}=\dfrac{9}{10}$

C) $\dfrac{2x+y}{y}=\dfrac{9}{10}$

D) $\dfrac{y}{x}=\dfrac{2}{5}$

2. If $\dfrac{a+2}{a-2}=5$, what is the value of a?

A) 3

B) 4

C) 5

D) 12

3. If $\dfrac{7}{r}=\dfrac{3}{r+12}$, what is the value of $\dfrac{r}{7}$?

A) -3

B) -21

C) 3

D) 7

4. If $6x-12\geq9$, what is the minimum possible value for $2x-9$?

A) -7

B) -2

C) 2

D) 5

5. $6y-(14-2y)=a(4y-7)$

If the equation shown has infinitely many solutions and a is a constant, what is the value of a?

A) -1

B) 1

C) 2

D) 7

6. If $2(x-1)+2x=\dfrac{1}{4}(16x-20)+3$, what is the value of x?

A) $x=1$

B) $x=4$

C) There is no value of x for which the equation is true.

D) There are infinitely many values of x for which the equation is true.

7. If $\dfrac{n-5}{n+5}=6$, what is the value of n?

A) -7

B) -5

C) 3

D) 6

8. If there are infinitely many solutions for the inequality $6x+7\geq 3(ax+2)$, what is the value of a?

A) -6

B) -2

C) 2

D) 6

9. If $\frac{1}{3}(3y)+4(y-2)=5(y-2)+7$, what is the value of y?

A) -8

B) -3

C) There is no value of y for which the equation is true.

D) There are infinitely many values of y for which the equation is true.

10. If $2(y+1)=\frac{x}{3}+2$, what is the value of $\frac{x}{y}$?

A) 2

B) 3

C) 6

D) It is impossible to determine the value in question because the information given is insufficient.

11. If $\frac{2(r+2)-7}{4}=\frac{14-(r+2)}{5}$, what is the value of r?

A) 2

B) 4.5

C) 6

D) 9

12. If $\dfrac{2x+7}{3} = \dfrac{3x+9}{4}$, what is the value of x?

A) 0

B) -1

C) 1

D) 55

13. If $x = ay$, where a is a constant, and $x = 56$ when $y = 4$, what is value of x when $y = 3$?

A) 3

B) 14

C) 28

D) 42

14. If $3x + 11 - 9(x+3) = 5x - 27$, what is the value of x?

A) 1

B) 5

C) 6

D) 11

15. If $\dfrac{3a+2}{5} = \dfrac{2a-8}{4}$, what is the value of a?

A) -48

B) -24

C) 12

D) 36

16. If $\dfrac{q}{3p}=7$, what is the value of $\dfrac{2q}{3p}$?

A) 7
B) 12
C) 14
D) 49

17. If $\dfrac{2k}{3r}=5$, what is the value of $\dfrac{15r}{2k}$?

A) 0
B) 1
C) 5
D) 6

18. If $9x-4\leq2x+11$, what is the maximum integer value of x?

A) -1
B) 2
C) 5
D) 8

A. Two Equations

1) A system of linear equations is a collection of linear equations involving the same set of variables.

2) n equations are needed to solve a system with n variables.

   Ex) two equations for two variables, three equations for three variables, etc.

3) Solve for y in terms of x:

   (i) Put y alone on left side.

   (ii) Put any other terms (that includes x and constants) on the right side.

B. Basic Principles of System of Equations/Inequalities

1) Solving for y in terms of x

   (i) Collect the terms, but put all the terms containing y on the left side.

   (ii) Divide by the coefficient of y to have the general form of the equation.

2) Plugging in

   (i) When plugging in, be sure to include parentheses first to avoid the common mistake of not distributing negative coefficients.

     ie. $y = -x + 3$ plugging in to $3x - y = 5$

$$3x - y = 5$$
$$3x - (-x + 3) = 5$$
$$3x + x - 3 = 5$$

Common Mistake! $\longrightarrow$

$3x - x + 3 = 5$

(wrong!)

You forgot to distribute the negative sign.

3) Subtracting Two Equations

   (i) Align the variables vertically and subtract terms by column.

$$\begin{array}{r} 6x + 2y = 14 \\ -\underline{\;4x + 2y = 6\;} \\ 2x \quad\;\; = 8 \end{array}$$

4) Number of solutions

Given $y = m_1 x + b_1$

$\quad y = m_2 x + b_2$

One Solution : if $m_1 \neq m_2$, $b_1 \neq b_2$

No Solution : if $m_1 = m_2$, $b_1 \neq b_2$

Infinitely many Solutions : if $m_1 = m_2$, $b_1 = b_2$

Exercise

The simplest kind of system equations involve two equations and two variables:

$4x + 2y = 6$

$3x + y = 7$

One method is called "Solve-and-Plug".

First, solve the top equation for y in terms of x:

$y = -2x + 3$

Now, plug this into the second equation as the y-value.

$3x + (-2x + 3) = 7$

The equation is now a single variable equation, and solving it will give the value of x.

$3x - 2x + 3 = 7$

$x = 4$

and also the value of y:

$y = -2x + 3 = -2 \times 4 + 3 = -5$

Another method is called "Align Variables".

Let's try with the same system of equations above and label them.

$4x+2y=6 \rightarrow$ ①

$3x+y=7 \rightarrow$ ②

Now align the coefficient of y by multiplying ② by 2.

② $\times 2 : 6x+2y=14$

since ② $\times 2$ and ① share the same coefficient for the variable y,

subtract the two equations to eliminate the variable y.

② $\times 2 -$ ① :

$$
\begin{array}{r}
6x+2y=14 \\
-\underline{4x+2y=6} \\
2x=8
\end{array}
$$

Solving the equation will give us $x=4$.

Plug the $x-$value into equation ②.

$3\times4+y=7$

$12+y=7$

$y=-5$

1. $2a+b=2$

    $4a-3b=19$

    Which of the following pairs of $(a,\ b)$ satisfies the system of equations above?

A) $(3,\ -2)$

B) $(2.5,\ -3)$

C) $(-2.5,\ 3)$

D) $(-3,\ -2)$

2. $45x - 27 = 173 + y$

$\dfrac{y}{x} = 9$

In the system of equations above, what is the value of y?

3. $5p - rq = 3$

$3p - 5q = 7$

In the system of equations above, r is a constant and p and q are variables. For what value of r will the system of equations have no solution?

A) $\dfrac{5}{3}$

B) $\dfrac{25}{3}$

C) $\dfrac{3}{7}$

D) 5

4. $5y - p = 7y - 11$

$5z - q = 7z - 11$

In the equations above, p and q are constants. If p is q minus 2, which of the following is true?

A) y is z minus 1.

B) z is y minus 1.

C) z is y plus 1.

D) z is y minus 2.

C. One Equation, One Inequality

Steps to Solve

1) Solve the equation.
2) Plug it into the equality.

Exercise

Let's take this question with an equation and an inequality as an example.

$x+2y=9$

$x+y\leq 6$

According to the given information, what is the minimum possible value of y?

Since the question is asking for the minimum possible value of y,

we should manipulate the inequality to read in terms of y.

In order to do so, let's collect the terms on the given equation.

$x+2y=9$

$x=9-2y$

Now we have the $x-$value's relationship with y. So the next step would be ...?

Plugging it into the inequality. Good thinking!

$x+y\leq 6$

Plug in the $x-$value:

$(9-2y)+y\leq 6$

$9-y\leq 6$

Collect the terms:

$9-6\leq y$

$\therefore 3\leq y$

Therefore, the minimum possible value of y would be 3.

Remember: − solve the equation
　　　　　　 − plug it into the inequality

Not the other way around.

(i.e. do not solve the inequality first.)

1. $2x+4\leq3y$

   $y=\dfrac{1}{3}x$

   According to the given information, what is the maximum possible value of x?

A) -5

B) -4

C) -3

D) 0

2. $3x+5\geq4y$

   $\dfrac{1}{2}x=2y-7$

   According to the given information, what is the minimum possible integer value of x?

SAT Questions

1. $kx+ry=13$

   $3x+7y=52$

   In the system of equations above, k and r are constants. If the system has infinitely many solutions, what is the value of $\dfrac{k}{r}$?

2. $3a-4b=-3$

   $4a-3b=-11$

   In the system of equations above, what is the value of $a+b$?

A) -8

B) -5

C) -3

D) 2

3. $\dfrac{z}{y}=9$

   $5(y+4)=z$

   In the system of equations above, what is the value of z?

   A) 4
   B) 5
   C) 9
   D) 45

4. $-2a+3b=9$

   $4a+2b=6$

   In the system of equations above, what is the value of a?

5. $5x+21=6y-4$

   $y+4=2x$

   In the system of equations above, what is the value of $y-x$?

   A) 3
   B) 7
   C) 10
   D) 14

6. $3r-a=5r-13$

   $3k-b=5k-13$

   In the equations above, a and b are constants. If b is a minus 6, which of the following is true?

   A) r is k minus 1.
   B) k is r plus 3.
   C) k is r minus 3.
   D) r is k plus 2.

7. $y = 7x + 5 - 2(x+1)$

   $y = -\dfrac{1}{2}x$

   If the system of equations above is satisfied by (p, q), what is the value of $11(p+q)$?

   A) $\dfrac{3}{11}$

   B) $-\dfrac{3}{11}$

   C) -3

   D) 6

8. $5a + 7 = 4b + 2$

   $2b = a + 3$

   In the system of equations above, what is the value of $6a$?

   A) 1

   B) 2

   C) 4

   D) 6

9. $3y + 2 = 5z$

   $2y = z + 8$

   In the system of equations above, what is the value of z?

   A) 2

   B) 4

   C) 6

   D) 8

10. $\dfrac{y}{x}=5$

  $3(x+2)=y$

  In the system of equations above, what is the value of y?

A) 3

B) 6

C) 15

D) 18

11. $4x+6=7y$

  $8x-3=9y$

  In the system of equations above, what is the value of x?

A) 3

B) 3.75

C) 6

D) 6.75

12. $2n+3m=4$

  $3n+4m=5$

  In the system of equations above, what is the value of $n+m$?

A) -1

B) 0

C) 1

D) 2

13. $5n-r=7n-9$

$3m-k=5m-9$

In the equations above, r and k are constants. If r is k minus 4, what is the value of $n-m$?

A) 2

B) 4

C) 5

D) 9

14. $6(x+3)-10=2(y+1)$

$y=\dfrac{1}{3}x$

In the system of equations above, what is the value of $8x$?

A) -9

B) $-\dfrac{9}{8}$

C) -6

D) 9

15. $6a+5b=26$

$2a-2b=5$

Which of the following pairs of $(a,\ b)$ satisfies the system of equations above?

A) $(3,\ -2)$

B) $(3.5,\ 1)$

C) $(3.5,\ -1)$

D) $(-3,\ -2)$

16. $4n - km = 9$

    $5n - 4m = 12$

    In the system of equations above, k is a constant and n and m are variables.

    For what value of k will the system of equations have no solution?

    A) 2.5
    B) 3.2
    C) 4
    D) 5

17. $2r - 5 = 9k$

    $r = 3k + 7$

    In the system of equations above, what is the value of r?

    A) 3
    B) 7
    C) 9
    D) 16

18. $4y + a = 9y - 11$

    $4z + b = 9z - 11$

    In the equations above, a and b are constants. If b is a minus 5, what is the value of $y - z$?

    A) -1
    B) 0
    C) 1
    D) 4

19. $7a+9=5b$

$2a+4=b+7$

In the system of equations above, what is the value of $\dfrac{a+b}{3}$?

A) 7

B) 8

C) 13

D) 21

Equations & Inequalities in Context

In the Math section of the SAT there sometimes are questions that don't seem like math questions. Instead, there're a bunch of words giving you context and asking you to answer in numbers. Ridiculous!

These questions are designed to test your ability to pick out the mathematical implications in the given context. As you master these questions, they might actually help you in real life situations whether you're trying to figure out how much to pay after a meal with your friends or calculate how many days it takes you to eat a bag of candy. (For me, probably not even a minute.)

Frequently Used Terms

x less than y : $y-x$

x more than y : $y+x$

a times bigger than x : ax

a times smaller than x : $\dfrac{x}{a}$

Careful not to confuse these two!

⟷

x minus y : $x-y$

x plus y : $x+y$

a times x : ax

Exercise

Schmidt has 23 more pairs of socks than Nick. If Schmidt and Nick have a total of 61 pairs of socks, how many pairs of socks does Nick have?

In this question, we want to know how many pairs of socks Nick has.
So, we set the number of Nick's pair of socks as x.

Schmidt has 23 more pairs of socks than Nick, which means he has:
(Pairs of socks Nick has) $+23=x+23$

It is given that Nick and Schmidt combined have 61 pairs of socks.

$x+(x+23)=61$

$2x+23=61$

We now have officially established a linear equation using the context given in the question!

Now simply collect the terms.

$2x=61-23$

$2x=38$

$x=19$

Therefore, Nick has 19 pairs of socks.

A mystery is solved and the world is a much safer place now, thanks to you!

Sometimes questions require you to create a mathematical expression based on the given constants and variables.

◄ **Exercise**

> In May, Sunny called s people every day for 10 days, and Khalim called k people every day for 5 days. Which of the following represents the total number of people called by Sunny and Khalim in May?

Let's break down the question step by step:

Sunny called s people per day for 10 days.

$$\frac{s \text{ people}}{\text{day}} \times 10 \text{ day(s)} = 10s \text{ people}$$

Khalim called k people per day for 5 days.

$$\frac{k \text{ people}}{\text{day}} \times 5 \text{ day(s)} = 5k \text{ people}$$

∴ The total number of people called by Sunny and Khalim is: $10s+5k$

Andy is a construction worker. Each day, he receives a pile of bricks to move. The number of bricks left to move at the end of the day can be estimated with the equation $B=253-20h$, where B is the number of leftover bricks and h is the number of hours he has worked that day.
What does the number 20 signify in this question?

It is given in the question that B signifies the number of leftover bricks and h is the number of hours Andy has worked.
Since the equation solves for the amount of leftover bricks by subtracting $20h$ from 253, we can deduce that 253 is the initial workload of the day.

$20 \times h$ is subtracted from the initial workload to solve how many bricks are left over.

Since h is the number of hours that Andy worked, the logical deduction for the value 20 would be the number of bricks Andy moves in an hour.

◢ **Exercise**

Here comes a tricky one.

> $g=13.76+1.37m$
> $d=10.01+2.12m$
> In the equations above, g and d represent the price per gallon, in dollars, of gasoline and diesel, respectively, m months after January 2014. What was the price per gallon of gasoline when it was equal to the price per gallon of diesel?

Since g and d each express the price per gallon of gasoline and diesel, when the price per gallon of gasoline and the price per gallon of diesel are equal to each other, $g=d$.
$13.76+1.37m=10.01+2.12m$

Collect the terms.
$-0.75m=-3.75$
$m=\dfrac{3.75}{0.75}=5$

Therefore, the price of gasoline and diesel equal each other after 5 months.

Oh, wait.

Double check what the question is asking you.

It's not the number of months, is it?

It's asking you to get the price of gasoline when the prices of gasoline and diesel are equal.

Plug $m=5$ into the equation for g.

$g=13.76+1.37m$

$g=13.76+1.37\times5$

$13.76+6.85=20.61(\text{dollars})$

It's very important to know what the question is actually asking. Doing math is important, but in the New SAT you have to think more carefully.

SAT Questions

1. James has 45 more dollars than Jacob. If James and Jacob have 173 dollars combined, how much money, in dollars, does Jacob have?

A) 45
B) 64
C) 109
D) 128

2. At a coffee shop, a serving of iced tea has 50 more milliliters than a serving of coke. If 3 orders of coke and 4 orders of iced tea is a total of 4400 milliliters, how many milliliters is a serving of iced tea?

3. Elizabeth has 32 less marbles than Andy. If Andy and Elizabeth have 218 marbles combined, how many marbles does Andy have?

A) 32

B) 125

C) 173

D) 250

4. When 2 is subtracted from 5 times the number x, the result is 38. What number is the result when 9 is subtracted from 3 times the number x?

A) 5

B) 8

C) 15

D) 24

5. Troy and Abed each ordered tacos at a taco food truck. The price of Troy's tacos was a dollars, and the price of Abed's tacos was $2 less than the price of Troy's tacos. If Troy and Abed evenly divided the payment for their tacos and paid 15 percent sales taxes, which of the following expressions represents the amount, in dollars, each of them paid?

A) $0.15a - 0.15$

B) $1.15a - 1.15$

C) $2.3a - 1.15$

D) $2.3a - 2.3$

6. A toy racing car is scaled to $\frac{2}{7}$ the size of the actual car. If the length of the real-life car is 7 feet, what would be the length, in feet, of the toy car?

A) $\frac{49}{2}$

B) $\frac{2}{49}$

C) 2

D) 7

7. Jeff is x centimeters tall and he is $\frac{1}{5}x$ centimeters taller than Britta. If Britta's height is 156 centimeters, how tall, in centimeters, is Jeff?

A) 39

B) 139

C) 195

D) 203

8. For a rectangular box to be shipped through air at an international delivery service, the height and the perimeter of the bottom side of the box must together be equal to or less than 105 inches. If Pierce is trying to send a box that is 27 inches in height and 15 inches in length of its bottom face, what is the maximum possible width, in inches, of the bottom face of box?

A) 15

B) 20

C) 24

D) 48

9. Henry is participating in a triathlon where the participants must run, bike, and kayak a total of 40 miles. If Henry ran and biked at the speed of 6 miles per hour and 10 miles per hour, respectively, for two hours each, and finished the race in 5 hours, at what speed, in miles per hour, did Henry kayak at?

A) 4
B) 6.2
C) 8
D) 11

10. In Springdale, taxi fares are charged with a $5.00 initial fee, $1.00 per person, and $0.50 per mile. If Dean called a cab with four other friends and was charged a total of $65.50 dollars, how many miles did Dean and his friends travel?

11. For a musical's premiere, tickets that were pre−purchased online cost $15.00 each while tickets bought at the box office on premiere night cost $20.00 each. The total profit of the premiere night was the same as if every ticket purchased cost $18.00 each. If 200 tickets were pre-purchased, how many tickets were sold at the box office?

A) 200
B) 300
C) 350
D) 500

12. Sam and Jeremy collect stamps, and Jeremy has 21 less stamps than 4 times the amount of stamps that Sam has. If Sam and Jeremy have a total of 94 stamps, how many more stamps does Jeremy have than Sam?

A) 21

B) 23

C) 48

D) 71

13. At a gas station near a highway, three bags of beef jerky and two cokes cost $19.00 and five bags of beef jerky and five cokes cost $37.50. What is the difference between the price, in dollars, of one bag of beef jerky and one can of coke?

A) 0.50

B) 3.50

C) 4.00

D) 18.5

14. On Tuesday, Rameez and Cameron have $23.00 and $15.50, respectively, in their bank accounts. Starting from Tuesday, if Rameez adds $0.50 per day and Cameron adds $2.00 per day to their bank accounts, on what day will Rameez and Cameron have the same amount of money in their bank accounts? (Assuming the bank does not close on weekends.)

A) Friday

B) Saturday

C) Monday

D) Tuesday

||

Chapter 1 | 49

15. In the children's section of a library, there is a total of 90 books in hardcover and paperback. If the amount of hardcovers is two times the amount of paperbacks minus nine, how many hardcover books are in the children's section?

A) 27

B) 33

C) 57

D) 66

16. A coffee shop has 21 tables that can seat a total of 71 people. If some of the tables can seat three people and the others seat four people, how many tables seat three people?

A) 5

B) 8

C) 13

D) 16

17. James is buying onions and garlic for $3.00 and $2.50, respectively, to prepare for Thanksgivings Day. If James spent a total of $72.50 from buying a total of 27 onions and garlic, how many onions did James buy?

A) 7

B) 10

C) 17

D) 20

18. In October, Turk ate t sandwiches every day for 13 days, and Carla ate c sandwiches every day for 3 days. Which of the following represents the total number of sandwiches eaten by Turk and Carla in October?

A) $13t + 3c$

B) $3t + 13c$

C) $16tc$

D) $39tc$

19. $a = 3.24 + 0.35n$

$o = 2.49 + 1.10n$

In the equations above, a and o represent the price per liter, in dollars, of apple juice and orange juice, respectively, n days after March 2015. What was the price per liter of apple juice when it was equal to the price per liter of orange juice?

A) $2.84

B) $3.24

C) $3.59

D) $4.34

20. Annie is buying 16GB and 32GB USBs that are priced at u and $2u$, respectively. If Annie bought 10 USBs and paid $17u$, how many 16GB USBs did Annie buy?

A) 2

B) 3

C) 4

D) 7

21. Archer bought 4 more sets of knives than sets of forks. There are 4 knives in each set of knives, and 5 forks in each set of forks. If the number of forks and knives Archer bought are the same, how many knives did Archer buy?

A) 16
B) 20
C) 80
D) 100

22. In a high school in Chapel Hill, there are four times as many football players as basketball players and twice as many basketball players as tennis players. If no student can play for two sports teams at the same time and there is a total of 66 athletes playing the three sports, how many students are football players?

23. On a two−section math test, the first section does not allow calculator use, and the other section allows calculators. The no−calculator questions are each worth 3 points, and have 20 questions. The calculator allowed questions are each worth 2 points and have 25 questions. A total score of 70 points is required to pass the test. If Fry got 8 questions wrong from the no−calculator section, what is the minimum amount of calculator allowed questions Fry must answer correctly in order to pass the test?

24. Lisa and Bart decide to open their piggy bank filled only with pennies. After dividing the pennies randomly, Lisa has 46 less pennies than Bart has. If Lisa and Bart have $13 in total, how many pennies does Bart have?   (1 dollar $=$ 100 pennies)

A) 627

B) 673

C) 1253

D) 1346

25. Bailey bakes cookies at a bakery. Each day, she receives an order of cookies to make. The number of cookies left to bake at the end of the day can be estimated by the equation $C=153-12h$, where C is the number of cookies left and h is the number of hours she has worked that day. What is the meaning of the value 153 in this equation?

A) Bailey will complete baking the cookies in 153 minutes.

B) Bailey bakes cookies at a rate of 153 per hour.

C) Bailey starts each day with 153 orders of cookies to bake.

D) Bailey bakes cookies at a rate of 47 per minute.

Equations/Inequalities in the Coordinate Plane

A. Basic Linear Equations on the Coordinate Plane

$y=ax+b$

a: slope of the line

b: y-intercept of the line

x-intercept : the intersection between the line and the x-axis (y-value is 0)

y-intercept : the intersection between the line and the y-axis (x-value is 0)

Exercise

A line in the xy-plane meets the x-axis at 1 and has a slope of -2.
Which of the following points lies on the line?

A) $(0,\ -1)$

B) $(3,\ 0)$

C) $(0,\ 2)$

D) $(1,\ -2)$

This question tests your knowledge on the nature of linear equations.
Using the information given by the question, establish a basic line equation.
Since the slope of the line is -2,

$y=-2x+b$

The x-intercept of the graph is 1. Therefore, plug in $(1,\ 0)$ to the equation above.

$0=-2\times1+b$

$0=-2+b$

Therefore, $b=2$.

Rewrite the line's equation.

$y=-2x+2$

Now, plug in the answer options to find what fits.

A} $-1=-2\times0+2$

$\quad -1=2$

This option does not belong on the given line.

B) $0 = -2 \times 3 + 2$

$0 = -6 + 2 = -4$

This option does not belong on the given line.

C) $2 = -2 \times 0 + 2$

$2 = 2$

This option belongs on the given line.

D) $-2 = -2 \times 1 + 2$

$-2 = -2 + 2 = 0$

This option does not belong on the given line.

B. Parallel and Perpendicular

If two lines are parallel to each other: slope is the same.

If two lines are perpendicular to each other: slopes are negative reciprocals of each other.

ex) $\quad y = 2x + 3$ and $y = 2x$ are parallel

$\quad y = 2x + 3$ is perpendicular to $y = -\dfrac{1}{2}x$

Exercise

In the xy-plane, lines $4x + 2y = 3$ and $ax + 3y = 3$ are parallel. What is the value of a?

Take the first equation and change it into a line equation form.

$2y = -4x + 3$

$y = -2x + \dfrac{3}{2}$

Take the second equation and change it into a line equation form.

$3y = -ax + 3$

$y = -\dfrac{a}{3}x + 1$

Since the two equations are parallel, the slope is the same.

$-\dfrac{a}{3} = -2$

$\therefore a = 6$

In the xy-plane, lines $4x+2y=3$ and $ax+3y=3$ are perpendicular. What is the value of a?

Take the first equation and change it into a line equation form.

$2y=-4x+3$

$y=-2x+\dfrac{3}{2}$

Take the second equation and change it into a line equation form.

$3y=-ax+3$

$y=-\dfrac{a}{3}x+1$

Since the two equations are perpendicular, the $-\dfrac{a}{3}$ is a negative reciprocal of -2.

$-\dfrac{a}{3}=\dfrac{1}{2}$

$\therefore a=-\dfrac{3}{2}$

C. Inequalities on the Coordinate Plane

$$y\leq 2x+5$$
$$y\leq -3x$$

In the xy-plane, if a point with coordinates $(p,\ q)$ lies in the solution set of the system of inequalities above, what is the maximum possible value of q?

The solution set of the inequalities will be the intersection of the areas below and including the boundary lines of $y=2x+5$ and $y=-3x$.

Drawing the two lines on the coordinate plane will form an 'X' shape since the slope of one equation is positive, and the other is negative.

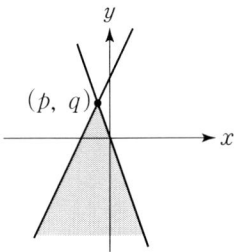

As you can see from the drawing, the greatest value of q will be at the point of intersection of the two lines.

Therefore, in order to get the greatest value of q, we must find the point where the two lines intersect.

$2x+5=-3x$

$5x=-5$

$x=-1$

Plug it into any of the inequalities.

$y\leq -3x$

$y\leq -3\times -1=3$

Therefore, the greatest value of q is 3.

Exercise

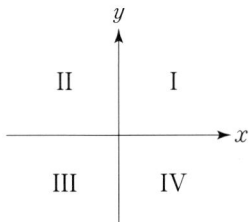

If the equation $6x+3y=9$ is drawn on the xy-plane above, which quadrant contains no solution to the line?

First we need to change the given equation to a line equation form.

Solve for y in terms of x.

$3y=-6x+9$

Divide both sides by 3.

$y=-2x+3$

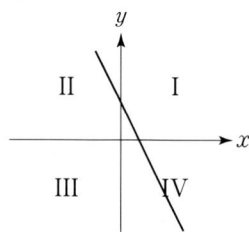

Above is the approximation of line $y = -2x + 3$ graphed out on the coordinate plane. Therefore, Quadrant IV does not contain a solution for the equation.

SAT Questions

1.

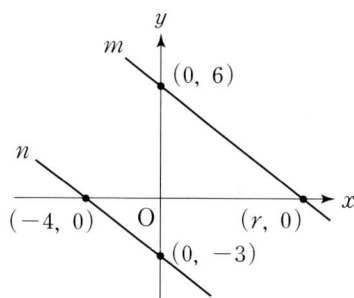

In the xy-plane above, line n is parallel to line m. What is the value of r?

A) 4

B) 6

C) 8

D) 11

2. The graph of a line in the xy-plane has slope -2 and contains the point $(1, 4)$. The graph of a second line passes through the points $(3, 0)$ and $(-3, -2)$. If the two lines intersect at (p, q), what is the value of $p - q$?

A) 6

B) 4

C) 3

D) 0

3. $y \leq 25x - 450$

   $y \leq -5x$

   In the xy-plane, if a point with coordinates $(p,\ q)$ lies in the solution set of the system of inequalities above, what is the maximum possible value of q?

4.

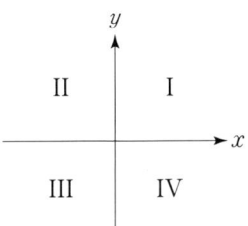

   If the system of inequalities $y \leq 2x+6$ and $y > x$ is graphed on the xy-plane, which quadrant contains no solution to the system?

   A) Quadrant I
   B) Quadrant III
   C) Quadrant IV
   D) There are solutions for every quadrant.

5. If the slope of a line is $\dfrac{7}{3}$ and a point on the line is $(3,\ 15)$, which of the following is the y-intercept?

   A) -8
   B) -1
   C) 8
   D) 12

6.

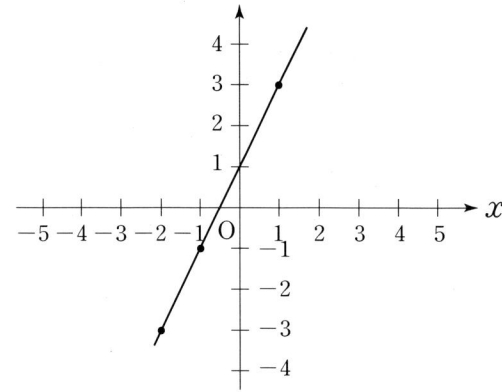

If the equation that represents the graph shown above is written in standard form $ax+by=c$, and $a=4$, what is the value of c?

7. In the xy-plane, lines $6x+2y=3$ and $9x+by=2$ are parallel. What is the value of b?

A) 1
B) 3
C) 4
D) 9

8.

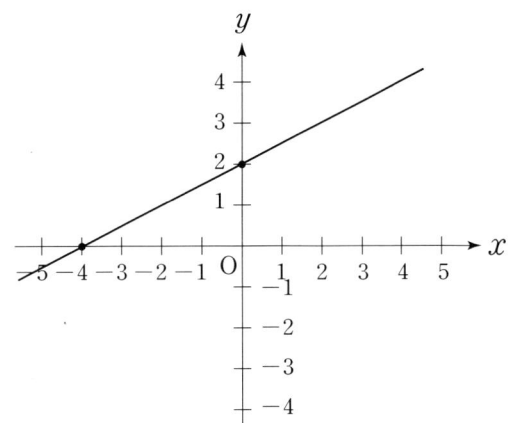

The graph of line l is drawn on the xy-plane above. Which of the following is the slope for a line that is perpendicular to line l ?

A) -2

B) -1

C) $\dfrac{1}{2}$

D) 2

9. If the slope of a line is -0.75 and a point on the line is $(16,\ 1)$, which of the following is the y-intercept?

A) -12

B) -1

C) 4

D) 13

10.

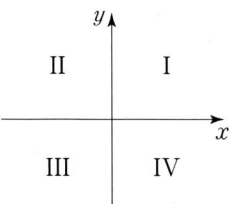

If the equation $2x+4y=3$ is drawn on the xy-plane above, which quadrant contains no solution to the line?

A) Quadrant I
B) Quadrant III
C) Quadrant IV
D) There are solutions for every quadrant.

11. A line on the xy-plane passes through the origin and has a slope of -2. Which of the following points lies on the line?

A) $(1, -2)$
B) $(1, 2)$
C) $(2, 4)$
D) $(4, 2)$

12. A line on the xy-plane passes through coordinates $(0, 2)$ and has a slope of $\frac{2}{3}$. Which of the following points DOES NOT lie on the line?

A) $(3, 4)$
B) $(-3, 0)$
C) $(6, 2)$
D) $(2, 0)$

13. A line on the xy-plane meets the y-axis at 5 and has a slope of -3. Which of the following points lies on the line?

A) $(2, -1)$
B) $(-4, 3)$
C) $(5, 3)$
D) $(3, 0)$

14.

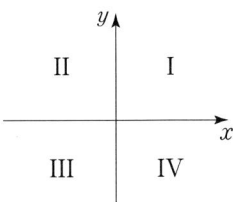

If the system of inequalities $y \leq -\frac{2}{3}x+6$ and $y>2x$ is graphed on the xy-plane, which quadrant contains no solution to the system?

A) Quadrant I
B) Quadrant III
C) Quadrant IV
D) There are solutions for every quadrant.

15.

If the system of inequalities $y>2x-5$ and $y \leq -x$ is graphed on the xy-plane, which quadrant contains no solution to the system?

A) Quadrant I
B) Quadrant III
C) Quadrant IV
D) There are solutions for every quadrant.

16. $y \leq 4x-7$
$y \leq -2x+5$
In the xy-plane, if a point with coordinates (a, b) lies in the solution set of the system of inequalities above, what is the maximum possible value of b?

17.

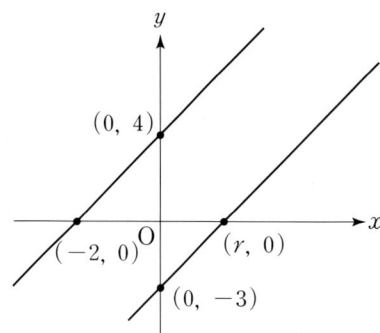

In the xy-plane above, the two lines are parallel. What is the value of r?

A) 1

B) 1.5

C) 2.5

D) 3

18.

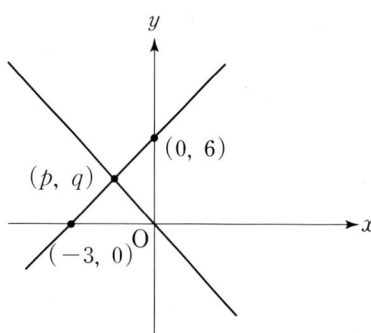

In the xy-plane above, the two lines are perpendicular and intersect at point $(p,\ q)$. What is the value of q?

19. In the xy-plane, lines $4x+2y=1$ and $2x+by=2$ are parallel. What is the value of b?

A) 1

B) 1.5

C) 2

D) 4

20. In the xy-plane, lines $ax+3y=1$ and $7x+y=9$ are parallel. What is the value of a?

A) -21

B) -3

C) 7

D) 21

21. In the $xy-$plane, $ax+2y=7$ and $x+2y=6$ are perpendicular to each other. What is the value of a?

A) -4

B) -2

C) 2

D) 4

22. In the $xy-$plane, $2y\leq4x+6$ and $3y\leq-6x+9$ meet at point $(p,\ q)$. What is the value of pq?

A) -3

B) 0

C) 2

D) 3

23.

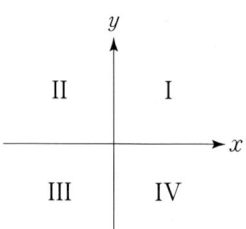

If the system of inequalities $y > 3x - 2$ and $2y \leq -4x$ is graphed on the xy-plane, which quadrant contains no solution to the system?

A) Quadrant I
B) Quadrant III
C) Quadrant IV
D) There are solutions for every quadrant.

24. The graph of a line on the xy-plane has slope -3 and contains the point $(1, \ 2)$. The graph of a second line passes through the points $(4, \ 0)$ and $(-4, \ -4)$. If the two lines intersect at $(r, \ k)$, what is the value of $r - k$?

A)   0
B)   1
C)   3
D)   7

25. $y \leq -11x + 169$

$y \leq 2x$

In the xy-plane, if a point with coordinates $(n, \ m)$ lies in the solution set of the system of inequalities above, what is the maximum possible value of m?

Chapter 2

Problem Solving and Data Analysis

Statistics

A. (Arithmetic) Mean : $\dfrac{\text{sum of values}}{\text{number of values}}$

B. Median : the middle number in a numerically ordered list of values

* When the number of values is even : find the arithmetic Mean of the two numbers in the middle.

*Increase the value of the numbers greater than the Median

*Decrease the value of the numbers smaller than the Median $\longrightarrow$ Doesn't affect the value of the Median

$\uparrow (\downarrow)$ all the numbers by $n \Rightarrow$ new Median $=$ old Median $+ (-)n$

C. Mode : the number that appears most frequently in a set of values

* Multiple Modes can exist.

ex} In Set $\{1,\ 2,\ 2,\ 3,\ 3,\ 4\}$, the Modes are $2,\ 3$.

D. Standard Deviation : a measure of how far the numbers are from the Mean

Standard Deviation of 0 means no spread at all

(ie. $\{2,\ 2,\ 2,\ 2,\ 2\}$ has a standard deviation of 0.

$\{2,\ 3,\ 4,\ 5,\ 6\}$ has a higher standard deviation.

$\{2,\ 12,\ 22,\ 32,\ 42\}$ has an even higher standard deviation)

E. Margins of Error & Confidence Intervals : a measure of precision of an estimate (i.e. how far from the actual value the estimates are likely to be)

ex) An average of 6 hours per week in the gym from the random sample of 300 college students has a margin of error of 1.5 hours at 95% confidence level. This means that in multiple random samples of size 300, the sample average will be within 1.5 hours of the population average in 95% of possible samples. In other words, you can be 95% confident that the interval from 4.5 hours to 7.5 hours includes the population average amount of time in the gym for all students at the college.

* When the confidence level is kept the same, the size of the margin of error is affected by two factors: sample size and the size of standard deviation

* Larger sample size → Smaller margin of error

Smaller sample size → Larger margin of error

Larger standard deviation → Larger margin of error

Smaller standard deviation → Smaller margin of error

* Margin of error and confidence interval does not apply to the value of the variable for particular individuals. In the example, we are 95% confident that the interval from 4.5 hours to 7.5 hours includes the true average amount of time in the gym for all students at the college. It does not imply that 95% of the students spend between 4.5 hours and 7.5 hours in the gym.

Exercise

1. What is the mean of {20, 30, 50}?

2. What is the median of {2, 4, 9, 7, 10, 5}?

3. What is the mode of {1, 1, 1, 2, 2, 2, 3, 3}?

1. 60 is the median of a set of values $2T$, $6T$, $10T$. What is the value of T?

2. $\begin{cases} y=x+6 \\ z=y+3 \end{cases}$

Based on the equations above, if x, y, z represent three numbers, what is the result when the average of the three numbers is subtracted from the median of the numbers?

A) 0

B) 0.5

C) 1

D) 1.5

3. Set X includes eight different numbers. All of the following can affect the value of the median EXCEPT

A) Squaring each number

B) Decreasing each number by 5

C) Decreasing the largest number only

D) Increasing the largest number only

4.

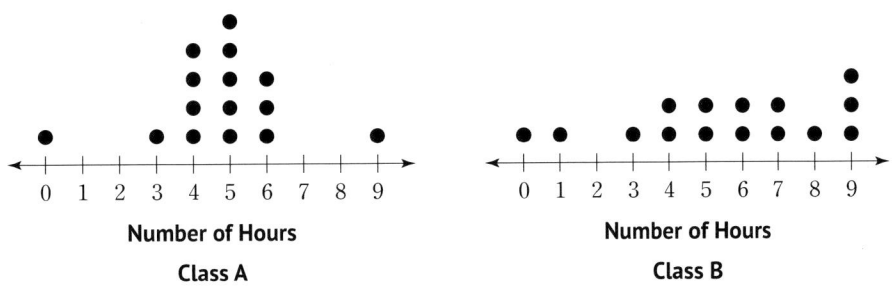

Exercising Hours per Week

Number of Hours
Class A

Number of Hours
Class B

The dot plots above summarize the number of exercising hours of students in Class A and Class B. Which of the following correctly compares the standard deviation of the scores in each of the classes?

A) The standard deviation of the hours in Class A is smaller.

B) The standard deviation of the hours in Class B is smaller.

C) The standard deviations of the scores in Class A and Class B are the same.

D) The relationship cannot be determined from the information given.

5. A quality control manager at an M&M factory is investigating the number of chocolates in one bag of M&Ms. The manager selects 300 bags at random from the daily output of the M&Ms and finds that the average number of chocolates in one bag of M&M has a 95% confidence interval of 41 to 49 chocolates. Which of the following conclusions is the most reasonable based on the confidence interval?

A) 95% of all the M&M bags produced by the factory that day have between 41 and 49 chocolates inside.

B) 95% of all the M&M bags ever produced by the factory have between 41 and 49 chocolates inside.

C) It is plausible that the true average number of chocolates in one bag of M&M produced by the factory that day is between 41 and 49 chocolates.

D) It is plausible that the true average number of chocolates in one bag of M&M ever produced by the factory is between 41 and 49 chocolates.

A. Using Venn Diagram

1) Intersection $(A \cap B)$: the Set of Elements that are in both Set A and Set B

2) Union $(A \cup B)$: the Set of Elements in either Set A or Set B

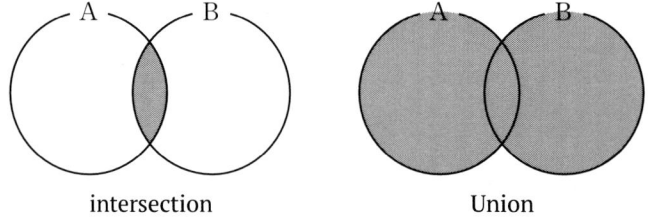

intersection   Union

3) # of Elements : # of Elements in $\{A \cup B)$

$\quad = [(\text{\# of Elements in } A) + (\text{\# of Elements in } B) - \text{\# of Elements in } (A \cap B)]$

B. Counting

1) Fundamental Counting Principle :

use when two INDEPENDENT cases occur at the same time.

When there are P different ways that case A can occur, and Q different ways that case B can occur $\Rightarrow P \times Q$ different ways, when cases A and B occur at the same time.

ex) There are 3 shirts and 4 jeans. How many different shirt-jean combinations are possible?

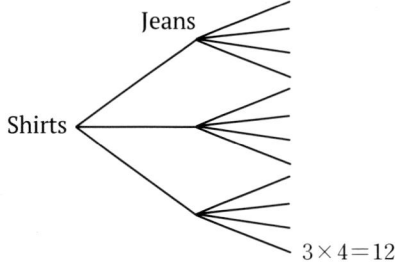

2) Permutation and Combination

(ⅰ) Permutation : the number of ways in selecting r objects in a definite order from n objects

* If order matters, when selecting r objects, Permutation is used.

ex} {**Electing the President, then the Vice-President** vs. electing 2 Board Members)

$$\text{Permutation} = \frac{n}{(n-4)!} = {}_nP_r$$

(ⅱ) Combination : the number of ways in selecting r objects from n objects

* As opposed to Permutation, the order of selecting r objects is not important.

ex} {**Electing 2 Board Members** vs. electing the President then the Vice$-$President)

$$\text{Combination} = \frac{n!}{(n-4)!r!} = {}_nC_r \text{ (dividing by } r! \text{ eliminates repeating outcomes)}$$

3) Probability :

a measure of the likeliness that an event will occur, under the premise that all events are equally likely to occur

$$\frac{\text{The Number of Ways Event } A \text{ Can Occur}}{\text{Total Number of Outcomes}}$$

* Basic Properties

1) Probability of an outcome A, or $P(A)$, is between 0 and 1, inclusively.

That is, $0 \leq P(A) \leq 1$. (Impossible outcome if $P(A)=0$; outcome <u>certain</u> to happen if $P(A) = 1$)

2) If we add together all probabilities of all outcomes, the answer is always 1.

ex} Probability {of dice as 1+ of dice as 2+$\cdots$+ of dice as 6) $=1$

3) When two events, Event A and Event B, don't affect each other, Probability of A and B happening at the same time $=$(probability of A)$\times$(probability of B)

That is, $P(A \cap B)=P(A) \times P(B)$, if A and B are independent.

* Geometric Probability In 2D : compare the areas of two regions to calculate the Probability of an event.

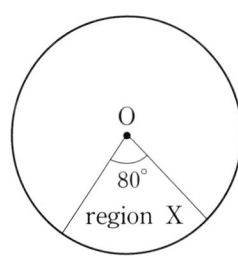

ex} The Probability that the spinner will land on region X?

Solution : $\dfrac{\text{Area in Question}}{\text{Total Area}} = \dfrac{80}{360}$

1. There are 4 elements in set A, 6 elements in set B, and 2 elements in both. How many elements are in either set A or set B?

2. Suppose there are 4 types of shirts and 3 types of ties. How many different combinations of a shirt and a tie are possible?

3. What is the probability of rolling an odd number on a fair 6-sided die?

4. We want to select one president and one vice-president from five candidates. How many different combinations of one president and one vice-president are possible?

5. Now we want to select a committee of three. How many different ways can this committee be selected from the five candidates?

1. 8 students are in a room. If everyone shakes hands with everyone else in a room once and only once, how many handshakes will take place?

2. By using each of the digits $5,\ 6,\ 7$ just once, different positive three-digit integers can be created. If the digits 5 and 6 must be adjacent, how many three-digit integers can be formed?

A) Two
B) Three
C) Four
D) Five

3. On a bookshelf, $\frac{1}{10}$ are non-fiction books, $\frac{1}{3}$ are fantasy books, and $\frac{1}{6}$ are science fiction books. If the 12 remaining books are romance, how many science fiction books are on the bookshelf?

A) 18
B) 30
C) 10
D) 5

4.

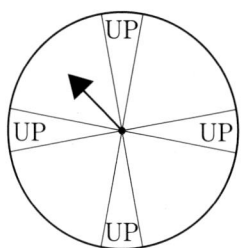

The spinner shown above is spun around its center and stops at a random position. The probability of a sector labeled 'up' ending up below the fixed arrow is $\frac{1}{9}$ (Assume that the arrow never points to any of the dividing lines). If the central angle of each sector labeled 'up' has the same degree measure x, what is the value of x?

A) 5
B) 7.5
C) 10
D) 30

5. A scoreboard contains two slots in which number cards ranging from 0 to 9 can be inserted. There are 12 cards available for each numeral. Assuming that each number card cannot be used more than once, how many scoreboards of consecutive scores, beginning with 01, can be formed?

A) 16
B) 17
C) 18
D) 20

6. Six students are sitting in a line in a classroom. If one student, A, never sits at either end, how many different sitting arrangements are possible?

7. In a certain game arcade, every 6th player is granted an extra life and every 8th player is given a gift token. A player is randomly selected from 100 consecutive players who will play at the arcade one day. What is the probability that the player will both gain an extra life and get a gift token?

A) $\dfrac{1}{100}$

B) $\dfrac{3}{100}$

C) $\dfrac{4}{100}$

D) $\dfrac{7}{100}$

Graphs and Data Analysis

A. Elements

1) <u>Unit</u> : a measurement of quantity. Indicates the size of the property

2) <u>Scaling</u> : the increments in which the data is represented

3) <u>Heading</u> : the title of the represented data

4) <u>Axes</u> : the variables (dependent or independent) involved in the data transformed into x and y axes; the x axis is horizontal, and the y axis is vertical

B. Tables

1) <u>A Table</u> is used to easily represent a list of data. Consisted of Columns and Rows. It will usually contain an independent variable and a dependent variable; a dependent variable changes due to the independent variable.

2) <u>Column</u> : the vertical arrangement of a Table

3) <u>Row</u> : the horizontal arrangement of a Table

* A Table may represent one independent variable, shared by two dependent variables.

ex} Table 1. Temperatures of Coffee and Green Tea at Various Hours

Time (h)	Temperature of Coffee $(^{\circ}C)$	Temperature of Green Tea $(^{\circ}C)$
0	34	38
1	32	30
2	29	29
3	28	27
4	24	26
5	25	24

1. Unit: How many minutes did it take for the coffee to cool to $28^{\circ}C$? (180 minutes)

2. Scaling: At which hour did the temperature of the green tea differ from the temperature of the coffee by $4^{\circ}C$ (0 hr)

C. Types of Graphs

1) <u>Bar Graph</u> : the most basic type of graph; shows how large each value is. May be horizontal or vertical. Usually derived from a Table of data with a single independent variable, with one or more dependent variables

   * In the case of multiple dependent variables, a Legend {key} will indicate which bar represents which variable.

ex} Bar graph : Temperature vs. Time

Exercise

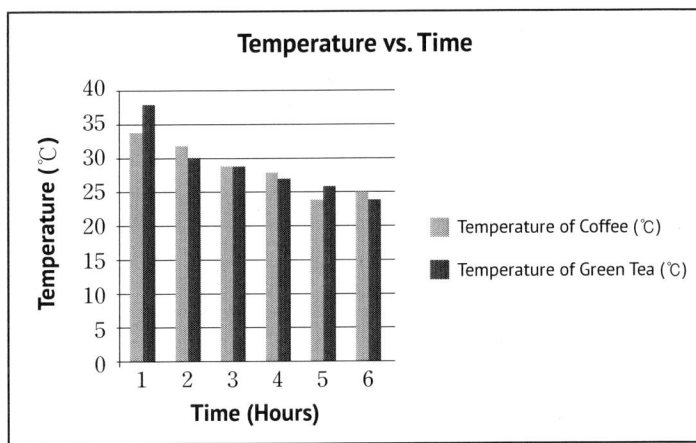

1. Unit: What temperature, in degrees Fahrenheit, is the coffee when the green tea reaches a temperature of 30 degrees Celsius? (degree Fahrenheit=1.80× degrees Celsius + 32.0; 89.6°F)

2. Scaling: What is the biggest temperature difference between the two drinks, and at which hour does this difference occur? (4°C; Hour 1)

3. Heading: What does the table represent? Explain in words. (The temperatures of coffee and green tea at various hours, from hour 1)

2) <u>Scatter Plot</u> : a graph of plotted points that shows the relationship between two sets of data.

  * Line of Best Fit : a line that best represents the trend of the data shown on the graph.

ex) Scatter plot : Y vs. X

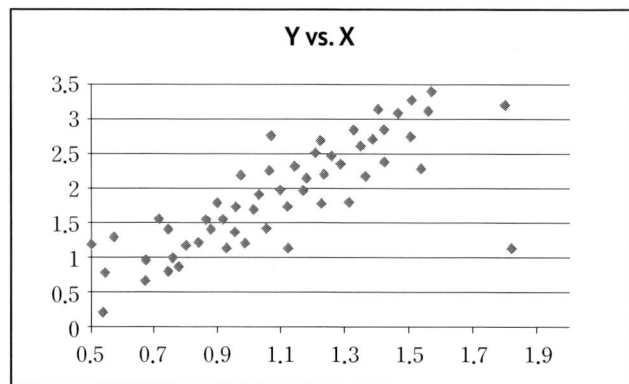

1. Heading : What could this graph be representing? (Various answers; situations in which the value of one variable increases with the other variable.)

2. Axes & Scaling : What is the coordinate of the point with the lowest x-value? $(0.5, \ 1.2)$

3. What type of equation would the line of best fit show for this graph? (Linear)

4. Looking at the graph, could you predict the next set of data? How? (Following the line of best fit would allow you to predict the next set of data.)

3) <u>Histogram</u> : a graph that is similar to the Bar Graph but groups its independent variable into ranges, showing how large each range of values is

ex) Histogram : Species A Survivability

Exercise

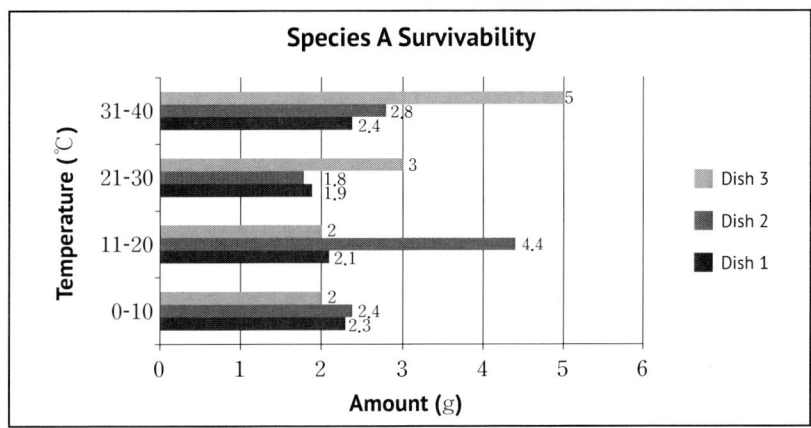

*Note that the graph is horizontal. However, the analytic method doesn't change.

1. Unit : If there was a total of 10 kg of species A in dish 2 at 11-20°C, what percentage survived? (0.044%)

2. Scaling : Which temperature range is the most suitable for species A to survive, if they were to live in dish 3's environment? (31−40°C)

4) <u>Line Graph</u> : a graph that connects individual points of data by lines; shows how the data changes in value (as time passes, etc.)

ex) Line Graph : Company Values over Time

Exercise

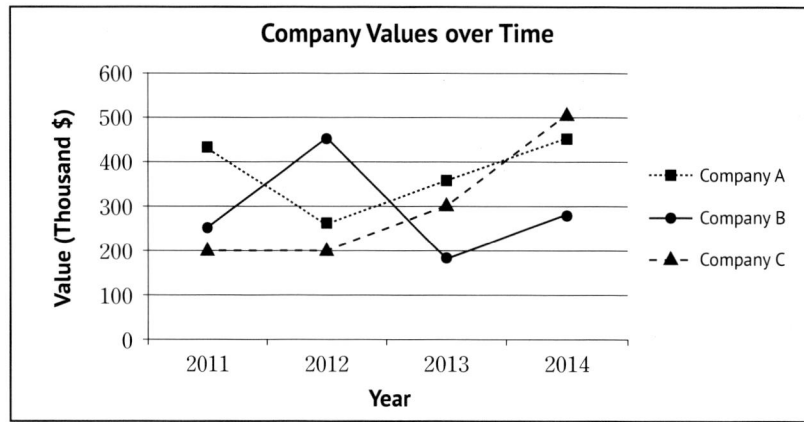

1. Unit : From 2011 to 2014, approximately how much did company C's value increase, in millions of dollars?
   ($0.3 Million)

5) <u>Pie Chart</u> : a type of graph, in the shape of a circle. Most commonly used to show the amount of portions in a whole

* As with a Bar Graph with multiple dependent variables, a Pie Chart will have a Legend to show what each part indicates.

ex) Pie Chart : Approval Rating: June 2014

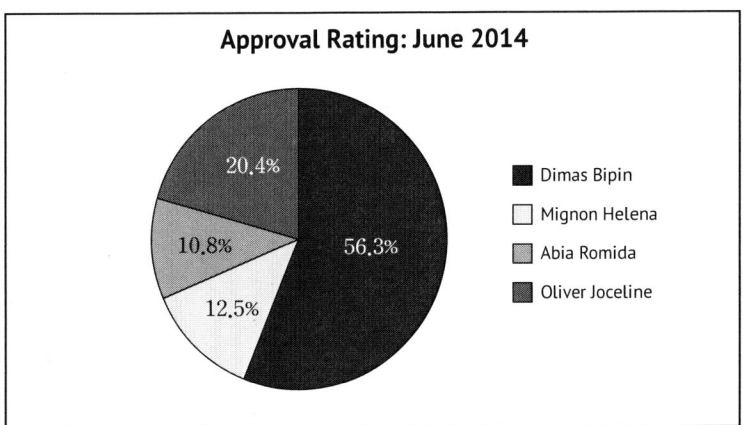

The following are the gas prices, for credit payment and for cash payment, per gallon.

	Regular	Plus	Premium
Credit	$2.11	$2.35	$2.47
Cash	$2.06	$2.29	$2.40

The following table shows the type of gas Tom and Barb purchased this year. Tom's car has a gas capacity of 18.5 gallons. Barb's car has a gas capacity of 17 gallons. Tom and Barb fill their tanks once a month, from zero gallons to the tank's full capacity.

Months	Tom	Barb
January - April	Plus	Premium
May - August	Regular	Plus
September - December	Regular	Regular

1. By how much is it more expensive to pay with credit? Round to the nearest hundredth percent.

A) Regular: 2.43% Plus: 2.62% Premium: 2.92%

B) Regular: 2.37% Plus: 2.55% Premium: 2.83%

C) Regular: 2.43% Plus: 2.18% Premium: 2.08%

D) Regular: 2.37% Plus: 2.13% Premium: 2.04%

2. If Tom fills his tank twice a month, by how much will his payments increase?

A) 100%, Tom originally only filled his tank once a month; if he filled his tank twice a month, he would spend double the original amount.

B) 50%, Tom only filled his tank twelve times this year.

C) 150%, Tom originally only filled his tank once a month; if he filled his tank twice a month, he would spend double the original amount.

D) 0%, nothing would change.

3. If Tom received $50,135 in wages this year and spent $474.34 on gas, what percent of his wage did he spend on gas, if he only paid in cash? Round to the nearest hundredth percent.

A) 9.5%

B) 0.95%

C) 0.97%

D) 9.7%

The following graph shows the number of students from the Class of 2014 and the majors they chose as they entered college.

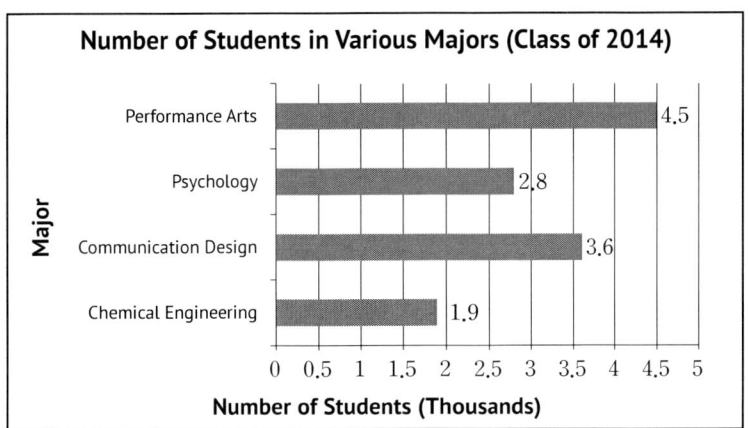

4. Of the students majoring in Chemical Engineering, about 23% change their major every year. For the Class of 2014, how many students changed their major from Chemical Engineering to something else at the end of their third year of college? Round to the nearest whole number.

A) 259

B) 867

C) 260

D) 337

Ratio

A. Direct Proportion:

When x increases by 2 or 3 times, y increases by 2 or 3 times.

e.g. 'x is directly proportional to y' can be expressed as:

$$x = ky \ (\ k \text{ is a constant})$$

B. Inverse Proportion:

When x increases by 2 or 3 times, y decreases by $\frac{1}{2}$ or $\frac{1}{3}$ times.

e.g. 'x is inversely proportional to y' can be expressed as:

$$x = k\frac{1}{y}$$

Exercise

1. If the ratio of A to B is $2:4$ and the ratio of B to C is $6:9$, what is the ratio of A to C?

2. If 4 pennies weigh 40 grams, what is the weight, in grams, of 80 pennies?

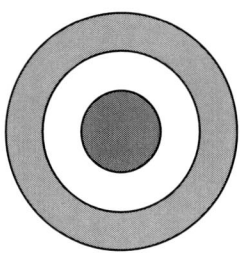

1. The three circles shown above are concentric and their radii are 2, 4, and 6, respectively. What is the ratio of the area of the small shaded circle to the area of the shaded ring?

A) 1 : 16

B) 1 : 9

C) 1 : 5

D) 1 : 4

2. The ratio of P to Q is 3 to 5 and the ratio of Q to R is 12 to 4. What is the ratio of R to P?

A) 5 to 4

B) 4 to 1

C) 5 to 9

D) 9 to 5

Rate

A. Motion Problem : Speed (Velocity) $\times$ Time $=$ Distance

$$\text{Average speed (velocity)} = \frac{\text{Total Distance}}{\text{Total Time}}$$

B. Work Problem : Rate of work $\times$ Time worked $=$ Amount of work done

Exercise

1. If a person travels 3 hours with an average speed of 25 miles per hour, what is the total distance of his / her trip?

2. 6 workers can build a bridge in 10 days. How many days would it take for 2 workers to build the same bridge?

1. When chasing prey, a cheetah can run x miles in 5 minutes. When relaxed, it will only walk at $\frac{1}{5}$ of that speed. How many minutes will it take for a cheetah to walk to a pond $\frac{x}{2}$ miles away?

A) 10
B) 12.5
C) 20
D) 25

2. An elephant needs to eat 100 kg of food to be one-third full. How many kilograms of food does it need to eat to be completely full?

A) 200
B) 100
C) 300
D) 250

3. Jenny climbed up a climbing wall at an average speed of 0.5 feet per second and descended at an average speed of 3 feet per second. If her total time spent on the climbing wall was 7 minutes, how many minutes did it take Jenny to climb up the climbing wall?

A) 5
B) 5.5
C) 6
D) 6.5

VI | Percentages

A. Percent : a number or ratio expressed as a fraction of 100

(If 5 people attended out of a pool of 20 people, $\frac{5}{20} \times 100 = 25\%$ attended)

B. Fraction, Decimal, Percent, Conversion, etc.

Fraction	$\frac{1}{10}$	$\frac{1}{8}$	$\frac{1}{6}$	$\frac{1}{5}$	$\frac{1}{4}$	$\frac{1}{3}$	$\frac{1}{2}$
Decimal	0.10	0.125	0.166$\cdots$	0.20	0.25	0.33$\cdots$	0.50
Percent	10%	12.5%	$16\frac{2}{3}\%$	20%	25%	$33\frac{1}{3}\%$	50%

C. Problem Types

1) x % of a number : $\dfrac{x}{100} \times \text{number} = \text{percent of that number}$

2) y % change : $\text{Percent change} = \dfrac{\text{amount of change}}{\text{original amount}} \times 100$

3) original amount :

① percent increase ($P\%$ Increase)

$$\text{original amount} = \frac{\text{new amount}}{1 + \dfrac{P}{100}}$$

② percent decrease ($P\%$ Decrease)

$$\text{original amount} = \frac{\text{new amount}}{1 - \dfrac{P}{100}}$$

1. What is $\frac{1}{8}$ in percentage?

2. What is 40% of 50?

3. midterm score: 70

   final score: 90

   What is the percent change from midterm to final?

4. If the price of a product, increased by 20%, is $60, what is its original price?

1. The percent increase from 8 to 14 is equal to the percent increase from 28 to x. What is the value of x?

A) 34

B) 42

C) 16

D) 49

2. A rise in the cost of corns caused the price of a bag of corn chips to increase by 20%. If the new price is $18, what was the original price of a bag of corn chips?

A) $3.6

B) $15

C) $14.4

D) $21.6

3. If a and b are positive numbers, what percent of $(2a+5)$ is b?

A) $\dfrac{1}{100b(2a+5)}\%$

B) $\dfrac{2a+5}{100b}\%$

C) $\dfrac{100b}{2a+5}\%$

D) $\left(\dfrac{100b}{2a+5}+1\right)\%$

Chapter 3

Passport to Advanced Math

Factoring

A. Factoring : method of writing numbers/polynomials as the product of their factors or divisors

Factor : a number/polynomial that divides another number/polynomial without remainders

B. Basic Laws

1) $ma + mb = m(a+b)$

2) $a^2 \pm 2ab + b^2 = (a \pm b)^2$

3) $a^2 - b^2 = (a+b)(a-b)$

C. Technique

1) Factoring by Greatest Common Divisor :

$$15x^2 + 3x = (3x \times 5x) + (3x \times 1)$$
$$= 3x(5x+1)$$

2) Factoring by Grouping :

$$(x^2 - x - 6) = x \times x + (2-3)x - 2 \times 3$$
$$= (x-3)(x+2)$$

Exercise

Factor the following.

1. $9x^2 + 6x + 3x^3$

2. $16x^2 + 32x + 16$

3. $25x^2 - 4$

4. $21x^2 - 22x - 8$

1.
$$ax^3 + bx^2 + cx + d = (5x + 13)(3x^2 + x - 2)$$
If the above equation is true for all values of x, what is the value of b?

2. The equation $(3x - n)^2 = 9x^2 - mx + 16$ is true for all values of x. If $n > 0$, what is the value of $m + n$?

A) 0

B) 4

C) 16

D) 28

3.
$$3\left(\frac{a}{b}+\frac{b}{a}\right)=k, \ 4\left(\frac{a}{b}-\frac{b}{a}\right)=m$$

If $a\neq0, b\neq0$ in the equations above, which of the following is equal to k^2-m^2?

A) $\left(\frac{7a}{b}-\frac{b}{a}\right)\left(-\frac{a}{b}+\frac{7b}{a}\right)$

B) $\left(\frac{7a}{b}+\frac{b}{a}\right)\left(\frac{a}{b}+\frac{7b}{a}\right)$

C) $-\left(\frac{7a}{b}+\frac{b}{a}\right)\left(\frac{a}{b}+\frac{7b}{a}\right)$

D) $7\left(\frac{a}{b}-\frac{b}{a}\right)\left(-\frac{a}{b}+\frac{b}{a}\right)$

4. If $\dfrac{2x+4x+6x+8x+10x}{10x}=3$, what are all possible values of x?

A) All real numbers except 0

B) 0 only

C) 1 only

D) 3 only

Equations

A. Quadratic Equation : an equation whose highest variable degree is 2

1) Zero-Product Rule : if the product of two or more factors is zero, then at least one of the factors must be zero

   ex) $(x-2)(x+4)=0$ means $x=2$ or $x=-4$

2) Solving by Factoring : simplify the equation using factorization and apply the zero-product rule

3) Using the Quadratic Formula

   If $ax^2+bx+c=0$, then $x=\dfrac{-b\pm\sqrt{b^2-4ac}}{2a}$

   (i) Sum and Product of Two Roots

   If $ax^2+bx+c=0$ and the two roots of the equation are x_1 and x_2,

   then $x_1+x_2=-\dfrac{b}{a}$ and $x_1\times x_2=\dfrac{c}{a}$

   (ii) Discriminant: expression that appears under the radical sign in the quadratic formula (i.e.); reveals the nature and number of solutions of a quadratic equation

   If $b^2-4ac>0$, then the equation has two distinct real solutions

   If $b^2-4ac=0$, then the equation has one real solution

   If $b^2-4ac<0$, then the equation has no real solution, or two distinct complex solutions

B. Polynomial Equation : an equation whose highest variable degree is larger than 2

   ex) $3x^5+x^3+8x^2+1=0$ is a polynomial equation with a highest degree of 5

1) Dividing Polynomials by a Linear Expression : when dividing polynomials by a linear expression, there are two ways to find the remainder. One is to perform long division and the other is to use the function form of the polynomial. For example, to find the remainder when $2x^2-5x^2+x+9$ is divided by $x-3$:

   (i) Long Division

$$
\begin{array}{r}
3x\ +x+4 \\
x-3\ )\overline{2x^3+5x^2+x+9} \\
\underline{2x^3-6x^2} \\
x^2\ +x \\
\underline{x^2-3x} \\
4x-\ 9 \\
\underline{4x-12} \\
21
\end{array}
$$

The remainder is 21.

(ii) Function form

Let $P(x)=2x^3-5x^2+x+9$

Since $x-3$ is the divisor, plug into $P(x)$ the solution to $x-3=0$ which is $x=3$.

$P(x)=2(3)^3-5(3)^2+3+9=21$

The remainder is 21.

As you can see, when trying to find the remainder of a polynomial divided by a linear expression, using the function form is the quickest method. On a related note, if a linear expression is a factor of a polynomial, let's say $Q(x)$, then the solution to $ax+b=0$, namely $x=-\dfrac{b}{a}$, will also be a solution to $Q(x)=0$.

In summary:

When polynomial $Q(x)$ is divided by $ax+b$, remainder is equal to $Q\left(-\dfrac{b}{a}\right)$.

If $ax+b$ is a factor of polynomial $Q(x)$, then $Q\left(-\dfrac{b}{a}\right)=0$.

C. Systems of Equations

In Chapter 1: Heart of Algebra, we learned to solve system of equations in which both equations were linear. In this section, we're going to look at systems of equations with two variables in which one equation is linear and the other is nonlinear.

D. Complex Equations in Context

Let's go back to Chapter 1: Heart of Algebra again. Remember those ridiculous questions that are filled with bunch of words but call themselves math questions? Well, here they are again except they're more complex than before. Ugh.

It's okay though. All the skills you learned until now are more than enough to get you through these tough-looking questions. In this section, you will be asked to manipulate equations to isolate a variable of interest, or use an equation regarding a context to figure out how one variable changes another variable, or even identify a new form of equation that will ultimately reveal new information about the context. Like before, these questions are designed to help you out in real life situations like figuring out how long it will take for your family to reach grandma's house during a holiday traffic jam. (Seems like never doesn't it?)

1. If $81-169x^2=0$, what are the possible values of x?

2. $2x^2-7x-10=0$

   What are the solutions to the equation above?

3. $(3x+4)(x+2)(x-5)=0$

   What are the zeroes of the given polynomial?

4. $k(x)=(3x-1)^5(x+7)^3(2x+5)^2(x-3)$

   The polynomial function k is defined above. How many distinct zeroes does k have?

5. What are the solution pairs $(x,\ y)$ to the system of equations shown below?

   $y=x^2+x-4$

   $y=-5x+8$

1. $(3x+7)(6-cx)=0$

   In the equation above, c is a constant. If the equation has the solutions $x=-\dfrac{7}{3}$ and $x=\dfrac{3}{2}$, what is the value of c?

2. $ty^2-6y=15$

   In the equation above, t is a constant. For what values of t does the equation have no real solution?

3. $x^3-9x^2-54x+216$

   The polynomial above has $(x-3)$ and $(x+6)$ as factors. What is the remaining factor?

4. $T(y)=(y-3)^3-7(y-3)^2+12(y-3)$

   The polynomial function T is defined above. What is the sum of the zeroes of T?

5. When $6x^3+x^2-29x+25$ is divided by $2x-3$, the result is $3x^2-5x-7+\dfrac{R}{2x-3}$, where R is a constant. What is the value of R?

6. What are the solution pairs (x, y) to the system of equations shown below?

$y=-(x+5)^2+4$

$y=x+3$

7. If (m, n) is a solution to the system of equations shown below and $m > 0$, what is the value of m?

$7x^2=(y+8)(y-8)$

$2y=8x$

8. Heather is selling homemade brownies for the school bake sale which happens every month. From her experience from last year, Heather predicts that for each $0.5 increase in brownie price, she will sell 10 less brownies. At the current price of $1.5 per brownie, an average of 80 brownies will be sold. Which of the following functions best models the amount of money that Heather expects to earn from the bake sale, y, based on an x increase in brownie price, assuming she only raises the price by units of $0.5?

A) $y=(1.5+x)\left(80-\dfrac{10x}{0.5}\right)$

B) $y=(1.5-x)\left(80+\dfrac{10x}{0.5}\right)$

C) $y=(1.5+x)\left(80-\dfrac{10}{x}\right)$

D) $y=(1.5+x)(80-10x)$

9. If an object of mass m is brought up to a height of h, the object's potential energy PE is given by the equation $PE=mgh$ where g is the gravitational constant. If the mass of the object is doubled and its height is halved, how does the potential energy change?

A) The potential energy is quartered (divided by 4).

B) The potential energy is halved.

C) The potential energy is unchanged.

D) The potential energy is doubled.

10. If an object starts moving in a straight line at an initial velocity v_0 and accelerates at a constant rate a for time t, the object's distance travelled s is given by the equation $s = v_0 t + \frac{1}{2} a t^2$. Which of the following correctly expresses a in terms of s, v_0, and t?

A) $a = \dfrac{2s}{t^2}$

B) $a = \dfrac{2v_0}{t}$

C) $a = \dfrac{2}{t^2}(s + v_0 t)$

D) $a = \dfrac{2}{t^2}(s - v_0 t)$

III   Absolute Value

A. Absolute Value : the absolute value of x is written as $|x|$. It shows how far x is from 0 on the real number line

　　ex) If $|x|=3$, x is 3 units away from 0, without considering the direction, therefore $x=\pm3$.

B. Absolute Value Equations : if $|expression\ with\ a\ variable|=a$, expression with a variable $=\pm a$

　　ex) If $|x-4|=8$, $x-4=\pm8 \rightarrow x=12,\ x=-4$

C. Absolute Value Inequalities : the inequality $|x-a|<d$ means "the distance between x and a is less than d"

　　1) $|ax-b|<d \ \rightarrow \ -d<ax-b<d$

　　2) $|ax-b|>d \ \rightarrow \ ax-b<-d$ or $ax-b>d$

Exercise

Solve the following equation or inequality.

1. $|4x|=8$

2. $|3x+2|=11$

3. $|10x|<10$

4. $|5x-2|>8$

IV Functions

A. Terms

1) Function: a function relates an input variable, often expressed with x, to an output variable, often expressed with y

ex) $y=f(x)$, where $f(x)=x^2+2$

2) Domain and Range

(i) Domain : the set of all possible input values of a function

(ii) Range : the set of all possible output values of a function

B. Types of Functions

1) Linear Function : expressed as $y=ax+b$, where a is the slope of the line, and b is the value of y where $x=0$ (y-intercept)

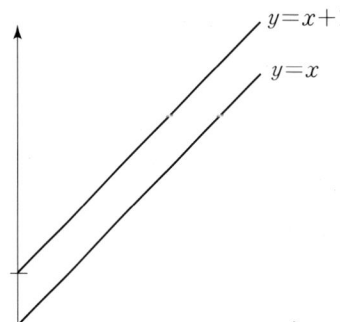

2) Absolute Value Function : expressed as $y=|x|$; has two parts : $y=x$ and $y=-x$

   *y can only have positive values.

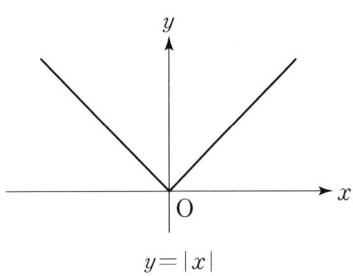

$$y=|x|$$

3) Quadratic Function : the graph of a quadratic function is a parabola whose axis of symmetry is parallel to the y-axis and goes through the vertex of the function. The graph is symmetric with respect to a line called the Axis of Symmetry

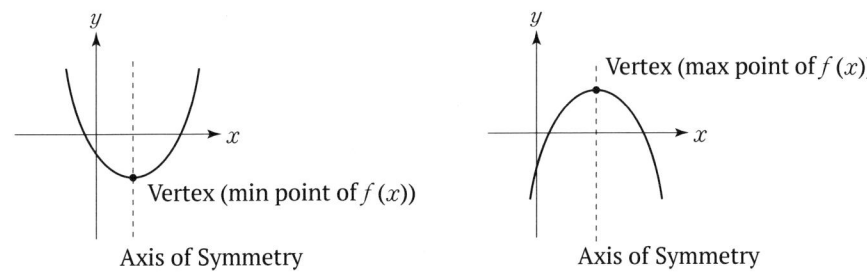

   * A standard formula for a quadratic function is $f(x)=ax^2+bx+c$. If $a>0$, the graph is concave up ($\cup$-shaped), and y's minimum value is its vertex. If $a<0$, the graph is concave down ($\cap$-shaped), and y's maximum value is its vertex.

4) Exponential Function : denoted by $y=a^x$ (a is a constant, greater than 0)

   Two cases exist: when a is $0<a<1$ and $a>1$

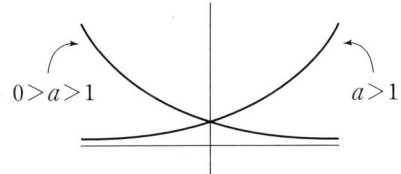

C. Transformations of Functions

1) Reflection

Action Taken in $y=f(x)$	Effect on Original Graph
Replace $f(x)=y$ with $-f(x)=y$	Reflects graph over the x axis
Replace x with $-x$	Reflects graph over the y axis

2) Shifting

Action taken in $y=f(x)$	Effect on Original Graph
Replace x with $x-(h)$	Shifts graph horizontally $\|h\|$ units If $h<0$, the shift is left If $h>0$, the shift is right
Add k to the function $y=f(x) \rightarrow y=f(x)+k$	Shifts graph vertically $\|k\|$ units If $k<0$, the shift is down If $k>0$, the shift is up

Exercise

1. Match each function with its graph.

(1) $y=ax+b$

(2) $y=|x|$

(3) $y=dx^2+ex+f$

(4) $y=g^x$

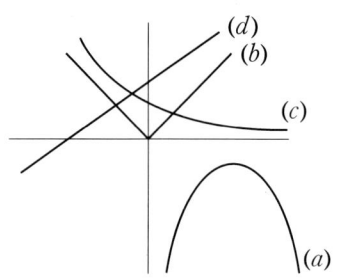

2. What happens to the graph of $f(x)$ if we replace x with $x-4$?

1. Function g is defined by $g(x)=\dfrac{3x-5}{2}$. For what value of x does $g(x)=5$?

2.

x	$f(x)$	$g(x)$
2	3	11
4	5	9
6	7	7
8	9	5
10	11	3

Functions f and g are defined by the table above. What is the value of x that satisfies the equation $g(x)+5=f(x)-3$?

A) 4

B) 6

C) 8

D) 10

3.

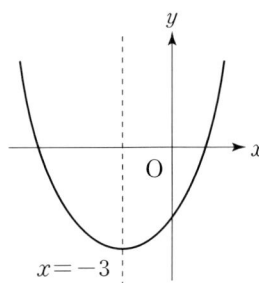

The line of symmetry of the parabola shown on the graph above has the equation $x=-3$.
The $x-$ intercepts of the parabola are $(-7,\ 0)$ and $(a,\ 0)$. What is the value of a?

A) 4

B) 5

C) 6

D) 1

4. The graph of the line $2x+5y-4=1$ on the xy-plane is reflected across the y-axis. What is the equation of the resulting reflection?

   A) $2x+5y=-5$
   B) $2x-5y=5$
   C) $-2x+5y=5$
   D) $-2x-5y=5$

5.

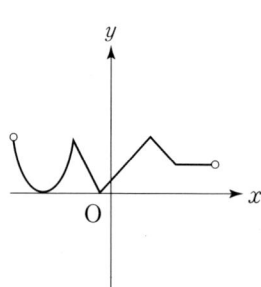

The complete graph of the function f is shown above. Function g is defined by $g(x)=-|f(x)|$. At how many points do the graphs of $f(x)$ and $g(x)$ intersect?

   A) None
   B) One
   C) Two
   D) Three

Powers & Roots

V

A. Power

1) Power : the value of a number or quantity raised to some exponent

2) Power Calculation Method

① $a^b \times a^c = a^{b+c}$

② $a^b \div a^c = a^{b-c}$

③ $(a^b)^c = a^{bc}$

④ $(a \cdot b)^c = a^c b^c$

⑤ $a^{-1} = \dfrac{1}{a}$

⑥ $a^0 = 1$

⑦ $a = (\sqrt[c]{a})^c$

B. Roots

1) Square Root : If A is multiplied by itself and results in B,

　　　　　　A is the Square Root of B

　　　　　　(± 3 is the square root of 9, ± 4 is the square root of 16, etc.)

　*$\sqrt{\ }$　is used to represent square root of positive numbers. (ex. $\sqrt{9}=3$, $\sqrt{16}=4$)

2) Cube Root : If A is multiplied twice by itself and results in B,

　　　　　　A is the Cube Root of B

　　　　　　(-3 is the cube root of -27)

3) Operations of Square Roots

① $\sqrt{a} \times \sqrt{b} = \sqrt{ab}$

② $\dfrac{\sqrt{a}}{\sqrt{b}} = \sqrt{\dfrac{a}{b}}$

③ $(\sqrt{a})^2 = a$

④ $a\sqrt{b} + c\sqrt{b} = (a+c)\sqrt{b}$

⑤ $\dfrac{a}{\sqrt{b}} = \dfrac{a \times \sqrt{b}}{\sqrt{b} \times \sqrt{b}} = \dfrac{a}{b}\sqrt{b}$

Simplify the following.

1. $(5 \cdot 3)^2$

2. $(4^0)^3$

3. $\sqrt{25}$

4. $2\sqrt{3} + 4\sqrt{3}$

5. $\dfrac{7}{\sqrt{8}}$

1. $(5 \times 10^k) + (3 \times 10^4) = (3.005 \times 10^4)$

   If the equation above is true, what is the value of k?

2. If $3^{t-2} = 27^2$, what is the value of t?

3. If $7x^3 = 56$, what is the value of $7x^6$?

4. If $m^2 = 3^{10}$, which of the following expressions represent 3^{11}?

   A) $6m^4$

   B) $9m^4$

   C) m^6

   D) $3m^2$

5. If q and x are real numbers for which $x^4 = -a$, which of the following could be true?

   I. $a > 0$

   II. $a = 0$

   III. $a < 0$

   A) I only

   B) III only

   C) I and II only

   D) II and III only

6. It is known that t is a positive integer. $5^t + 5^t$ is equal to which of the following?

A) $2 \cdot 5^t$

B) 5^{2t}

C) 10^t

D) 10^{2t}

7. If x is a non-negative integer, then all of the following can be unit digit of 7^x EXCEPT?

A) 9

B) 1

C) 3

D) 5

8. If $x = 3^3$, which of the following expressions is equal to 3^8?

A) $27x$

B) $243x$

C) x^3

D) $3x^2$

Chapter 4

Additional Topics

I | Triangles

A. Types

1) Isosceles Triangle : a triangle with two equal angles and two equal sides

2) Equilateral Triangle : a triangle with three equal sides (all three angles are 60°)

3) Right Triangle : a triangle with one angle of 90°

B. Pythagorean Theorem : $(\text{opposite})^2 + (\text{adjacent})^2 = (\text{hypotenuse})^2$

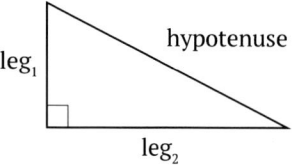

ex) $3^2 + 4^2 = 5^2$, $5^2 + 12^2 = 13^2$

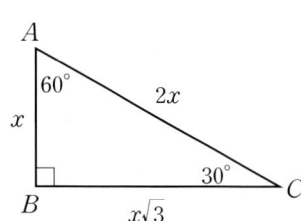

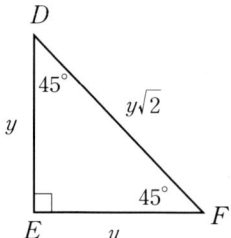

C. Special Triangles

1) $30° - 60° - 90°$
$$\overline{AB} : \overline{BC} : \overline{AC} = 1 : \sqrt{3} : 2$$

2) $45° - 45° - 90°$
$$\overline{DE} : \overline{EF} : \overline{DF} = 1 : 1 : \sqrt{2}$$

D. Triangle Inequality

Given that $a < b < c$,

1) One side of a triangle is longer than the difference between the other two sides.

$a > c - b$

$b > c - a$

$c > b - a$

2) One side of a triangle is shorter than the sum of both sides.

$a + b > c$

$a + c > b$

$b + c > a$

3) The longest side is at the opposite side of the greatest angle. The shortest side is at the opposite side of the smallest angle.

E. Similar Triangles

1) <u>Characteristics</u>
   (ⅰ) Three equal angles
   (ⅱ) Same ratio of corresponding sides

2) <u>Similarity Rules</u> : at least one of the following must be satisfied for the triangles to be similar
   (ⅰ) Angle Angle : two of the angles of a triangle are the same
   (ⅱ) Side Angle Side : the ratio between one side of a triangle and the corresponding side of another triangle is equal to the ratio between another side of the first triangle and the corresponding side of the second triangle. The angle made between both these sides in both triangles must be the same
   (ⅲ) Side Side Side : the ratio between all three corresponding sides of two triangles are equal

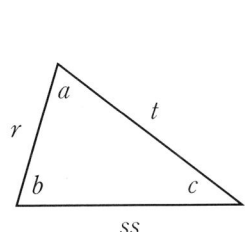
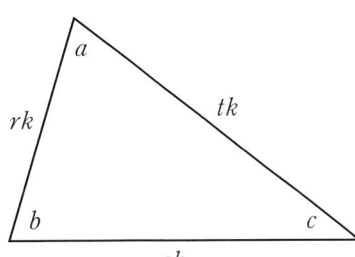

1. If △ABC is an equilateral triangle, find the ratio $x : y : z$.

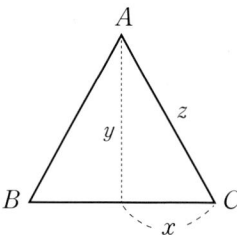

2. If □ABCD is a square, find the ratio $x : y : z$.

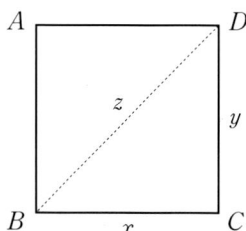

3. If △ABC > 90°, what is one possible value of $\overline{AC}$?

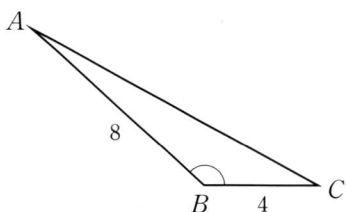

4. Find the length of $\overline{DF}$.

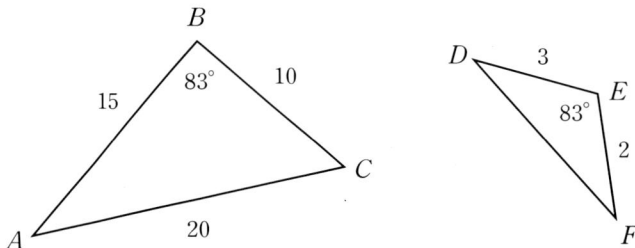

5. What are the values of x and y?

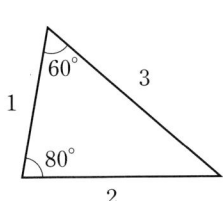 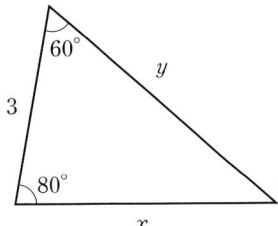

1. In the figure below, $z>95$ and $x=y+15$. If y is an integer, what is the greatest possible value of y?

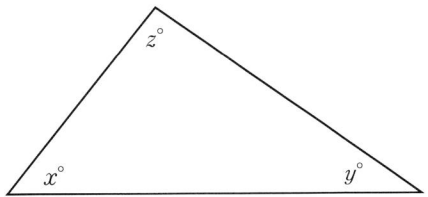

A) 70

B) 68

C) 35

D) 34

2. In the figure below, $\overline{CP}=\sqrt{3}$. What is the length of AB?

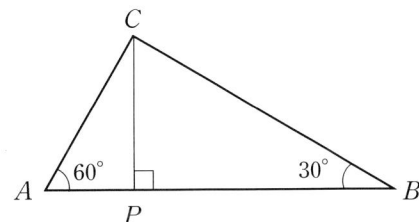

3. In the figure below, points O, A, B, C are equally spaced on line *l* and points O, P, Q, R are equally spaced on line *m*. If $\overline{OC}=12$, $\overline{OR}=15$, and $\overline{AP}=3$, what is the perimeter of the quadrilateral BCRQ?

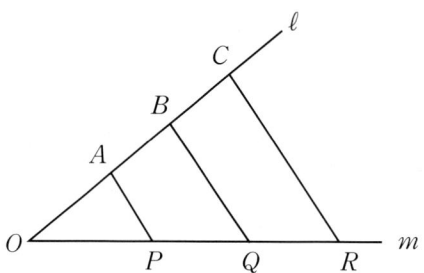

A) 23

B) 24

C) 26

D) 27

4. In the figure below, all of the following are isosceles triangles EXCEPT

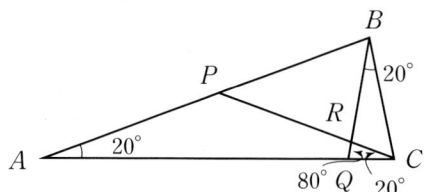

A) △APC

B) △CRQ

C) △ABC

D) △BPC

5. If the perimeter of the triangle below is 30, what is the length of the longest side?

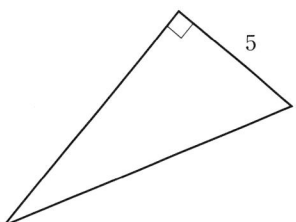

A) 12

B) $5\sqrt{3}$

C) 11

D) 13

6. In the figure below, $\triangle$PQR is an isosceles triangle and $\triangle$XYZ is an equilateral triangle. If $\angle$PQR is 30 degrees and $\angle$QXZ is 60 degrees, what is the degree measure of $\angle$XYP?

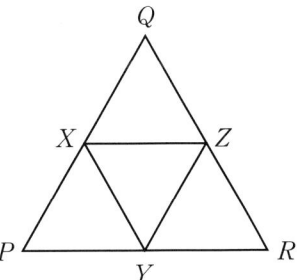

A) 30

B) 35

C) 45

D) 50

Polygons

Angles

1) <u>Sum of the Interior Angles</u> : $(n-2) \times 180$ where n is the number of sides.

2) <u>Sum of the Exterior Angles</u> : $360°$

3) <u>Regular Polygon</u> (regular $n-$polygon)

Each exterior angle $= \dfrac{360°}{n}$

Each interior angle $= 180° - \dfrac{360°}{n}$

A. Terms

1) <u>Acute</u> : any angles greater than $0°$ and smaller than $90°$

2) <u>Obtuse</u> : any angle greater than $90°$ and smaller than $180°$

3) <u>Right</u> : an angle of $90°$

4) <u>Adjacent Angles</u> : angles placed next to each other that share a common vertex/side, but do not overlap

B. Intersecting Lines

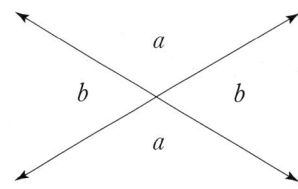

1) Opposite angles are equal in measure

2) The sum of Adjacent Angles is $180°$

C. Parallel Lines

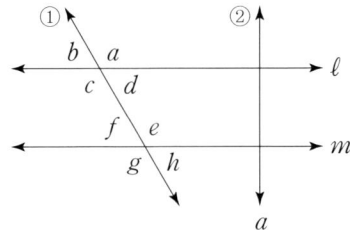

1) $\angle a = \angle c = \angle e = \angle g$
   $\angle b = \angle d = \angle f = \angle h$

2) When line n passes through either one of two parallel lines ℓ and m perpendicularly, then line n passes through the other line perpendicularly as well. (Since n and ℓ are vertical to each other, m and n are vertical as well.)

D. Exterior Angles

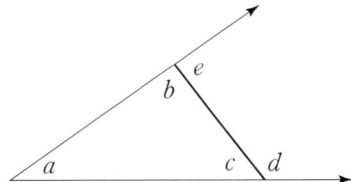

1) $\angle a + \angle b = 180 - \angle c = \angle d$

2) $\angle a + \angle c = 180 - \angle b = \angle e$

Special Types of Polygons

A. Parallelogram : a quadrilateral whose opposite sides are parallel

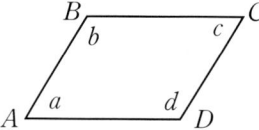

* Properties : (i) AB=CD, BC=AD
                  (ii) $a=c, b=d$
                  (iii) $a+b=b+c=c+d=d+a$
                  (iv) each diagonal cuts the other diagonal in half

B. Rectangle : quadrilateral with four right angles

* Properties : (i) a rectangle is a type of parallelogram, so it has the properties of a parallelogram
                  (ii) its two diagonals have the same length

C. Rhombus : a parallelogram with four equal sides

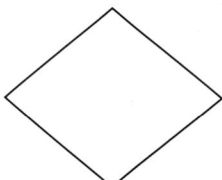

*Properties : (i) has all the properties of a parallelogram
                 (ii) its two diagonals are perpendicular to each other

D. Square : a parallelogram with four equal sides and four right angles

* Properties : (i) has all the properties of a parallelogram

            (ii) has all the properties of a rectangle and a rhombus

Exercise

1. Find the values of a,b,c,d,and e if $\ell \parallel m$.

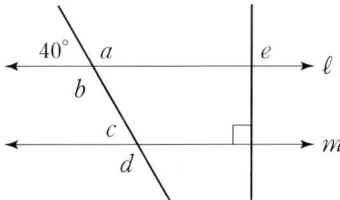

Questions 2 and 3 refer to the following regular polygon.

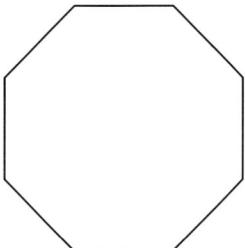

2. What is the sum of the interior angles of the given polygon?

3. What is the value of each exterior angle of the given polygon?

4. If □ABCD is a parallelogram, what is the value of $a+b$?

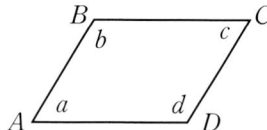

5. If □ABCD is a rhombus, what is the value of a?

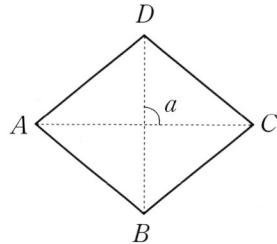

6. If □ABCD is a rectangle and the length of $\overline{AC}$ is 6, what is the length of $\overline{DE}$?

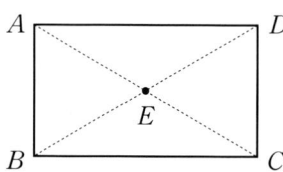

1. In the figure below, point O is the intersection of the line segments $\overline{AC}$ and $\overline{BE}$. If $\overline{OD}$ bisects $\angle EOC$ and $x=140$, what is the value of y?

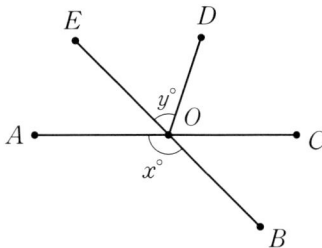

2. In the figure below, ℓ and m are parallel and $2b=e$. Which of the following is equal to c?

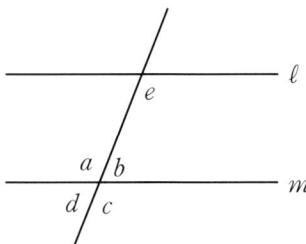

A) $a+b$

B) $a-b$

C) $3b-d$

D) $2b+d$

3. In the figure below, if $z=70$, what is the value of $3y-3x$?

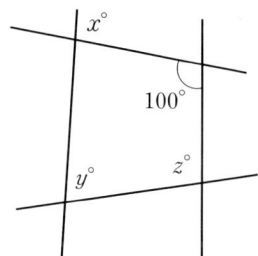

A) 0

B) 10

C) 15

D) 30

4. In the hexagon below, what is the sum of x, y, z, and w?

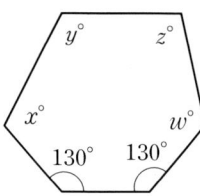

5. In the figure below, if $\square$ABCD is a trapezoid and $h=2\sqrt{3}$, what is the length of $\overline{AB}$?

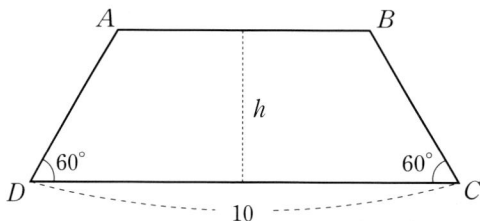

6. A large solid cube is made using identical small white cubes. All six faces of the large cube are painted yellow. If exactly 125 of the small cubes making up the large cube have no yellow paint on them, how many small cubes were used to make the large cube?

III Perimeter and Area

A. Rectangle

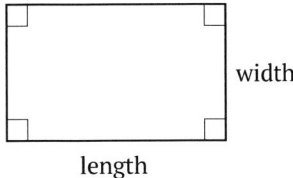

1) <u>Perimeter</u>$=2\times(\text{length}+\text{width})$

2) <u>Area</u>$=\text{length}\times\text{width}$

B. Parallelogram

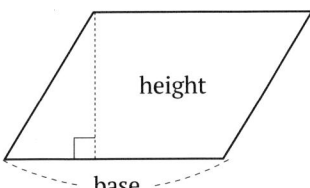

1) <u>Area</u>$=\text{base}\times\text{height}$

C. Rhombus

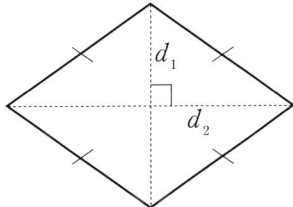

1) <u>Area</u>$=\dfrac{(\text{diagonal}_1\times\text{diagonal}_2)}{2}$

D. Square

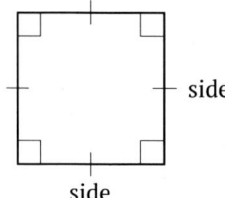

1) $\underline{\text{Area}} = \text{side} \times \text{side} = \dfrac{(\text{diagonal})^2}{2}$

E. Triangle

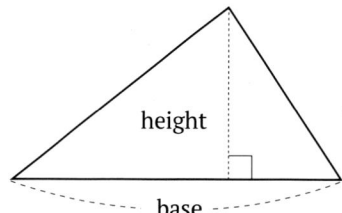

1) $\underline{\text{Area}} = \dfrac{1}{2}(\text{height} \times \text{base})$

F. Trapezoid

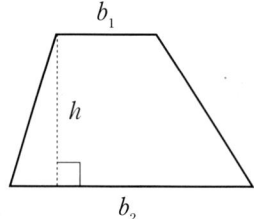

1) $\underline{\text{Area}} = \text{height} \times \dfrac{b_1 + b_2}{2}$

1. If □ABCD is a rhombus, what is the area of □ABCD?

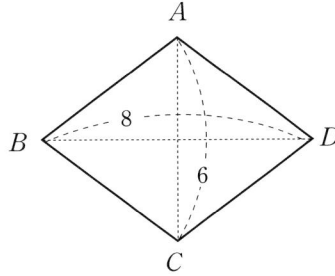

2. If □ABCD is a trapezoid, what is the area of □ABCD?

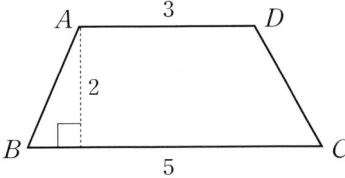

1. The area of the shaded region in the rectangle □ABCD is 160. What is the perimeter of △EFG?

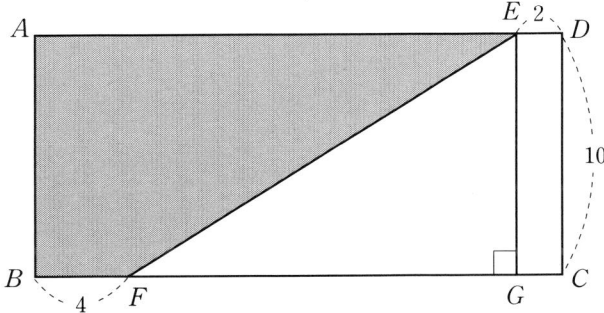

2. In the figure below, the base of the four regular hexagons lie alongside each other on a straight line. What is the distance between point A and point B?

A) 12

B) 21

C) 18

D) $10\sqrt{3}$

3. A piece of land is surrounded by a rectangular fence. If the length of the rectangle created by the fence is 60 m and the area of the land is 300 m^2, what is the total perimeter of the fence?

4. In the figure below, squares A, B, and C are constructed on each side of the right triangle. If the area of A and B are 25 and 144 each, what is the perimeter of the right triangle?

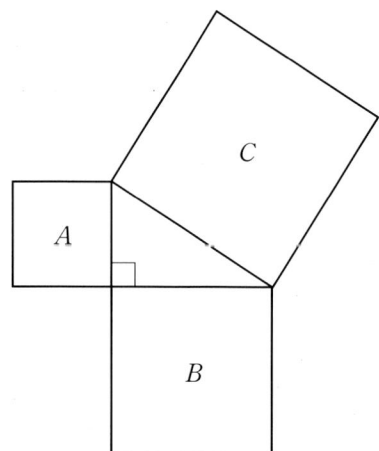

A) 17

B) 25

C) 30

D) 60

5. In the cone below, the radius of the circular base is 3 inches and the length of AB is 12 inches. If a piece of string is looped around the side of the cone as shown above from point B to point M, where M is the midpoint of AB, what is the length of the string?

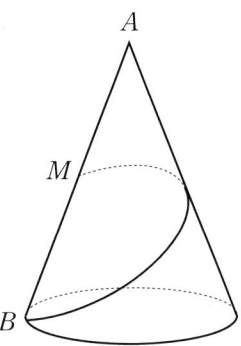

A) $3\sqrt{5}$

B) $6\sqrt{5}$

C) 18

D) 6π

Circles

A. Circles : the locus of all points that are at an equal distance (Radius) from the center

1) Radius : the distance from the center of a circle to its edge (or that line segment itself)

2) Chord : a line segment on the interior of a circle with both its endpoints lying on its edges

3) Diameter : a Chord that passes through the center of a circle

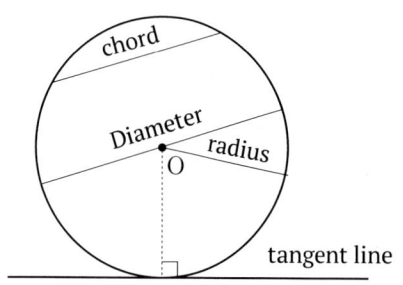 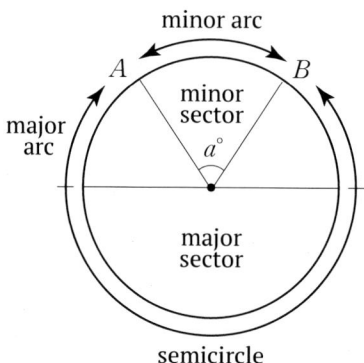

4) Arc : a part of the Circumference of a circle

5) Sector : a pie−shaped part of a circle bounded by an Arc and two Radii

6) Tangent Line : when a line is Tangent to a circle, that line touches the circle at exactly one point
(A line segment that connects the center of a circle and a tangential point is always perpendicular to a Tangent Line)

B. Circumference and Area

1) Circumference : $2\pi \times \text{radius}$

2) Arc Length : $2\pi \times \text{radius} \times \dfrac{\text{degree of arc}}{360}$

3) Area of a Circle : $\pi \times (\text{radius})^2$

4) Area of a Sector : $\pi \times (\text{radius})^2 \times \dfrac{\text{degree of arc}}{360}$

C. Circles with Polygons

1) <u>Inscribed Rectangles</u> : the diagonal of a rectangle becomes the diameter of a circle

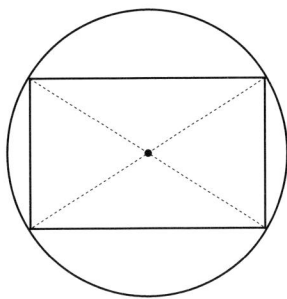

2) <u>Inscribed Circles</u> : the length of one side of a square = the diameter of a circle

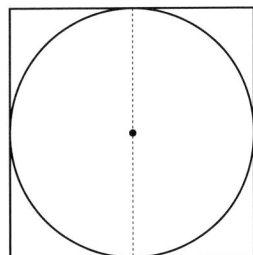

3) <u>Shaded Regions</u> : subtract the area of an unshaded part from the whole

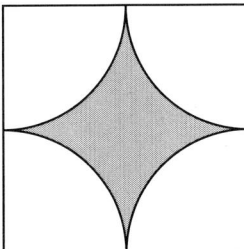

1. If the radius of the circle is 3, what is the area of the minor sector AOC? What is the length of the minor arc $\overset{\frown}{AC}$?

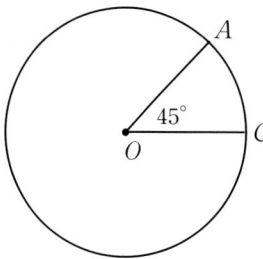

2. If the radius of the circle is 4, what is the length of the diagonal of the rectangle?

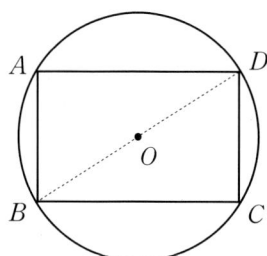

3. If ☐ABCD is a square and the length of its side is 10, what is the radius of the circle?

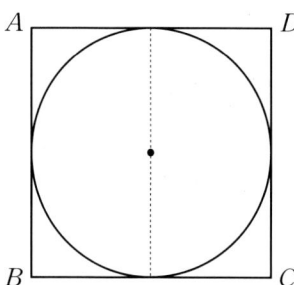

4. If □ABCD is a square whose side is 10, and a, b, c, d are midpoints of $\overline{AB}$, $\overline{BC}$, $\overline{CD}$, $\overline{AD}$, respectively, what is the area of the shaded region?

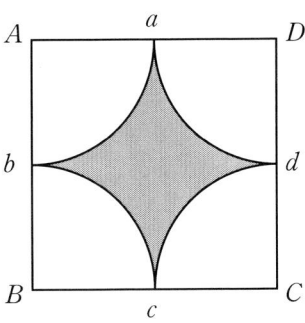

1. In the circle below, O is the center of the circle of radius 6. If M is the midpoint of $\overline{XY}$ and $\angle XOY = 120°$, what is the area of △MOX?

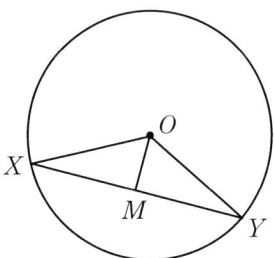

A) $\dfrac{9\sqrt{3}}{2}$

B) $9\sqrt{3}$

C) 9π

D) $\dfrac{9\pi}{2}$

2. Points X, Y, Z, and W are the centers of identical circles with radii of r. What is the perimeter of the rectangle □ABCD in terms of r?

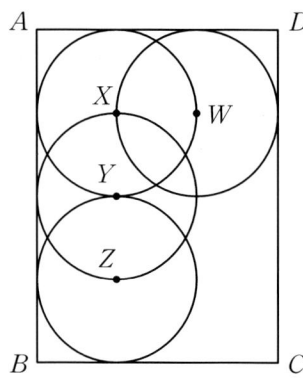

3. In the circle below, $\overline{AB}$, $\overline{CD}$, and $\overline{EF}$ are diameters. If the area of the shaded sector is $\frac{1}{10}$ of the area of the circle, what is the value of x?

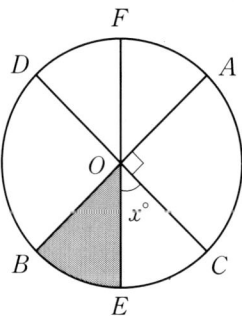

4. In the figure below, □ABCD is a square with a side length of 8. Semicircles are constructed by using the sides of the square as their diameters. If M and N are midpoints of $\overline{BC}$ and $\overline{AD}$, what is the total length of the darkened outline of the figure?

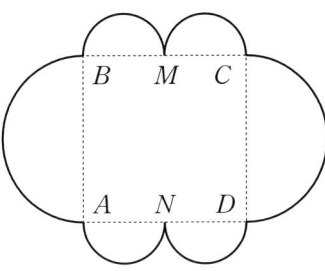

A) 12π

B) 14π

C) 16π

D) 18π

5. In the figure below, $\overset{\frown}{XY}$ is the arc of a circle with center O. If the length of arc $\overset{\frown}{XY}$ is 10π, what is the area of sector XOY?

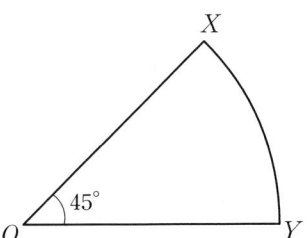

A) 144π

B) 169π

C) 196π

D) 200π

6. In the figure below, six small circles of equal radius are inside a large circle so that they are tangent to the large circle and three other small circles. A seventh circle with the same radius is tangent to each of the six small circles. If O is the center of the large circle, the area of the shaded region is how many times the area of one of the small circles?

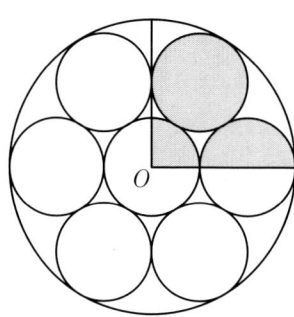

7. In the figure below, a square with side length 16 is divided into 16 squares. If each dot represents the center of the four corner squares, what is the area of the circle (not shown) that passes through the four dots?

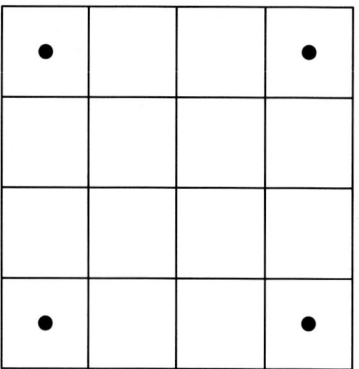

A) $36\sqrt{2}\pi$

B) 36π

C) 72π

D) $72\sqrt{2}\pi$

V   **Solids**

A. Rectangular Solid

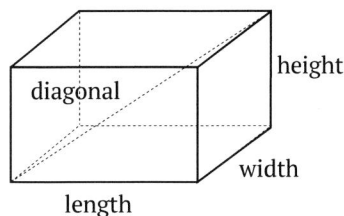

1) <u>Volume</u>＝length×width×height

2) <u>Surface Area</u>＝2×[(length×width)＋(height×width)＋(height×length)]

3) <u>Length of a Diagonal</u>＝$\sqrt{(\text{length})^2+(\text{width})^2+(\text{height})^2}$

B. Cube

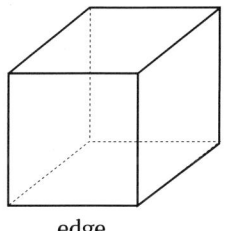

edge

1) <u>Volume</u>＝(edge)^3

2) <u>Surface Area</u>＝6×(edge)^2

C. Cylinder

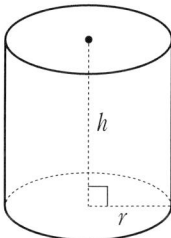

1) <u>Volume</u>＝π×(radius)^2×height

2) <u>Surface Area</u>＝2×[π×(radius)^2]＋[height×(2×π×radius)]

D. Cone

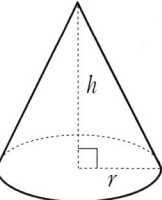

1) <u>Volume</u> $= \dfrac{1}{3} \times [\pi \times (\text{radius})^2 \times \text{height}]$

◢ **Exercise**

1. Find the length of the diagonal.

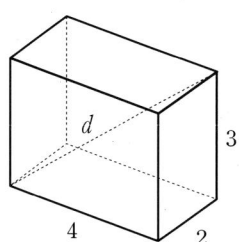

2. Find the volume and surface area of the cube.

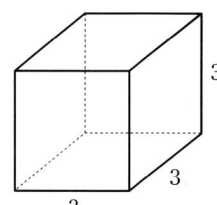

3. Find the volume and surface area of the cylinder.

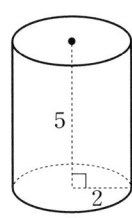

4. Find the volume of the cone.

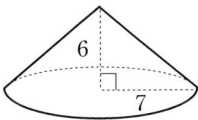

1. In the cube below, X and Y are the midpoints of two of the edges. If the length of each edge is 6, what is the length of the line segment $\overline{XY}$?

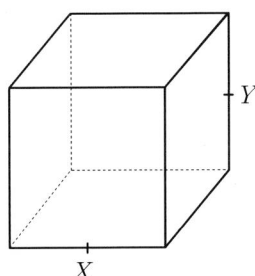

2. What is the surface area of a cube if its volume is 216 cubic inches?

VI Coordinate Geometry

A. Basic Formulas

1) <u>Distance</u> : the Distance between $(x_1, \; y_1)$ and $(x_2, \; y_2)$ is $\sqrt{(x_2-x_1)^2+(y_2-y_1)^2}$

2) <u>Midpoint</u> : the Midpoint of a line that has $(x_1, \; y_1)$ and $(x_2, \; y_2)$ as endpoints is $\left(\dfrac{x_1+x_2}{2}, \; \dfrac{y_1+y_2}{2} \right)$

B. Finding the Slope of a Line

1) <u>Slope</u> : the change in y for a unit change in x along the line

2) <u>Slope Formula</u> : $\dfrac{y_2-y_1}{x_2-x_1}$ for the Slope of a line that passes through $(x_1, \; y_1)$ and $(x_2, \; y_2)$

3) <u>Properties</u>

   (i) Horizontal Line : Slope is zero

   (ii) Vertical Line : Slope is not defined

   (iii) "two different lines never intersect"="the lines are parallel"="they have the same slope and different y-intercepts"

   (iv) Perpendicular Lines=product of their Slopes is -1

4) <u>Equation of a Line</u>: $y=mx+b$

   (i) m is the slope, b is the y-intercept (value of y when $x-0$)

     * If you know the two points that a line passes through, or if you know one point and its slope, you can get the equation.

1. Find the distance between $(2, -1)$ and $(-3, 4)$.

2. If $A = (3, 2)$ and $B = (1, 0)$, find the midpoint of $\overline{AB}$.

3. Find the slope of a line that passes through $(3, 2)$ and $(5, 4)$.

4. Find the equation of a line that passes through $(4, 2)$ and $(10, 5)$.

SAT Questions

1. If the points $A(2, 6)$ and $B(-1, 6)$ and $C(2, 2)$ are vertices of a triangle, what is the area of the triangle?

2. In the figure below, OABC, ADEF, and DGHI are squares with sides of length 9, 3, and 6, respectively. What is the difference between the slopes of line segments $\overline{OI}$ and $\overline{OH}$?

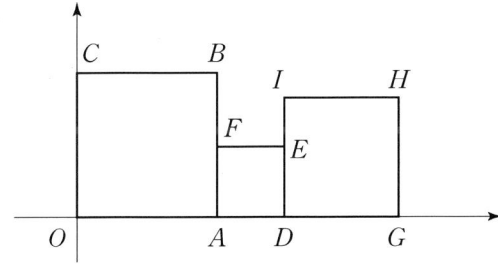

3. On the linear scales below, 20 and 120 on the X-scale corresponds to 80 and 140, respectively, on the Y-scale. Which of the following linear equations can be used to convert an X-scale value to a Y-scale value?

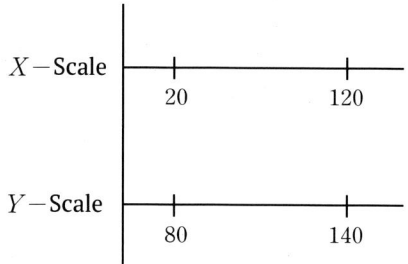

A) $Y=X+20$

B) $Y=1.2X+12$

C) $Y=0.6X+68$

D) $Y=X+60$

VII   Circle Equation

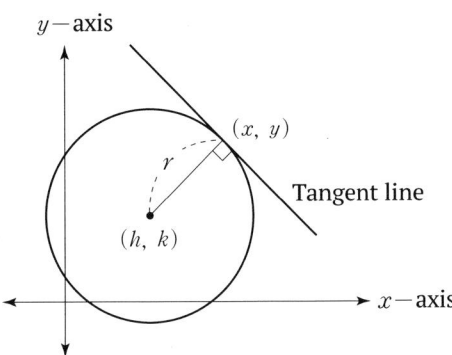

A. Equation

1) On a coordinate plane, the equation of a circle is :

$$(x-h)^2+(y-k)^2=r^2$$

2) Sometimes it is necessary to complete the square of a given expression in order to identify the equation of the circle.

ex) $x^2+4x+y^2-6y-12=0$
$(x^2+4x)+(y^2-6y)-12=0$
$(x^2+4x+4)+(y^2-6y+9)-12-4-9=0$
$(x+2)^2+(y-3)^2-25=0$
$(x+2)^2+(y-3)^2=5^2$

B. Intersection

1) If a line with known equation intersects a circle at any point, simply solve for x and y to identify the points of intersections.

C. Tangent

1) Perpendicular : a line segment drawn from the center of a circle to the point at which the tangent meets the circumference is Perpendicular to the tangent

2) Slopes : when two lines are Perpendicular to each other, the product of their Slopes is -1

1. What is the equation of a circle with center $(-2,\ 3)$ and radius 6?

2. A circle with its center at the origin has point A $(3,\ 4)$ on its circumference. What is the radius of the circle?

SAT Questions

1. The slope of line l is tangent to a circle at point $(1,\ 5)$. Given that the slope of the line is $\frac{2}{5}$ and that the circle is centered at $(s,\ 2)$, find the value of s.

2. A circle with a known radius of 5 has a circumference that passes through the points $(1,-1)$. The y-coordinate of the center of the circle is 3. Given that the x-coordinate is positive, find the value of the center's x-coordinate.

3. The center of circle A lies on the x-axis where $x=-1$. A point on the circumference also lies on the x-axis where $x=3$. Given that a line is tangent to the circle at point $(1, \, p)$, at which point does the tangent intersect the x-axis?

A) $(4, \, 0)$

B) $\left(\dfrac{17}{4}, \, 0\right)$

C) $(7, \, 0)$

D) $\left(\dfrac{19}{3}, \, 0\right)$

4. A circle is known to have diameter $\overline{AB}$ with $A(7,-2)$ and $B(-1, \, 10)$ being points on the circumference. Rachel wants to construct an equation based on the coordinates $(a, \, b)$ also found on the circumference. Which of the following options shows the correct equation?

A) $(a-4)^2+(b-6)^2=208$

B) $(a-4)^2+(b+6)^2=104$

C) $(a-3)^2-(b-4)^2=104$

D) $(a-3)^2+(b-4)^2=52$

VIII   Trigonometry

A. Radians

1) The radian (θ) is a different way to measure the angle other than degrees $(°)$.

2) <u>Formulas</u> : Arc length $(l)=r\theta$

$$\text{Area of sector}=\frac{1}{2}r^2\theta=\frac{1}{2}rl$$

3) <u>Conversion</u> : $180°=\pi$ rad

$$360°=2\pi \text{ rad}$$

$$1 \text{ rad}=\frac{180°}{\pi}$$

ex) In rad, $72°=\dfrac{72°}{180}\times\pi$ rad

$$=1.257 \text{ rad}$$

B. Trigonometry

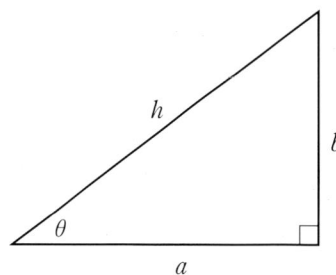

1) <u>Formulas</u> :

$$\sin\theta=\frac{b}{h}$$

$$\cos\theta=\frac{a}{h}$$

$$\tan\theta=\frac{b}{a}$$

2) Special Angles :

θ	Sine	Cosine	Tangent
0°	0	1	0
30°	$\dfrac{1}{2}$	$\dfrac{\sqrt{3}}{2}$	$\dfrac{1}{\sqrt{3}}$
45°	$\dfrac{1}{\sqrt{2}}$	$\dfrac{1}{\sqrt{2}}$	1
60°	$\dfrac{\sqrt{3}}{2}$	$\dfrac{1}{2}$	$\sqrt{3}$
90°	1	0	Not defined

3) Other Angles

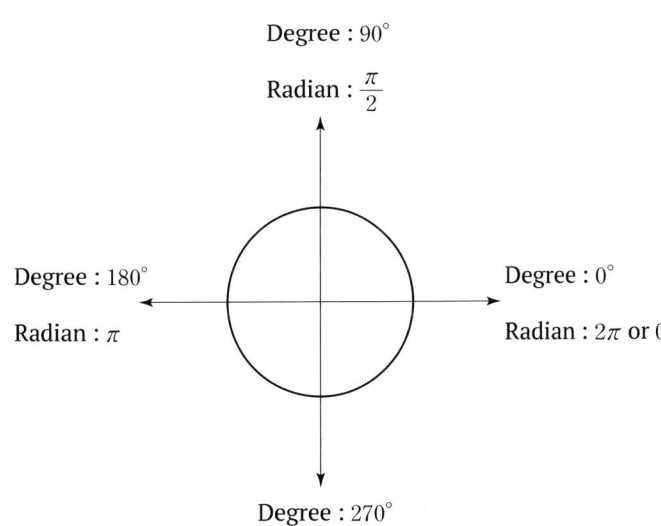

Degree : 90°
Radian : $\dfrac{\pi}{2}$

Degree : 180°
Radian : π

Degree : 0°
Radian : 2π or 0

Degree : 270°
Radian : $\dfrac{3\pi}{2}$

0° to 90° : all is positive

90° to 180° : $\sin x$ is positive, $\cos x$ and $\tan x$ are negative

180° to 270° : $\tan x$ is positive, $\sin x$ and $\cos x$ are negative

270° to 360° : $\cos x$ is positive, $\sin x$ and $\tan x$ are negative

4) Graphs

(ⅰ) **Sine Graph** $(y=\sin x)$

Amplitude : 1

Period : 2π

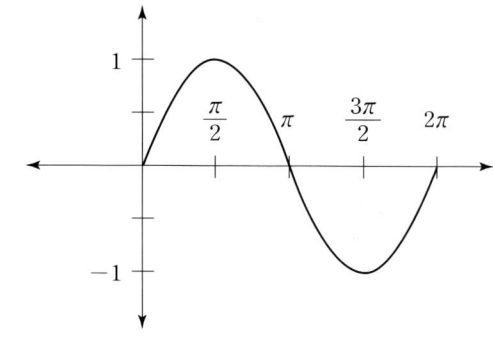

(ⅱ) **Cosine Graph** $(y=\cos x)$

Amplitude : 1

Period : 2π

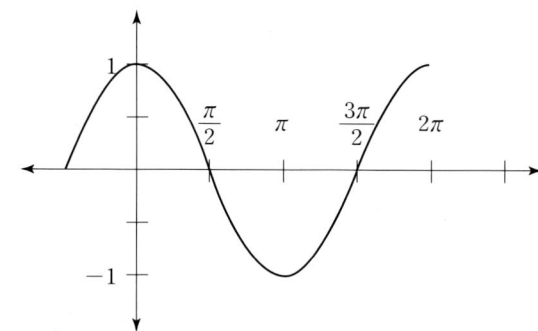

(ⅲ) **Tangent Graph** $(y=\tan x)$

Amplitude : $-\infty$ to ∞

Period : π

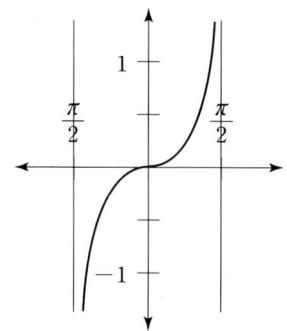

Exercise

1. What is $200°$ in radians?

2. In which quadrant are both $\cos x$ and $\sin x$ negative?

3. What is the period of $y=\sin x$?

SAT Questions

1. In a right triangle, an angle measures x, where $\sin x=\dfrac{5}{13}$. What is $\cos (90°-x)$?

2. An isosceles right triangle ABC and $<$ B = 90° If the area of the right triangle was doubled, what is the value of $\tan A$?

Complex Numbers

A. Complex Numbers : numbers that can be expressed in the form of $a+bi$, where a and b are Real Numbers, and i is the Imaginary Unit

1) Imaginary Unit i : number that satisfies $i^2=-1$

2) For all $a>0$, $\sqrt{-a}=\sqrt{a}\,i$

   Therefore, the square roots of $-a$ are $\pm\sqrt{-a}=\pm\sqrt{a}\,i$

3) Equality of Complex Numbers

   $a+bi=0 \iff a=0,\ b=0$

   $a+bi=c+di \iff a=c,\ b=d$

   $(a, b, c,$ and d are Real Numbers$)$

4) Complex Number Operations

   If a, b, c, and d are Real Numbers,

   A. If $a<0,\ b<0$, then $\sqrt{a}\cdot\sqrt{b}=-\sqrt{ab}$

   B. If $a>0,\ b<0$, then $\dfrac{\sqrt{a}}{\sqrt{b}}=-\sqrt{\dfrac{a}{b}}\,i$

   C. $(a+bi)+(c+di)=(a+c)+(b+d)i$

   D. $(a+bi)-(c+di)=(a-c)+(b-d)i$

   E. $(a+bi)(c+di)=(ac-bd)+(ad+bc)i$

   F. $\dfrac{a+bi}{c+di}=\dfrac{a+bi}{c+di}\cdot\dfrac{c-di}{c-di}=\dfrac{ac+bd}{c^2+d^2}+\dfrac{bc-ad}{c^2+d^2}i\ \ (c+di\neq0)$

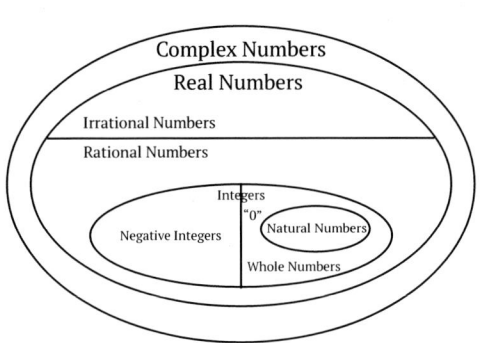

SAT Questions

1. What's the value of $(4+i)-(3-8i)$? $(i^2=-1)$

2. What's the value of $3+7i-(2-3i)\times i$? $(i^2=-1)$

3. What is the value of $(1+i)(2-i)(1+2i)$? $(i^2=-1)$

Extra Topics

A. Rewriting Expressions

There are several SAT questions that ask you to simply rewrite an existing expression. Skills involved in solving these problems include but are not limited to: expansion, grouping by common factors, equalizing denominators. The patterns involved with them aren't very varied so the more you solve them, the more you will get used to them.

B. Designing & Interpreting Experiments

1) Types of Studies
   (i) Observational Study: the investigator observes subjects and measures the possible changes in the variables without assigning treatments to the subjects

   (ii) Controlled Experiment: the investigator separates subjects into a control group that does not receive any treatment and an experimental group that receives a treatment and observes and measures the possible changes in the variables

   (iii) Sample Survey: the investigator uses methods such as a questionnaire or an interview to obtain data from a sample in order to estimate a population parameter of interest

2) Interpreting Data
   Back in Chapter 2, you learned basic skills involved with the analysis of tables and graphs. Those examples mostly asked you to estimate or calculate some characteristics of the sample or the population. However, another focus of gathering data from surveys and experiments is to investigate relationships between variables. Researchers use the data to draw conclusions about cause and effect. The credibility of the conclusion depends mainly on two factors: random sampling and random assignment.

   (i) Random Sampling: a group of subjects (a sample) is chosen randomly from a larger group (a population). Each individual has the same probability of being selected for the sample. Random sampling ensures that the result from the experiment can be appropriately generalized to the entire population.

   (ii) Random Assignment: individuals in the sample are randomly assigned to different treatments. Each treatment has the same probability of being assigned to an individual. Random assignment ensures that the treatment groups are relatively equivalent at the beginning of the experiment apart from the treatment they receive. Thus, it can be appropriate to draw conclusions about the cause and effect between the variables.

The following table summarizes the results of random sampling and assignment:

	Random Sampling	Non-random Sampling
Random Assignment	Result can be appropriately generalized to the population. Conclusion about cause and effect can be appropriately drawn.	Result cannot be appropriately generalized to the population. Conclusion about cause and effect can be appropriately drawn.
Non-random Assignment	Result can be appropriately generalized to the population. Conclusion about cause and effect cannot be appropriately drawn.	Result cannot be appropriately generalized to the population. Conclusion about cause and effect cannot be appropriately drawn.

1. $(4mn^3)^2 - (x-7) + \sqrt{49l^6}$

   Which of the following is equivalent to the expression above?

   A) $-(x-7) + (7l^3) + (4mn^6)$

   B) $-(x-7) + (7l^3) + (16m^2n^6)$

   C) $(16m^2n^6) - (7-x) + (7l^3)$

   D) $(7l^6) - (x-7) + (16m^2n^6)$

2. $\dfrac{3x}{5x+15} + \dfrac{x+4}{x^2+3x}$

   Which expression is equivalent to the above sum?

   A) $\dfrac{3x^2+5x+20}{5x^2+15x}$

   B) $\dfrac{3x^2+12x}{5x^3+30x^2+45x}$

   C) $\dfrac{4x+4}{x^2+8x+15}$

   D) $\dfrac{4x+4}{x+3}$

3. $\dfrac{45p^2q^4r^5+15p^5q^3r^6-25p^3q^5r^2}{5p^2q^3r^4}$

Which expressions is equivalent to the above for all $p>1$, $q>1$, and $r>1$?

A) $9pqr^3+3pr^2-5q$

B) $9q+3r^4-5p$

C) $\dfrac{9qr+3p^2r-5pq}{r^2}$

D) $\dfrac{9qr^3+3p^3r^4-5pq^2}{r^2}$

4. The expression $(x^2+t^2)^2$ can be written as $(1+a-b)x^4+2bx^2+ab$ where t, a, and b are constants. What is one possible value of a?

A) 1

B) t

C) t^2

D) t^4

5. The school swimming pool allows registered members to enter the pool one hour before opening time. The coach for the school swimming team found out that more than three quarters of the team was made up of students who were registered members of the swimming pool. Which of the following is an appropriate conclusion?

A) Registered members of the swimming pool perform better at athletics than non−registered students.

B) Registered members of the swimming pool are better at swimming than non-registered students.

C) Registering for the swimming pool was the cause of admission into the school swimming team.

D) No conclusion about cause and effect can be made regarding students in the school swimming team who registered for the swimming pool and their performance in the team.

6. A scientist wants to investigate the relationship between level of adrenaline in a mouse's body and the mouse's reaction time by randomly injecting small amount of adrenaline into some mouse and water into others and then observing how fast different treatment groups react to the sound of a cat's meow from behind them. Which of the following is the best description of the research design for this study?

A) Observational study
B) Sample survey
C) Controlled experiment
D) None of the above

7. A researcher conducted a survey to determine the average amount of time high school students in a certain large city spend playing computer games. The researcher asked 300 students who attended a local high school for boys, and 33 students refused to respond. Which of the following factors makes it least likely that a reliable conclusion can be drawn about the average time spent on computer games for all high school students in the city?

A) Sample size
B) Population size
C) The number of people who refused to respond
D) Where the survey was given

Question Answers & Explanations

Chapter 1. Heart of Algebra

1-1   Linear Equations/Inequalities

Example Questions 1

1. Linear Equations/Inequalities

$4a+8=24$

$4a=24-8=16$

$a=4$

$\therefore\ 8a-9=32-9=23$

Therefore, the answer is (C).

2. Linear Equations/Inequalities

$\dfrac{3}{a}=\dfrac{6}{a+15}$

$3(a+15)=6a$

$3a+45=6a$

$3a=45$

$\therefore\ a=15$

Therefore, $\dfrac{a}{3}=\dfrac{15}{3}=5$

Therefore, the answer is {B).

3. Linear Equations/Inequalities

$\left(\dfrac{5}{6}a-\dfrac{1}{6}a=\dfrac{1}{2}+\dfrac{1}{6}\right)\times 6$

$5a-a=3+1$

$4a=4$

$\therefore\ a=1$

Therefore, the answer is 1.

Example Questions 2

1. Linear Equations/Inequalities

$4x-2\geq 6\ \rightarrow\ ①$

$①\div 2:$

$2x-1\geq 3$

$\therefore\ 2x+3\geq 7$

Therefore, the answer is 7.

2. Linear Equations/Inequalities

$2x+7+5(x-2)\geq 6x+7$

$2x+7+5x-10\geq 6x+7$

$7x-3\geq 6x+7$

$\therefore\ x\geq 10$

Therefore, the answer is (C).

3. Linear Equations/Inequalities

$3a-5\leq 2$

$3a\leq 7$

$6a\leq 14$

$\therefore\ 6a-9\leq 5$

Therefore, the answer is (B).

SAT Questions

1. Linear Equations/Inequalities

$\dfrac{2x-y}{2y}=\dfrac{2}{5}$

$5(2x-y)=4y$

$10x-5y=4y$

$10x=9y$

$\therefore\ \dfrac{x}{y}=\dfrac{9}{10}$

Therefore, the answer is (B).

2. Linear Equations/Inequalities

$\dfrac{a+2}{a-2}=5$

$a+2=5(a-2)$

$a+2=5a-10$

$4a=12$

$\therefore\ a=3$

Therefore the answer is (A).

3. Linear Equations/Inequalities

$$\frac{7}{r}=\frac{3}{r+12}$$

$$7(r+12)=3r$$

$$7r+84=3r$$

$$4r=-84$$

$$\therefore r=-21$$

$$\frac{r}{7}=-3$$

Therefore, the answer is (A).

4. Linear Equations/Inequalities

$$6x-12\geq 9$$

$$6x\geq 21$$

$$2x\geq 7$$

$$\therefore 2x-9\geq -2$$

Therefore, the answer is (B).

5. Linear Equations/Inequalities

$$6y-(14-2y)=a(4y-7)$$

$$6y-14+2y=4ay-7a$$

$$(8-4a)y=14-7a$$

For the equation to have infinitely many solutions,

$8-4a$ and $14-7a$ must be 0.

Both $8-4a$ and $14-7a$ is 0 when $a=2$.

Therefore, the answer is {C}

6. Linear Equations/Inequalities

$$2(x-1)+2x=\frac{1}{4}(16x-20)+3$$

$$2x-2+2x=4x-5+3$$

$$4x-2=4x-2$$

$$\therefore x=x$$

which means there are infinitely many values for this equation.

Therefore, the answer is (D).

7. Linear Equations/Inequalities

$$\frac{n-5}{n+5}=6$$

$$n-5=6(n+5)$$

$$n-5=6n+30$$

$$5n=-35$$

$$\therefore n=-7$$

Therefore, the answer is (A).

8. Linear Equations/Inequalities

$$6x+7\geq 3(ax+2)$$

$$6x+7\geq 3ax+6$$

$$(6-3a)x\geq -1$$

In order for there to be infinitely many solutions to the inequality above,

$$6-3a=0$$

$$\therefore a=2$$

Therefore, the answer is (C).

9. Linear Equations/Inequalities

$$\frac{1}{3}(3y)+4(y-2)=5(y-2)+7$$

$$y+4y-8=5y-10+7$$

$$5y-8=5y-3$$

$$5y-5y=5$$

$$\therefore 0\times y=5$$

Therefore, there is no value of y where this equation is true.

Therefore, the answer is (C).

10. Linear Equations/Inequalities

$$2(y+1)=\frac{x}{3}+2$$

$$2y+2=\frac{x}{3}+2$$

$$2y=\frac{x}{3}$$

$$\therefore \frac{x}{y}=6$$

Therefore, the answer is (C).

11. Linear Equations/Inequalities

$$\frac{2(r+2)-7}{4}=\frac{14-(r+2)}{5}$$

$$\frac{2r+4-7}{4}=\frac{14-r-2}{5}$$

$$\frac{2r-3}{4}=\frac{12-r}{5}$$

$$5(2r-3)=4(12-r)$$

$$10r-15=48-4r$$

$$14r=63$$

$$\therefore\ r=\frac{9}{2}(=4.5)$$

Therefore, the answer is (B).

12. Linear Equations/Inequalities

$$\frac{2x+7}{3}=\frac{3x+9}{4}$$

$$4(2x+7)=3(3x+9)$$

$$8x+28=9x+27$$

$$\therefore\ x=1$$

Therefore, the answer is (C).

13. Linear Equations/Inequalities

In the given equation $x=ay$, $x=56$ when $y=4$.

$$56=4a$$

$$a=14$$

$$\therefore\ x=14y$$

Therefore, when $y=3$,

$$x=14\times3=42$$

Therefore, the answer is (D).

14. Linear Equations/Inequalities

$$3x+11-9(x+3)=5x-27$$

$$3x+11-9x-27=5x-27$$

$$-6x+11=5x$$

$$11x=11$$

$$\therefore\ x=1$$

Therefore, the answer is (A).

15. Linear Equations/Inequalities

$$\frac{3a+2}{5}=\frac{2a-8}{4}$$

$$4(3a+2)=5(2a-8)$$

$$12a+8=10a-40$$

$$2a=-48$$

$$\therefore\ a=-24$$

Therefore, the answer is (B).

16. Linear Equations/Inequalities

$$\frac{q}{3p}=7$$

$$q=21p$$

$$\therefore\ \frac{2q}{3p}=\frac{2(21p)}{3p}=14$$

Therefore, the answer is (C).

17. Linear Equations/Inequalities

$$\frac{2k}{3r}=5$$

$$2k=15r$$

$$\therefore\ \frac{15r}{2k}=\frac{15r}{15r}=1$$

Therefore, the answer is (B).

18. Linear Equations/Inequalities

$$9x-4\le2x+11$$

$$7x\le15$$

$$x\le\frac{15}{7}\approx2.14$$

Therefore, the answer is (B).

1-2　System of Equations/Inequalities

Example Questions 1

1. System of Equations/Inequalities

$2a+b=2 \rightarrow$ ①

$4a-3b=19 \rightarrow$ ②

②$-$①$\times 2$:

$-5b=15$

$b=-3$

Plug $b=-3$ into ①

$2a-3=2$

$2a=5$

$a=\dfrac{5}{2}=2.5$

$\therefore (a,\ b)=(2.5,\ -3)$

Therefore, the answer is (B).

2. System of Equations/Inequalities

From the second equation, $y=9x$

Substitute into the first equation,

$45x-27=173+9x$

$36x=200$

$9x=50$

$\therefore y=50$

Therefore, the answer is 50.

3. System of Equations/Inequalities

$5p-rq=3 \rightarrow$ ①

$3p-5q=7 \rightarrow$ ②

①$\times 3$: $15p-3rq=9$

②$\times 5$: $15p-25q=35$

①$\times 3-$②$\times 5$: $(3-r+25)q=-26$

For the system of equations to have no solution,

$-3r+25=0$

$3r=25$

$\therefore r=\dfrac{25}{3}$

Therefore, the answer is (B).

4. System of Equations/Inequalities

$5y-p=7y-11 \Rightarrow -2y-p=-11$

$5z-q=7z-11 \Rightarrow -2z-q=-11$

$\therefore -2y-p=-2z-q$

Since it is given that $p=q-2$

$-2y-(q-2)=-2z-q$

$-2y-q+2=-2z-q$

$-2y+2=-2z$

$\therefore y-1=z$

Therefore, the answer is (B).

Example Questions 2

1. System of Equations/Inequalities

Plug the second equation, $y=\dfrac{1}{3}x$, into the first inequality.

$2x+4\le 3\left(\dfrac{1}{3}x\right)$

$2x+4\le x$

$\therefore x\le -4$

Therefore, the answer is (B).

2. System of Equations/Inequalities

If we solve the equation for y,

$2y=\dfrac{1}{2}x+7$

Plug $2y$ into the inequality.

$3x+5\ge 2\left(\dfrac{1}{2}x+7\right)$

$3x+5\ge x+14$

$2x\ge 9$

$x\ge \dfrac{9}{2}=4.5$

$\therefore$ The minimum possible integer value of x is 5.

Therefore, the answer is 5.

1. System of Equations/Inequalities

$kx + ry = 13 \; \rightarrow \; ①$

$3x + 7y = 52$

$① \times 4 : 4kx + 4ry = 52$

For this system of equation to have infinitely many solutions, the coefficients of the two equations must match.

$4k = 3, \; 4r = 7$

$\therefore \; \dfrac{4k}{4r} = \dfrac{k}{r} = \dfrac{3}{7}$

Therefore, the answer is $\dfrac{3}{7}$.

2. System of Equations/Inequalities

$3a - 4b = -3 \; \rightarrow \; ①$

$4a - 3b = -11 \; \rightarrow \; ②$

$① \times 3 : 9a - 12b = -9$

$② \times 4 : 16a - 12b = -44$

$① \times 3 - ② \times 4 :$

$-7a = 35$

$\therefore \; a = -5$

Plug $a = -5$ into $①$

$-15 - 4b = -3$

$4b = -12$

$\therefore \; b = -3$

Therefore, $a + b = -5 - 3 = -8$

Therefore, the answer is (A).

3. System of Equations/Inequalities

$\dfrac{z}{y} = 9$

$z = 9y \; \rightarrow \; ①$

$5(y + 4) = z$

$5y + 20 = z \; \rightarrow \; ②$

$\therefore 5y + 20 = 9y$

$4y = 20$

$y = 5$

From $②$,

$\therefore \; z = 9 \times 5 = 45$

Therefore, the answer is (D).

4. System of Equations/Inequalities

$-2a + 3b = 9 \; \rightarrow \; ①$

$4a + 2b = 6 \; \rightarrow \; ②$

$① \times 2 : -4a + 6b = 18$

$② + ① \times 2 :$

$8b = 24$

$b = 3$

Plug $b = 3$ into $①$

$-2a + 9 = 9$

$\therefore \; a = 0$

Therefore, the answer is 0.

5. System of Equations/Inequalities

$y + 4 = 2x$

$y = 2x - 4$

Plug y into the first equation

$5x + 21 = 6(2x - 4) - 4$

$5x + 21 = 12x - 24 - 4$

$5x + 21 = 12x - 28$

$7x = 49$

$x = 7$

$y = 2 \times 7 - 4 = 10$

$\therefore \; y - x = 10 - 7 = 3$

Therefore, the answer is (A).

6. System of Equations/Inequalities

$3r - a = 5r - 13 \; \Rightarrow \; -2r - a = -13$

$3k - b = 5k - 13 \; \Rightarrow \; -2k - b = -13$

$\therefore \; -2r - a = -2k - b$

Since it is given that $b = a - 6$,

$-2r - a = -2k - (a - 6)$

$-2r - a = -2k - a + 6$

$-2r = -2k + 6$

$2k - 2r = 6$

$k - r = 3$

$\therefore \; k = r + 3$

Therefore, the answer is (B).

7. System of Equations/Inequalities

$y=7x+5-2(x+1)$

$\quad =7x+5-2x-2$

$\quad =5x+3 \; \rightarrow \; ①$

$y=-\dfrac{1}{2}x \; \rightarrow \; ②$

To solve for $(p, \; q)$

$5x+3=-\dfrac{1}{2}x$

$10x+6=-x$

$11x=-6$

$x=p=-\dfrac{6}{11}$

$q=-\dfrac{1}{2}\times-\dfrac{6}{11}=\dfrac{3}{11}$

From ②,

$\therefore \; 11(p+q)=11\left(-\dfrac{6}{11}+\dfrac{3}{11}\right)=-3$

Therefore, the answer is (C).

8. System of Equations/Inequalities

$2b=a+3$

Plug $2b$ into the first equation.

$5a+7=2(2b)+2$

$5a+7=2(a+3)+2$

$5a+7=2a+6+2$

$3a=1$

$\therefore \; 6a=2$

Therefore, the answer is (B).

9. System of Equations/Inequalities

$2y=z+8$

$2y-8=z \; \rightarrow \; ②$

Plug z into the first equation.

$3y+2=5(2y-8)$

$3y+2=10y-40$

$7y=42$

$y=6$

From ②

$\therefore \; z=2\times6-8=4$

Therefore, the answer is (B).

10. System of Equations/Inequalities

From the first equation, $y=5x$

Substitute into the first equation,

$3(x+2)=5x$

$3x+6=5x$

$2x=6$

$x=3$

$\therefore \; y=5\times3=15$

Therefore, the answer is (C).

11. System of Equations/Inequalities

$4x+6=7y \; \rightarrow \; ①$

$8x-3=9y \; \rightarrow \; ②$

$①\times2 : 8x+12=14y$

$①\times2-② :$

$5y=15$

$y=3$

Plug $y=3$ into ①

$4x+6=21$

$4x=15$

$\therefore \; x=\dfrac{15}{4}=3.75$

Therefore, the answer is (B).

12. System of Equations/Inequalities

$2n+3m=4 \; \rightarrow \; ①$

$3n+4m=5 \; \rightarrow \; ②$

$①\times3 : 6n+9m=12$

$②\times2 : 6n+8m=10$

$①\times3-②\times2$

$m=2$

Substitute into ①,

$2n+3\times2=4$

$2n=-2$

$n=-1$

$\therefore \; n+m=-1+2=1$

Therefore, the answer is (C).

13. System of Equations/Inequalities

$5n-r=7n-9 \Rightarrow -2n-r=-9$

$3m-k=5m-9 \Rightarrow -2m-k=-9$

$\therefore -2n-r=-2m-r$

Since it is given that $r=k-4$,

$-2n-(k-4)=-2m-k$

$-2n-k+4=-2m-k$

$-2n+4=-2m$

$4=2n-2m$

$\therefore n-m=2$

Therefore, the answer is (A).

14. System of Equations/Inequalities

Plug $y=\frac{1}{3}x$ into the first equation,

$6(x+3)-10=2\left(\frac{1}{3}x+1\right)$

$6x+8=\frac{2}{3}x+2$

$\frac{16}{3}x=-6$

$x=-6\times\frac{3}{16}=-\frac{9}{8}$

$\therefore 8x=-9$

Therefore, the answer is (A).

15. System of Equations/Inequalities

$6a+5b=26 \rightarrow ①$

$2a-2b=5 \rightarrow ②$

$②\times 3 : 6a-6b=15$

$①-②\times 3 :$

$11b=11$

$b=1$

Plug into ②,

$2a-2=5$

$a=\frac{7}{2}=3.5$

$\therefore (a, b)=(3.5, 1)$

Therefore, the answer is (B).

16. System of Equations/Inequalities

$4n-km=9 \rightarrow ①$

$5n-4m=12 \rightarrow ②$

$①\times 5 : 20n-5km=45$

$②\times 4 : 20n-16m=48$

$①\times 5-②\times 4 :$

$(-5k+16)m=-3$

For this system of equation to have no solution,

$-5k+16=0$

$5k=16$

$\therefore k=\frac{16}{5}=3.2$

Therefore, the answer is (B).

17. System of Equations/Inequalities

Plug the second equation $r=3k+7$ into the first equation.

$2(3k+7)-5=9k$

$6k+14-5=9k$

$3k=9$

$k=3$

$r=3\times 3+7$

$\therefore r=16$

Therefore, the answer is (D).

18. System of Equations/Inequalities

$4y+a=9y-11 \Rightarrow 5y=11+a \rightarrow ①$

$4z+b=9z-11 \Rightarrow 5z=11+b \rightarrow ②$

Since it is given that b=a-5, plug into ②,

$5z=11+(a-5)$

$5z+5=11+a=5y$ (From ①)

$\therefore 5y=5z+5$

$5(y-z)=5$

$\therefore y-z=1$

Therefore, the answer is (C).

19. System of Equations/Inequalities

If we solve the second equation for b,

$b = 2a - 3$

Plug $b = 2a - 3$ into the first equation.

$7a + 9 = 5(2a - 3)$

$7a + 9 = 10a - 15$

$3a = 24$

$a = 8$

$b = 2 \times 8 - 3 = 13$

$\therefore \dfrac{a+b}{3} = \dfrac{21}{3} = 7$

Therefore, the answer is (A).

1-3   Equations/Inequalities in Context

SAT Question

1. Equalities/Inequalities in Context

If the amount of money Jacob has is x, James has $x + 45$ dollars.

Since Jacob and James have a combined amount of 173 dollars,

$x + (x + 45) = 173$

$2x + 45 = 173$

$2x = 128$

$\therefore x = 64$

Therefore, the answer is (B).

2. Equalities/Inequalities in Context

If one serving of Coke is x milliliters, one serving of Iced Tea is $x + 50$ milliliters.

Since 3 Cokes and 4 Iced Teas are 4400 milliliters,

$3x + 4(x + 50) = 4400$

$7x + 200 = 4400$

$7x = 4200$

$x = 600$

$\therefore$ One serving of Iced Tea $= x + 50 = 650$ milliliters.

Therefore, the answer is 650.

3. Equalities/Inequalities in Context

If the number of marbles Andy has is x, the number of marbles Elizabeth has is $x - 32$.

Since Andy and Elizabeth have a combined number of 218 marbles,

$x + (x - 32) = 218$

$2x = 250$

$\therefore x = 125$

Therefore, the answer is (B).

4. Equalities/Inequalities in Context

$5x - 2 = 38$

$5x = 40$

$x = 8$

$\therefore 3x - 9 = 24 - 9 = 15$

Therefore, the answer is (C).

5. Equalities/Inequalities in Context

Troy's tacos: a dollars

Abed's tacos: $a - 2$ dollars

Total payment :

$(a + (a - 2))(1.15) = (2a - 2)(1.15) = 2.30a - 2.30$

Since Troy and Abed evenly divided the bill in two,

$\dfrac{2.30a - 2.30}{2} = 1.15a - 1.15$

Therefore, the answer is (B).

6. Equalities/Inequalities in Context

If the real-life car's length is x, the length of the toy car is $\dfrac{2}{7}x$.

Since it is given that $x = 7$

$7 \times \dfrac{2}{7} = 2$

Therefore, the answer is (C).

7. Equalities/Inequalities in Context

If Jeff is x centimeters tall, Britta is $x - \frac{1}{5}x$ centimeters tall.

Britta's height is 156 centimeters.

$x - \frac{1}{5}x = 156$

$\frac{4}{5}x = 156$

$\therefore \ x = 195$

Therefore, the answer is (C).

8. Equalities/Inequalities in Context

Height of the box is 27 inches, and the perimeter of the bottom side of the box consists of the width, w, and length, 15 inches.

$27 + 2(w + 15) \leq 105$

$27 + 2w + 30 \leq 105$

$2w \leq 48$

$\therefore \ w \leq 24$

Therefore, the answer is (C).

9. Equalities/Inequalities in Context

Henry finished the race in 5 hours, in which he ran and biked a total of 4 hours.

Therefore, he kayaked for 1 hour.

If Henry kayaked in x miles per hour,

$(6 \times 2) + (10 \times 2) + (x \times 1) = 40$

$12 + 20 + x = 40$

$\therefore \ x = 8$

Therefore, the answer is (C).

10. Equalities/Inequalities in Context

Number of miles Dean and friends traveled: x

Total number of people riding cab is 5.

$5 + 1 \times 5 + 0.5x = 65.50$

$0.5x = 55.50$

$\therefore \ x = 111$

Therefore, the answer is 111.

11. Equalities/Inequalities in Context

Number of tickets sold at box office : x

Number of pre-purchased tickets: 200

$15 \times 200 + 20x = 18(200 + x)$

$3000 + 20x = 3600 + 18x$

$2x = 600$

$\therefore \ x = 300$

Therefore, the answer is (B).

12. Equalities/Inequalities in Context

Number of Sam's stamps: x

Number of Jeremy's stamps: $4x - 21$

$x + (4x - 21) = 94$

$5x = 115$

$x = 23$

$\therefore \ (4x - 21) - x = 3x - 21 = 3 \times 23 - 21 = 48$

Therefore, the answer is (C).

13. Equalities/Inequalities in Context

Bags of beef jerky : j

Number of cokes : c

$3j + 2c = 19 \ \rightarrow \ ①$

$5j + 5c = 37.5 \ \rightarrow \ ②$

$① \times 2 : \ 6j + 4c = 38$

$① \times 2 - ②$

$j - c = 0.50$

Therefore, the answer is (A).

14. Equalities/Inequalities in Context

Rameez : $23 + 0.50d$

Cameron: $15.50 + 2d$

$23 + 0.50d = 15.50 + 2d$

$1.5d = 7.5$

$\therefore \ d = 5$

Therefore, 5 days after Tuesday (including Tuesday) is Saturday.

Therefore, the answer is (B).

15. Equalities/Inequalities in Context

Paperback books: x

Hardcover books: $2x-9$

$x+(2x-9)=90$

$3x=99$

$x=33$

$\therefore \ 2x-9=66-9=57$

Therefore, the answer is (C).

16. Equalities/Inequalities in Context

3-people table: x

4-people table: y

$x+y=21 \ \rightarrow \ ①$

$3x+4y=71 \ \rightarrow \ ②$

$①\times3: \ 3x+3y=63$

$②-①\times3$

$y=8$

$\therefore \ x=21-8=13$

Therefore, the answer is (C).

17. Equalities/Inequalities in Context

Onions: x

Garlic: $27-x$

$3x+2.5(27-x)=72.50$

$0.5x+67.5=72.50$

$0.5x=5$

$x=10$

Therefore, the answer is (B).

18. Equalities/Inequalities in Context

Turk ate t sandwiches per day for 13 days: $13t$

Carla ate c sandwiches per day for 3 days: $3c$

Total number of sandwiches eaten by Turk and Carla during the month: $13t+3c$

Therefore, the answer is (A).

19. Equalities/Inequalities in Context

When the price per liter of apple juice and orange juice is the same,

$3.24+0.35n=2.49+1.10n$

$0.75n=0.75$

$\therefore \ n=1$

The price per liter of apple juice when $n=1$,

$\therefore \ 3.24+0.35=3.59$

Therefore, the answer is (C).

20. Equalities/Inequalities in Context

If the number of 16GB USBs and 32GB USBs is a and b respectively,

$a+b=10$

Plug in $b=10-a$ into the second equation.

$ua+2u(10-a)=17u$

$a+20-2a=17$

$\therefore \ a=3$

Therefore, the answer is (B).

21. Equalities/Inequalities in Context

Sets of forks: x

Sets of knives: $x+4$

$5x=4(x+4)$

$5x=4x+16$

$x=16$

$\therefore \ 4(x+4)=4(16+4)=80$

Therefore, the answer is (C).

22. Equalities/Inequalities in Context

Basketball players: x

Football players: $4x$

Tennis players: $\dfrac{1}{2}x$

$4x+x+\dfrac{1}{2}x=66$

$5.5x=66$

$x=12$

$\therefore \ $ Number of football players $=4x=48$

Therefore, the answer is 48.

23. Equalities/Inequalities in Context

No-Calculator questions are worth 3 points and Calculator using questions are worth 2 points.

Fry got 12 No-Calculator questions right.

If we set the number of Calculator-allowed questions that Fry answered correctly as x,

$12 \times 3 + 2x \geq 70$

$36 + 2x \geq 70$

$2x \geq 34$

$\therefore x \geq 17$

Therefore, the answer is 17.

24. Equalities/Inequalities in Context

Pennies Bart has: b

Pennies Lisa has: $b - 46$

13 dollars $= 1300$ pennies

$b + (b - 46) = 1300$

$2b = 1346$

$\therefore b = 673$

Therefore, the answer is (B).

25. Equalities/Inequalities in Context

In the given equation $C = 153 - 12h$,

C represents the number of cookies left to bake, and h is the number of hours Bailey has worked.

Therefore, the number 12 represents the number of cookies Bailey bakes in an hour.

From the information above, we can infer that the number 153 represents the initial number of cookies to bake daily.

Therefore, the answer is (C).

1-4   Equations/Inequalities on the Coordinate Plane

1. Equations/Inequalities in the Coordinate Plane

Slope of line n:

$$\frac{-3 - 0}{0 - (-4)} = -\frac{3}{4}$$

y-intercept of line n is -3.

$\therefore$ Equation of line n is $y = -\frac{3}{4}x - 3$

Since line m is parallel to line n and has a y-intercept of 6,

Equation of line m is $y = -\frac{3}{4}x + 6$

r is the x value of line m when the y value is 0.

$0 = -\frac{3}{4}r + 6$

$\frac{3}{4}r = 6$

$\therefore r = 8$

Therefore, the answer is (C).

2. Equations/Inequalities in the Coordinate Plane

The equation for the line with slope -2 and point (1, 4) is,

$y = -2x + a$

$4 = -2 + a$

$a = 6$

$\therefore y = -2x + 6$

The equation for the line with points (3, 0), (-3, -2) is,

slope: $\frac{0 - (-2)}{3 - (-3)} = \frac{2}{6} = \frac{1}{3}$

$y = \frac{1}{3}x + b$

$0 = \frac{1}{3} \times 3 + b$

$b = -1$

$\therefore y = \frac{1}{3}x - 1$

The two lines intersect at point (p, q), therefore,

$\frac{1}{3}x - 1 = -2x + 6$

$$\frac{7}{3}x=7$$

$p=3, \ q=0$

$\therefore \ p-q=3$

Therefore, the answer is (C).

3. Equations/Inequalities in the Coordinate Plane

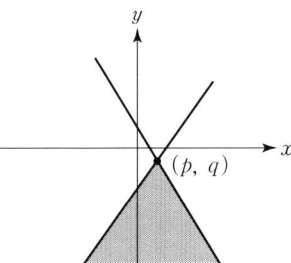

The solution set of the inequalities will be the intersection of the areas below and including the boundary lines $y=25x-450$ and $y=-5x$. Because the slope of one equation is positive (25) and the other is negative (-5), the graph will look like an 'X'. The greatest value of q will be the point of intersection of the two lines.

$25x-450=-5x$

$30x=450$

$x=15$

$\therefore \ y=-5\times15=-75$

Therefore, the answer is -75.

4. Equations/Inequalities in the Coordinate Plane

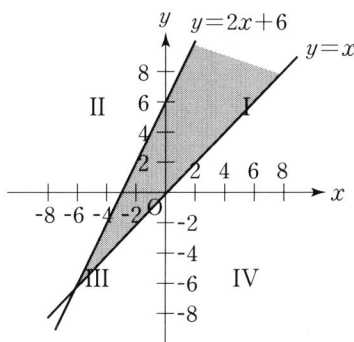

Above is the given system of inequalities drawn on the xy-plane. The colored area shows the solution set to the system of inequalities. There are no solutions in Quadrant IV.

Therefore, the answer is (C).

5. Equations/Inequalities in the Coordinate Plane

If we set the y-intercept of the line as b,

$$y=\frac{7}{3}x+b$$

Since the line passes through point $(3, \ 15)$,

$$15=\frac{7}{3}\times3+b$$

$\therefore \ b=15-7=8$

Therefore, the answer is (C).

6. Equations/Inequalities in the Coordinate Plane

If we write the equation of the line from the given figure, $y=2x+1$.

$ax+by=c$

$by=-ax+c$

$$y=-\frac{a}{b}x+\frac{c}{b}=2x+1$$

It is given that $a=4$,

$$-\frac{4}{b}=2$$

$b=-2$

$$\frac{c}{b}=\frac{c}{(-2)}=1$$

$\therefore \ c=-2$

Therefore, the answer is -2.

7. Equations/Inequalities in the Coordinate Plane

Rewrite the given equations to a standard line equation.

$6x+2y=3$

$2y=-6x+3$

$$y=-3x+\frac{3}{2}$$

$9x+by=2$

$by=-9x+2$

$$y=-\frac{9}{b}x+\frac{2}{b}$$

Since the two lines are parallel to each other, they share the same slope.

$$-3=-\frac{9}{b}$$

$\therefore \ b=3$

Therefore, the answer is (B).

8. Equations/Inequalities in the Coordinate Plane

From the given graph, it is shown that the graph passes points $(-4, 0)$ and $(0, 2)$.

Therefore, the slope of line l:

$$\frac{2-0}{0-(-4)} = \frac{1}{2}$$

The slope of a perpendicular line is the negative reciprocal of given line.

$\therefore$ slope of line perpendicular to line $l = -2$

Therefore, the answer is (A).

9. Equations/Inequalities in the Coordinate Plane

Create a standard line equation based on the given information.

$y = -0.75x + b$

Since the line passes point $\{16, 1\}$,

$$1 = -\frac{3}{4} \times 16 + b$$

$$1 = -12 + b$$

$\therefore b = 13$

Therefore, the answer is (D).

10. Equations/Inequalities in the Coordinate Plane

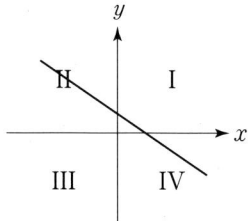

Rewrite $2x + 4y = 3$ as a line equation.

$4y = -2x + 3$

$\therefore t = -\frac{1}{2}x + \frac{3}{4}$

When the equation above is graphed on the xy-plane, it does not pass through quadrant III.

Therefore, the answer is (B).

11. Equations/Inequalities in the Coordinate Plane

A line that passes through the origin and has a slope of -2 is,

$y = -2x$

If every answer option is plugged into the equation, the only point that fits is $\{1, -2\}$.

Therefore, the answer is (A).

12. Equations/Inequalities in the Coordinate Plane

A line that passes through the point $(0,2)$ and has a slope of $\frac{2}{3}$ is,

$$y = \frac{2}{3}x + 2$$

If every answer option is plugged into the equation, the only point that does not fit is $\{2, 0\}$.

Therefore, the answer is (D).

13. Equations/Inequalities in the Coordinate Plane

A line that meets the y-axis at $+5$ and has a slope of -3 is,

$y = -3x + 5$

If every answer option is plugged into the equation, the only point that fits is $(2, -1)$.

Therefore, the answer is (A).

14. Equations/Inequalities in the Coordinate Plane

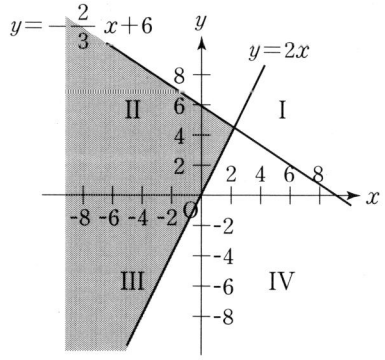

Above is the given system of inequalities drawn on the xy-plane. The colored area shows the solution set to the system of inequalities. There are no solutions in Quadrant IV.

Therefore, the answer is (C).

15. Equations/Inequalities in the Coordinate Plane

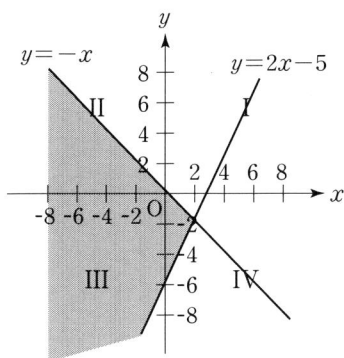

Above is the given system of inequalities drawn on the xy-plane. The colored area shows the solution set to the system of inequalities. There are no solutions in Quadrant I.

Therefore, the answer is (A).

16. Equations/Inequalities in the Coordinate Plane

The solution set of the inequalities will be the intersection of the areas below and including the boundary lines $y=4x-7$ and $y=-2x+5$.

The greatest value of (a, b) will be the point of intersection of the two lines.

$4x-7=-2x+5$

$6x=12$

$x=2$

$\therefore\ y=4\times2-7=1$

Therefore, the answer is 1.

17. Equations/Inequalities in the Coordinate Plane

Slope of line with points $(0, 4)$ and $(-2, 0)$:

$\dfrac{4-0}{0-(-2)}=2$

y-intercept of this line is 4.

$\therefore$ Equation of this line is $y=2x+4$

Since the two lines are parallel and the line below has a y-intercept of -3,

Equation of the line below is $y=2x-3$

r is the x value of the line below when the y value is 0.

$0=2x-3$

$2x=3$

$\therefore\ x=\dfrac{3}{2}=1.5$

Therefore, the answer is (B).

18. Equations/Inequalities in the Coordinate Plane

Let's set the line with points $(0, 6)$ and $(-3, 0)$ as line 1 and the other as line 2.

Slope of line 1:

$\dfrac{6-0}{0-(-3)}=2$

y-intercept of line 1 is 6.

$\therefore$ Equation of line 1 is $y=2x+6$

Since the two lines are perpendicular and line 2 passes through the origin,

Equation of line 2 is $y=-\dfrac{1}{2}x$

Point (p, q) is where the two lines intersect.

$2x+6=-\dfrac{1}{2}x$

$\dfrac{5}{2}x=-6$

$x=-\dfrac{12}{5}$

$y=-\dfrac{12}{5}\times-\dfrac{1}{2}=\dfrac{6}{5}=1.2$

Therefore, the answer is 1.2.

19. Equations/Inequalities in the Coordinate Plane

Rewrite the given equations to a standard line equation.

$4x+2y=1$

$2y=-4x+1$

$y=-2x+\dfrac{1}{2}$

$2x+by=2$

$by=-2x+2$

$y=-\dfrac{2}{b}x+\dfrac{2}{b}$

Since the two lines are parallel to each other, they share the same slope.

$$-2=-\frac{2}{b}$$

$\therefore\ b=1$

Therefore, the answer is (A).

20. Equations/Inequalities in the Coordinate Plane

Rewrite the given equations to a standard line equation.

$7x+y=9$

$y=-7x+9$

$ax+3y=1$

$3y=-ax+1$

$y=-\frac{a}{3}x+\frac{1}{3}$

Since the two lines are parallel to each other, they share the same slope.

$-7=-\frac{a}{3}$

$\therefore\ a=21$

Therefore, the answer is (D).

21. Equations/Inequalities in the Coordinate Plane

Rewrite the given equations to a standard line equation.

$x+2y=6$

$2y=-x+6$

$y=-\frac{1}{2}x+3$

$ax+2y=7$

$2y=-ax+7$

$y=-\frac{a}{2}x+\frac{7}{2}$

Since the two lines are perpendicular to each other,

$-\frac{a}{2}$ would be the negative reciprocal of $-\frac{1}{2}$.

$2=-\frac{a}{2}$

$\therefore\ a=-4$

Therefore, the answer is (A).

22. Equations/Inequalities in the Coordinate Plane

The solution set of the inequalities will be the intersection of the areas below and including the boundary lines $2y=4x+6$ and $3y=-6x+9$.

The greatest value of $(p,\ q)$ will be the point of intersection of the two lines.

Rewrite the equations as: $y=2x+3$ and $y=-2x+3$

$2x+3=-2x+3$

$4x=0$

$x=0$

$y=2\times0+3=3$

$\therefore\ pq=3\times0=0$

Therefore, the answer is (B).

23. Equations/Inequalities in the Coordinate Plane

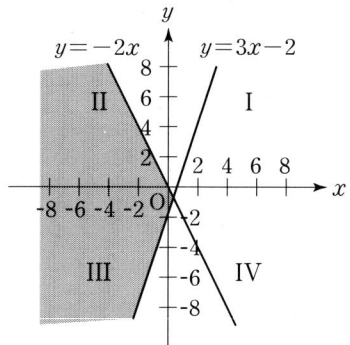

$2y\leq-4x$ can be rewritten into $y\leq-2x$

Above is the given system of inequalities drawn on the xy-plane. The colored area shows the solution set to the system of inequalities. There are no solutions in Quadrant I.

Therefore, the answer is (A).

24. Equations/Inequalities in the Coordinate Plane

Let's set the line with the slope of -3 and point $(1,\ 2)$ line 1 and the other as line 2.

$y=-3x+b$

Line 1 passes the point $\{1, 2\}$ so,

$2=-3\times1+b$

$b=5$

$\therefore$ Equation of line 1 is $y=-3x+5$

Line 2 passes the point {4, 0} and {-4, -4}.

Slope of line 2:

$$\frac{0-(-4)}{4-(-4)} = \frac{4}{8} = \frac{1}{2}$$

$$y = \frac{1}{2}x + c$$

$$0 = \frac{1}{2} \times 4 + c$$

$$c = -2$$

∴ Equation of line 2 is $y = \frac{1}{2}x - 2$

Point (r, k) is where the two lines intersect.

$$-3x + 5 = \frac{1}{2}x - 2$$

$$\frac{7}{2}x = 7$$

∴ $x = r = 2$

$$k = \frac{1}{2} \times 2 - 2 = -1$$

∴ $r - k = 2 - (-1) = 3$

Therefore, the answer is (C).

25. Equations/Inequalities in the Coordinate Plane

The solution set of the inequalities will be the intersection of the areas below and including the boundary lines $y = 2x$ and $y = -11x + 169$.

The greatest value of $\{n, m)$ will be the point of intersection of the two lines.

$$2x = -11x + 169$$

$$13x = 169$$

$$x = 13$$

∴ $y = 2 \times 13 = 26$

Therefore, the answer is 26.

I. Statistics

Exercise

1. $\dfrac{20+30+50}{3}=\dfrac{100}{3}$

2. $\{2,\ 4,\ 5,\ 7,\ 9,\ 10\}\ \Rightarrow$ median

$=\dfrac{5+7}{2}=6$

3. 1, 2

SAT Question

1. $60=6T$

$T=10$

The answer is 10.

2. $x<y<z$

$x<x+6<x+9\ \Rightarrow$ median$=x+6$

average$=\dfrac{x+(x+6)+(x+9)}{3}$

$=\dfrac{3x+15}{3}=x+5$

$x+6-(x+5)=1$

Therefore, the answer is (C).

3. (A), (B), (C) all change the median. However, even if the biggest number in Set X gets bigger, the increase has no impact on the median.

Therefore, the answer is (D).

4. The dots in the plot on the left (Class A) are more concentrated towards a specific number, around 5.

Therefore, the answer is (A).

5. In this question, a 95% confidence interval of 41 to 49 chocolates means that when multiple samples of 300 bags of M&Ms are investigated for the average number of chocolates inside them, 95% of them will be between 41 and 49. It does not mean 95% of the bags produced have between 41 and 49 chocolates inside. Also, be careful not to confuse the answer for (D) as this result applies to only the particular day that the investigation was carried out and not for all the M&Ms the factory produced.

Therefore, the answer is (C).

II. Probability

Exercise

1. $4+6-2=8$

2. $4\times3=12$

3. $\dfrac{3}{6}=\dfrac{1}{2}$

4. $\dfrac{5!}{(5-2)!}=20$

5. $\dfrac{5!}{(5-2)!2!}=\dfrac{5\cdot4\cdot3}{3\cdot2}=10$

1. # of handshakes the 1st person has:

once with 7 other people → 7 handshakes

# of handshakes the 2nd person has:

once with 6 remaining people → 6 handshakes

$\vdots$

# of handshakes the 7th person has:

once with 1 remaining person → 1 handshake

total=7+6+5+4+3+2+1=28 handshakes

Therefore, the answer is 28.

2. 5+6+7

7+5+6

6+5+7

7+6+5

Therefore, the answer is (C).

3. $x=$fraction of romance books

$$\frac{3}{30}+\frac{10}{30}+\frac{5}{30}+x=1$$

$$x=\frac{2}{5}$$

12 romance books=$\frac{2}{5}\times$total number of books

Total number of books=30

SF books=$30\times\frac{1}{6}=5$ books.

Therefore, the answer is (D}.

4. $4x=\frac{1}{9}\times360$

$4=40$

$x=10$

Therefore, the answer is (C).

5. 12 cards for each numeral ranging from 0 to 9

01 ✓   11 ✓ → 1 is used two times.

02   12 ✓

03   13 ✓

04   14 ✓

05   15 ✓

06   16 ✓

07   17 ✓

08   18 ✓

09   19 ✓ → 1 is used 12 times up to here.

10 ✓   20

Therefore, the answer is (D).

6. $6\times5\times4\times3\times2\times1=720$

$5\times4\times3\times2\times1=120$

(2 exists at the beginning and at the end)

$720-(2\times120)=480$

Therefore, the answer is 480.

7. LCM of 6 and 8=24

$$\frac{100}{24}=4(\text{remainder } 2)$$

Probability=$\frac{4}{100}$

Therefore, the answer is (C).

III. Graphs and Data Analysis

1. Credit vs. cash for regular:

$$\frac{2.11}{2.06}=1.02427=102.43\%$$

which means that credit is 2.43 % more expensive

Credit vs. cash for plus:

$$\frac{2.35}{2.29}=1.0262=102.62\%$$

credit is 2.62% more expensive

$$\frac{2.47}{2.40}=1.02917=102.917\%$$

Credit vs. cash for premium:

credit is 2.92% more expensive

Therefore, the answer is (A).

2. If Tom fills his tank twice a month, he will have to pay for twice the number of gallons. Thus, his gas payments will increase by 100%.
Therefore, the answer is (A).

3. $\frac{474.34}{50,135}=0.00946\approx0.95\%$
Therefore, the answer is (B).

4. To begin with there were 1,700 Chemical Engineering students.

The number of students who stayed in Chemical Engineering until the beginning of their third year
$=1,900\times0.77\times0.77$
The number of students who changed from Chemical Engineering to something else at the end of their third year
$=1,900\times0.77\times0.77\times0.23=259.0973$
Therefore, the answer is (A).

IV. Ratio

1. $6:12:18=A:B:C \rightarrow A:C=1:3$

2. $4:40=80:x \rightarrow 4x=3200 \rightarrow x=800$

1. small circle's area: 4π
largest circle's area: 36π
middle circle's area: 16π
outer ring's area: $36\pi-16\pi=20\pi$
small circle's area: outer ring's area$=4\pi:20\pi=1:5$
Therefore, the answer is (C).

2. $P:Q=3:5 \qquad Q:R=12:4$
$\quad P:Q=36:60 \qquad Q:R=60:20$
$\quad R:P=20:36=5:9$
Therefore, the answer is (C).

V. Rate

1. $25\times3=75$

2. If it takes 10 days for 6 workers to build one bridge, it will take 60 days for one worker to build one bridge. Since there are two workers, it will take 30 days to build one bridge.

1. 1) When the cheetah runs: travels x miles in 5

minutes $\rightarrow \dfrac{x}{5}$ miles per minute

2) When the cheetah walks: travels at $\dfrac{1}{5}$ of its

running speed $\rightarrow \dfrac{x}{25}$ miles per minute

$$\dfrac{x}{2} \div \dfrac{x}{25} = 12.5 \text{ miles}$$

Therefore, the answer is (B).

2. $\dfrac{1}{3} : 100 = 1 : x$

$100 = \dfrac{1}{3}x$

$300 = x$

Therefore, the answer is (C).

3. $A \rightarrow B \ (0.5f/\text{min}) \mid A \leftarrow B \ (3f/\text{min})$

$\text{time} = \dfrac{\text{distance}}{\text{speed}}$

$\dfrac{x}{0.5} + \dfrac{x}{3} = 7$

$\dfrac{6x}{3} + \dfrac{x}{3} = 7$

$\dfrac{7x}{3} = 7$

$7x = 21$

$x = 3$ (Be careful! $x=$ distance)

$\dfrac{3}{0.5} = 6 \text{ min.}$

Therefore, the answer is (C).

VI. Percentages

Exercise

1. $\dfrac{1}{8} \times 100(\%) = 12.5(\%)$

2. $50 \times \dfrac{40}{100} = 20$

3. $\dfrac{90-70}{70} \times 100(\%) = \dfrac{20}{70} \times 100(\%)$

$\quad = 28.571... \approx 28.6(\%)$

4. $x \times \dfrac{120}{100} = 60$

$\quad x = 60 \times \dfrac{120}{100} = 50$

SAT Question

1. $\dfrac{14-8}{8} \times 100 = 75\%$

$\dfrac{x-28}{28} = 0.75$

$x = 49$

Therefore, the answer is (D).

2. $1.2x = 18$

$x = 15$

Therefore, the answer is (B).

3. 1) Let the percentage be $k \rightarrow \dfrac{k}{100} \times (2a+5) = b$

$\dfrac{k}{100} = \dfrac{b}{2a+5} \rightarrow k = \left(\dfrac{b}{2a+5}\right) \times 100$

$\therefore \ \dfrac{100b}{2a+5}\%$

2) Simply put, what percentage of 10 is 1?

It's $\dfrac{1}{10} \times 100\%$.

Likewise, just substitute with $(2a+5)$ and b.

$\dfrac{b}{2a+5} \times 100\%$

$\therefore \ \dfrac{100b}{2a+5}\%$

Therefore, the answer is (C).

Chapter 3. Passport to Advanced Math

I. Factoring

Exercise

1. $3x(x+2)(x+1)$

2. $16(x+1)^2$

3. $(5x+2)(5x-2)$

4. $(7x+2)(3x-4)$

▲ **SAT Question**

1. $15x^3+44x^2+3x-26$

$b=44$

Therefore, the answer is 44.

2. $9x^2-6nx+n^2=9x^2-mx+16$

$n=4,\ m=24$

$n+m=28$

Therefore, the answer is (D).

3. $k^2-m^2=(k+m)(k-m)$

$$=\left[3\left(\frac{a}{b}+\frac{b}{a}\right)+4\left(\frac{a}{b}-\frac{b}{a}\right)\right]$$
$$\times\left[3\left(\frac{a}{b}+\frac{b}{a}\right)-4\left(\frac{a}{b}-\frac{b}{a}\right)\right]$$
$$=\left(\frac{3a}{b}+\frac{3b}{a}+\frac{4a}{b}-\frac{4b}{a}\right)$$
$$\times\left(\frac{3a}{b}+\frac{3b}{a}-\frac{4a}{b}+\frac{4b}{a}\right)$$
$$=\left(\frac{7a}{b}+\frac{-b}{a}\right)\times\left(\frac{-a}{b}+\frac{7b}{a}\right)$$

Therefore, the answer is (A).

4. $\dfrac{2x+4x+6x+8x+10x}{10x}=\dfrac{30x}{10x}=3\ (x\in R)$

But! Denominator must not be 0.

Thus, $x\neq0$

Therefore, the answer is (A).

II. Equations

▲ **Exercise**

1. $81-169x^2=0$

$(9+13x)(9-13x)=0$

$x=-\dfrac{9}{13}$ or $\dfrac{9}{13}$

2. $2x^2-7x-10=0$

$x=\dfrac{7\pm\sqrt{(-7)^2-4(2)(-10)}}{2(2)}$

$=\dfrac{7\pm\sqrt{49+80}}{4}$

$=\dfrac{7\pm\sqrt{129}}{4}$

$x=\dfrac{7}{4}+\dfrac{\sqrt{129}}{4}$ or $\dfrac{7}{4}-\dfrac{\sqrt{129}}{4}$

3. $\left(-\dfrac{4}{3},\ -2.5\right)$

4. 4

5. $y=x^2-x-4$

$y=-5x+8$

$x^2-x-4=-5x+8$

$x^2+4x-12=0$

$(x-2)(x+6)=0$

$x=2,\ y=-2$ or $x=-6,\ y=38$

$(2,\ -2)$ and $(-6,\ 38)$

1. Solution to $+-cx=0$ is $x=\dfrac{3}{2}$.

$6-\dfrac{3}{2}c=0$

$6=\dfrac{3}{2}c$

$c=4$

Therefore, the answer is 4.

2. $ty^2-6y=15$

In order for the equation to have no real solution, the determinant has to be less than zero.

$ty^2-6y-15=0$

Determinant $=(-6)^2-4t(-15)$

$\qquad\qquad\quad =36+60t<0$

$t<-\dfrac{36}{60}\left(=-\dfrac{3}{5}\right)$

Therefore, the answer is $t<-\dfrac{3}{5}$.

3. Here, the constant of the polynomial is the negative product of all the zeroes of the polynomial. Since $(x-3)$ and $(x+6)$ are two of the factors, 3 and -6 are two of the zeroes.

If the remaining zero is k, then:

$3\times(-6)\times k=-18\ k=-216$

$k=12$

Therefore, the answer is $(x-12)$.

4. $T(y)=(y-3)^3-7(y-3)^2+12(y-3)$

$T(y)=(y-3)[(y-3)^2-7(y-3)+12]$

$\qquad =(y-3)\{[(y-3)-3][(y-3)-4]\}$

$\qquad =(y-3)(y-6)(y-7)$

$3+6+7=16$

Therefore, the answer is 16.

5. Let $P(x)=6x^3+x^2-29x+25$.

$P\left(\dfrac{3}{2}\right)=6\left(\dfrac{3}{2}\right)^3+\left(\dfrac{3}{2}\right)^2-29\left(\dfrac{3}{2}\right)+25$

$\qquad\quad =\dfrac{81}{4}+\dfrac{9}{4}-\dfrac{87}{2}+25$

$\qquad\quad =4$

Therefore, the answer is 4.

6. $x+3=-(x+5)^2+4$

$x+3=-x^2-10x-25+4$

$x^2+11x+24=0$

$(x+3)(x+8)=0$

$x=-3,\ y=0$ or $x=-8,\ y=-5$

Therefore, the answer is (-8, -5) and (-3, 0).

7. $7x^2=(y+8)(y-8)$

$y=4x$

$7x^2=(4x+8)(4x-8)$

$7x^2=16x^2-64$

$9x^2-64=0$

$(3x+8)(3x-8)=0$

$x=\dfrac{8}{3}$ or $-\dfrac{8}{3}$

Since $m>0$, $m=\dfrac{8}{3}$

Therefore, the answer is $\dfrac{8}{3}$.

8. $y=(1.5+x)\left(80-\dfrac{10x}{0.5}\right)$

9. Initil PE $=mgh$

Changed PE $=(2m)(g)\left(\dfrac{1}{2}h\right)=mgh$

Therefore, the answer is (C).

10. $s=v_0t+\dfrac{1}{2}at^2$

$a=\dfrac{2}{t^2}(s-v_0t)$

Therefore, the answer is (D).

III. Absolute Value

1. $4x=8$ or $4x=-8$

$x=2$ or $x=-2 \to x=-2$ or 2

2. $3x+2=11$ or $3x+2=-11$

$3x=9$ or $3x=-13 \to x=-\dfrac{13}{3}$ or 3

3. $-10<10x<10 \to -1<x<1$

4. $|5x-2|>8 \to 5x-2<-8$ or $5x-2>8$

$5x<-6$ or $5x>10 \to x<-\dfrac{6}{5}$ or $x>2$

IV. Functions

Exercise

1. (d), (b), (a), (c)

2. Shifts the original graph to the right by 4 units.

SAT Question

1. $\dfrac{3x-5}{2}=5$

$3x-5=10$

$3x=15$

$x=5$

Therefore, the answer is 5.

2. When $x=10$, $g(x)+5=8$, $f(x)-3=8$. Use substitution.

Therefore, the answer is (D).

3. The "left" x-intercept is 4 units away from $(-3,\ 0)$ $\to$ the "right" x-intercept should be 4 units away as well.

$\to a=1$

Therefore, the answer is (D).

4. Reflecting across the y-axis $\to$ change x to $-x$

$\to -2x+5y-4=1$

Therefore, the answer is (C).

5.

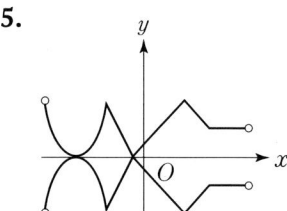

Two points

Therefore, the answer is {C}.

V. Powers & Roots

Exercise

1. 225

2. 1

3. 5

4. $6\sqrt{3}$

5. $\dfrac{7}{8}\sqrt{8}=\dfrac{7}{4}\sqrt{2}$

1. $3.005 \times 10^4 = 30050$

$\qquad = 30000 + 5 \times 10^1$

$\qquad = (3 \times 10^4) + (5 \times 10^k)$

$\qquad \rightarrow k = 1$

Therefore, the answer is 1.

2. $3^{t-2} = 3^6$

$t - 2 = 6$

$t = 8$

Therefore, the answer is 8.

3. $7x^3 = 56$

$x^3 = 8$

$7x^6 = 7 \times (x^3)^2 = 7 \times 64$

Therefore, the answer is 448.

4. $3^{11} = 3^{10} \cdot 3 = m^2 \cdot 3$

Therefore, the answer is (D).

5. x^4 cannot be negative $\rightarrow a \le 0$

Therefore, the answer is (D).

6. Substitute 5^t with a

$5^t + 5^t = a + a = 2a = 2 \cdot 5^t$

Therefore, the answer is (A).

7. $7^x \rightarrow$ Power numbers of 7

Find out the pattern of the unit digits

$\rightarrow \underline{7}, 4\underline{9}, 34\underline{3}, 240\underline{1}, \dots \underline{7}, \underline{9} \dots$

Unit digits of 7, 9, 3, 1 repeat.

Therefore, the answer is (D).

8. $3^8 = 3^3 \times 3^3 \times 3^2 = 9x^2 = x \times 3^3 \times 3^2 = 243x$

Therefore, the answer is (B).

Chapter 4. Additional Topics in Math

I. Triangles

Exercise

1. $x : y : x = 1 : \sqrt{3} : 2$

2. $x : y : z = 1 : 1 : \sqrt{2}$

3. $4\sqrt{5} < \overline{AC} < 12$

4. 4

5. $x = 6$, $y = 9$

SAT Question

1. $z > 95$, $x + y < 85$ (Substitute x with $y + 15$)

$2y + 15 < 85$

$2y < 70$

$y < 35$

$y = 34°$

Therefore, the answer is (D).

2. Apply the special ratio of a right triangle

$1 : \sqrt{3} : 2 (30°, 60°, 90°)$

$\overline{PB} = 3$, $\overline{AP} = 1$

Therefore, the answer is 4.

3. $BC = 4$, $QR = 5$

$\overline{OA} : \overline{AP} = \overline{OC} : \overline{CR} \rightarrow 4 : 3 = 12 : \overline{CR}$

$\overline{CR} = 9$

$4 : 3 = 8 : \overline{BQ} \rightarrow \overline{BQ} = 6$

$5 + 4 + 6 + 9 = 24$

Therefore, the answer is (B).

4. $\triangle APC(O)$, $\angle A$, $\angle PCA = 20°$

$\triangle CRQ(O)$, $\angle BQC$, $\angle CRQ = 80°$

$\triangle ABC(O)$, $\angle B$, $\angle C = 80°$

$\triangle BPC(X)$, no $\angle$ match

$\triangle QBC(O)$, $\angle BQC$, $\angle C = 80°$

Therefore, the answer is (D).

5.

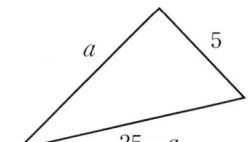

Let the three sides be 5, a, and $25 - a$ and use the Pythagorean Theorem

$a^2 + 5^2 = (25 - a)^2$

$a^2 + 5^2 = 625 - 50a + a^2$

$25 = 625 - 50a$

$50a = 600$

$a = 12$

$25 - 12 = 13$

Therefore, the answer is (D).

6.

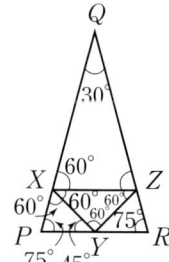

$\angle XYP = 45°$

Therefore, the answer is (C).

II. Polygons

1. $a=140°$
$b=140°$
$c=40°$
$d=140°$
$e=90°$

2. $(8-2)\cdot180°=1080$

3. $\dfrac{360°}{8}=45°$

4. $180°$

5. $90°$

6. 3

1. $\angle EOC$ is the opposite angle of x
*Opposite angles always have the same value
$\angle DOC, \angle DOE=70°$
$y=70°$
Therefore, the answer is $70°$.

2. $e=2b$
$3b=180°$
$b=60°$
$a=e=c=120°$
(Applying the nature of opposite angles and adjacent angles)
$b=d=60°$
$3b-d=c \ (180°-60°=120°)$
Therefore, the answer is (C).

3. Sum of the interior angles of the quadrilateral is $360°$
$(180°-x)+y+100+70°=360°$
$y-x+350=360$
$\therefore \ 3y-3x=30$
Therefore, the answer is (D).

4. Sum of the interior angles of a hexagon: $720°$
$\because$ Polygon Interior Angles Sum Theorem:
$180(n-2) \ \rightarrow \ n=$the number of vertices
$\because \ 720-(130+130)=460$
Therefore, the answer is 460.

5.

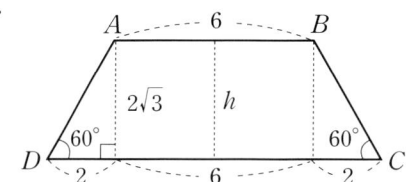

Draw a perpendicular line from A to DC
Use $1:\sqrt{3}:2 \ (30°, \ 60°, \ 90°)$
$\therefore \ \overline{AB}=10-2-2=6$
Therefore, the answer is 6.

6. $125=5\times5\times5$ is the number of small cubes with no paint on them.
$\therefore \ 7\times7\times7=343$ is the total number of cubes
Therefore, the answer is 343.

III. Perimeter and Area

1. 24

2. 8

1. $(\overline{AE}+\overline{BF})\overline{AB}/2=160$

$\overline{AE}=28$, $\overline{FG}=24$, $\overline{EG}=10$

Using Pythagorean Theorem,

$\overline{EF}^2=\overline{FG}^2+\overline{EG}^2$ and thus $\overline{EF}=26$

$\therefore 26+10+24=60$

Therefore, the answer is 60.

2. Each hexagon is equilateral $\rightarrow \overline{AB}=7\times3=21$

Therefore, the answer is (B).

3. area$=300$, length$=60$

Let width$=x \rightarrow 60x=300$

$x=5$

$120+10=130$

Therefore, the answer is 130m.

4.

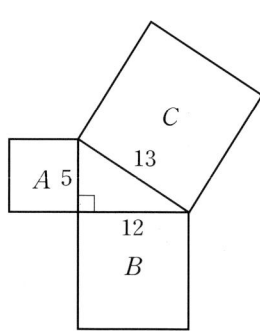

one side of A$=5$

one side of B$=12$

$5^2+12^2=13^2 \rightarrow$ one side of C

$12+5+13=30$

Therefore, the answer is (C).

5.

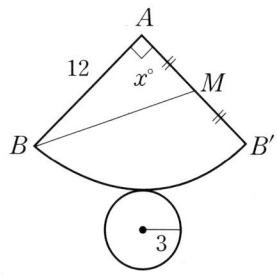

$\overset{\frown}{BB'}=2\pi r=6\pi$

$=12\times\pi\times2\times\dfrac{x}{360}$

$=24\pi\times\dfrac{x}{360}$

$=\dfrac{x}{15}\pi$

$x=90°$, $\overline{AM}=6$

$\overline{BM}=\sqrt{6^2+12^2}$

$=\sqrt{180}=6\sqrt{5}$

Therefore, the answer is (B).

IV. Circles

1. area: $9\pi\cdot\dfrac{45}{360}=\dfrac{9}{8}\pi$

arc length: $6\pi\cdot\dfrac{45}{360}=\dfrac{3}{4}\pi$

2. $2r=$diagonal $\rightarrow$ 8

3. $\dfrac{10}{2}=5$

4. $100-\pi(5^2)=100-25\pi$

1. $\triangle OXY=$Isosceles triangle

$\angle X$, $\angle Y=30°$, $\angle M=90°$

$\overline{OM}=3$, $\overline{XM}=3\sqrt{3}$

area$=\dfrac{3\times3\sqrt{3}}{2}=\dfrac{9\sqrt{3}}{2}$

Therefore, the answer is (A).

2. $\overline{AD}=3r$, $\overline{AB}=4r$

Perimeter is $14r$.

Therefore, the answer is $14r$.

3. $\dfrac{360}{10}=36 \rightarrow 180-90-36=54$

$\therefore \ 54°$

Therefore, the answer is $54°$.

4. radius of small semicircle$=2$

radius of large semicircle$=4$

$4\pi\times2=8\pi$

$8\pi\times1=8\pi$

$8\pi+8\pi=16\pi$

Therefore, the answer is (C).

5. $2\pi r\times\dfrac{45}{360}=10\pi$

$2\pi r\times\dfrac{1}{8}=10\pi$

$\dfrac{r}{4}=10, \ r=40$

area of a circle$=\pi r^2$

$40\times40\times\pi\times\dfrac{45}{360}=200\pi$

Therefore, the answer is (D).

6. Let small circle's radius be r.

area of semicircle$=\dfrac{\pi r^2}{2}$

3 semicircles$=\dfrac{3\pi r^2}{2}$

1 quarter-circles$=\dfrac{\pi r^2}{4}$

$\dfrac{3\pi r^2}{2}+\dfrac{\pi r^2}{4}=\dfrac{7\pi r^2}{4}$

$\therefore \ \dfrac{7}{4}$ times

Therefore, the answer is $\dfrac{7}{4}$ times.

7.

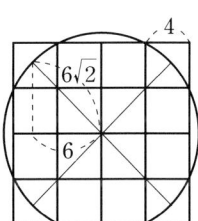

$r=6\sqrt{2} \rightarrow A=\pi r^2=72\pi$

Therefore, the answer is (C).

V. Solids

1.

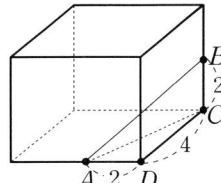

$4^2+2^2=16+4=20$

$\rightarrow (\sqrt{20})^2+3^2=29 \rightarrow d=\sqrt{29}$

2. volume$=27$

SA$=54$

3. volume$=\pi\times4\times5=20\pi$

SA$=2(\pi\cdot2^2)+5(2\cdot\pi\cdot2)=8\pi+20\pi=28\pi$

4. $\dfrac{1}{3}(7^2\times\pi\times6)=98\pi$

1. $3^2+6^2=\sqrt{45}$

$\sqrt{(\sqrt{45})^2+3^2}=XY$

$\sqrt{45+9}=\sqrt{54}=3\sqrt{6}$

Therefore, the answer is $3\sqrt{6}$.

2.

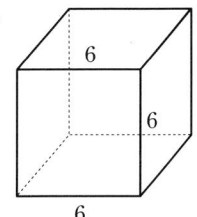

Area of each surface is 36.

$\rightarrow$ There are 6 faces.

Surface Area$=36\times6=216$

Therefore, the answer is SA$=216$.

VI. Coordinate Geometry

Exercise

1. $\sqrt{(-3-2)^2+(4+1)^2}=\sqrt{25+25}=5\sqrt{2}$

2. $\left(\dfrac{3+1}{2},\ \dfrac{2+0}{2}\right)=(2,\ 1)$

3. $\dfrac{4-2}{5-3}=\dfrac{2}{2}=1$

4.
$\begin{aligned}2&=4m+b\\5&=10m+b\end{aligned}\ \Rightarrow\ \begin{aligned}5&=10m+2.5b\\5&=10m+b\end{aligned}$

$\Rightarrow\ 0=1.5b\ \rightarrow\ b=0$

$\Rightarrow\ m=\dfrac{1}{2}\ \rightarrow\ y=\dfrac{1}{2}x$

SAT Question

1.

$B(-1,\ 6)$ $A(2,\ 6)$

$C(2,\ 2)$

$\overline{AC}=6-2=4$

$\overline{AB}=2-(-1)=3$

$\dfrac{3\times4}{2}=6$

Therefore, the answer is 6.

2.

slope of $\overline{OI}=\dfrac{6-0}{12-0}=\dfrac{1}{2}$

slope of $\overline{OH}=\dfrac{6-0}{18-0}=\dfrac{1}{3}$

$\dfrac{1}{2}-\dfrac{1}{3}=\dfrac{1}{6}$

Therefore, the answer is $\dfrac{1}{6}$.

3. $x=20,\ y=80\ \rightarrow\ (20,\ 80)$

$x=120,\ y=140\ \rightarrow\ (120,\ 140)$

$\Rightarrow\ y=mx+c$

$m(slope)=\dfrac{140-80}{120-20}=\dfrac{60}{100}=\dfrac{3}{5}$

$y=0.6x+c\,(20,\ 80)\ \rightarrow\ c=68$

$y=0.6x+68$

Therefore, the answer is (C).

VII. Circle Equation

Exercise

1. $(x+2)^2+(y-3)^2=36$

2. Center: $(0,\ 0)$

Point: $(3,\ 4)$

Radius

$=\sqrt{\text{distance between center and a point on circumference}}$

$=\sqrt{3^2+4^2}=5$

Therefore, the answer is 5.

SAT Question

1.

$T(1,\ 5)$ line ℓ

$C\left(\dfrac{11}{5},\ 2\right)$

Slope of line $l=\dfrac{2}{5}$

Slope of $\overline{CT}=\dfrac{-3}{s-1}$

Since the two slopes are perpendicular,

$\dfrac{2}{5} \times \dfrac{-3}{s-1} = -1$

$5s - 5 = 6$

$5s = 11$

$s = \dfrac{11}{5}$

Therefore, the answer is $\dfrac{11}{5}$.

2.

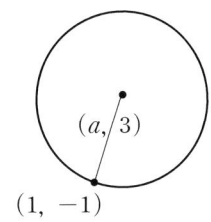

$(1-a)^2 + (-1-3)^2 = 5^2$

$(a-1)^2 + 16 = 25$

$(a-1)^2 = 9$

$a - 1 = \pm 3$

$a = 4, \ -2$

Since a must be positive,

$a = 4$

Therefore, the answer is 4.

3.

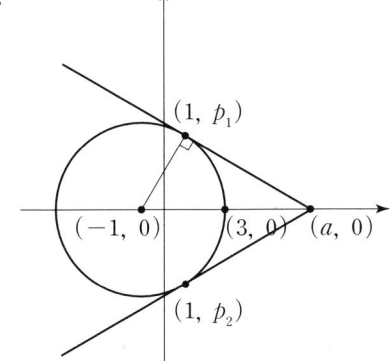

Circle equation:

$(x+1)^2 + y^2 = 16$

Plug $x = 1$ into the equation, and you will get p.

$4 + p^2 = 16$.

$p^2 = 12$

$p = \pm 2\sqrt{3}$

It doesn't matter whether p is positive or negative

because the value of a is the same for both cases.

So let's just go with

$p = 2\sqrt{3}$

Slope of the segment that connects $\{-1, 0\}$ and $\{1, 2\sqrt{3}\}$

$= \dfrac{2\sqrt{3}-0}{1-(-1)} = \sqrt{3}$

Since this segment is perpendicular to the tangent line,

$\sqrt{3} \times \dfrac{-2\sqrt{3}}{a-1} = -1$

$6 = a - 1$

$a = 7$

Therefore, the answer is (C).

4. Center of the circle

$\left(\dfrac{7-1}{2}, \ \dfrac{10-2}{2} \right) = (3, \ 4)$

Radius

=Distance between center and any point on the circle

$= \sqrt{(7-3)^2 + (-2-4)^2}$

$= \sqrt{4^2 + 6^2}$

$= \sqrt{52}$

Thus, the equation of the circle is

$(a-3)^2 + (b-4)^2 = 52$

Therefore, the answer is (D).

VIII. Trigonometry

Exercise

1. π rad $= 180°$

$\dfrac{\pi}{180}$ rad $= 1°$

$200° = 200 \times \dfrac{\pi}{180}$ rad

$\quad = \dfrac{10}{9}\pi$

Therefore, the answer is $\dfrac{10}{9}\pi$.

2.

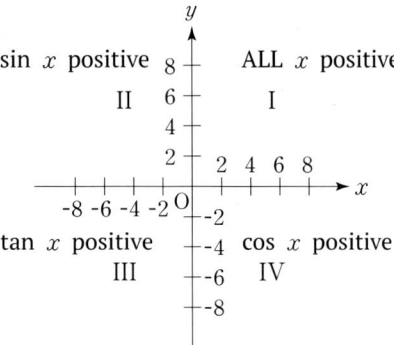

Only $\tan x$ is positive in Quadrant III.

Therefore, the answer is Quadrant III.

3. 2π

1. $\cos(90° - x°) = \sin x°$

$$= \frac{5}{13}$$

Therefore, the answer is $\dfrac{5}{13}$.

2.

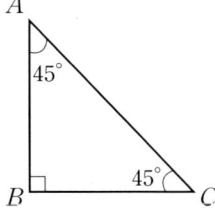

The angles of the triangle stay the same even if it's enlarged.

$\tan 45° = 1$

Therefore, the answer is 1.

IX. Complex Numbers

1. $4 + i - 3 + 8i$

$\quad = 1 + 9i$

Therefore, the answer is $1 + 9i$

2. $3 + 7i - (2i - 3i^2)$

$\quad = 3 + 7i - 2i + 3(-1)$

$\quad = 3 + 5i - 3$

$\quad = 5i$

Therefore, the answer is $5i$

3. $(1 + i)(2 - i)(1 + 2i)$

$\quad = (2 - i + 2i + 1)(1 + 2i)$

$\quad = (3 + i)(1 + 2i)$

$\quad = 3 + 6i + i - 2$

$\quad = 1 + 7i$

Therefore, the answer is $1 + 7i$

X. Extra Topics

1. $(4mn^3)^2 - (x - 7) + \sqrt{49l^6}$

$\quad = (16m^2n^6) - (x - 7) + 7l^3$

Therefore, the answer is (B).

2. $\dfrac{3x}{5x + 15} + \dfrac{x + 4}{x^2 + 3x}$

$\quad = \dfrac{3x}{5(x + 3)} + \dfrac{x + 4}{x(x + 3)}$

$\quad = \dfrac{3x^2 + 5x + 20}{5x(x + 3)}$

$\quad = \dfrac{3x^2 + 5x + 20}{5x^2 + 15x}$

Therefore, the answer is (A).

3. $\dfrac{45p^2q^4r^5+15p^5q^3r^6-25p^3q^5r^2}{5p^2q^3r^4}$

$=\dfrac{5p^2q^3r^2(9qr^3+3p^3r^4-5pq^2)}{5p^2q^3r^4}$

$=\dfrac{9qr^3+3p^3r^4-5pq^2}{r^2}$

Therefore, the answer is (D).

4. $(x^2+t^2)^2$

$=x^4+2x^2t^2+t^4$

$=(1+a-b)x^4+2bx^2+ab$

$1+a-b=1$

$a-b=0$

$\therefore\ a=b$

$2b=2t^2$

$b=t^2$

$\therefore\ a=t^2$

Therefore, the answer is (C).

5. Just because there are more registered members than non-registered members in the swimming team does not mean the former is better at swimming than the latter. The registered members might be more passionate about swimming which may be why they joined the swimming team or they might have joined the team to improve their swimming skills. There is no evidence of relationship between being a member of the swimming pool and being in the swimming team. Therefore, the answer is (D).

6. The researcher is creating a control group and an experimental group by randomly assigning different treatments to the mice. This experiment is called a controlled experiment.
Therefore, the answer is (C).

7. In order for a result of an experiment to be valid, two factors must be met: random sampling and random assignment. In this survey, the researcher only interviewed high school boys and not girls. Hence, the sample was not randomly selected and the result cannot be generalized to the whole population. Therefore, the correct answer is (D).

SAT Math Practice Test 1

Math Test (No Calculator)

25 MINUTES, 20 QUESTIONS

Turn to Section 3 of your answer sheet to answer the questions in this section.

DIRECTIONS

For questions 1-15, solve each problem, choose the best answer from the choices provided, and fill in the corresponding circle on your answer sheet. **For questions 16-20,** solve the problem and enter your answer in the grid on the answer sheet. Please refer to the directions before question 16 on how to enter your answers in the grid. You may use any available space in your test booklet for scratch work.

NOTES

1. The use of a calculator **is not permitted.**
2. All variables and expressions used represent real numbers unless otherwise indicated.
3. Figures provided in this test are drawn to scale unless otherwise indicated.
4. All figures lie in a plane unless otherwise indicated.
5. Unless otherwise indicated, the domain of a given function f is the set of all real numbers x for which $f(x)$ is a real number.

REFERENCE

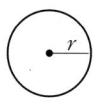

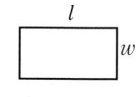

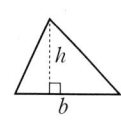

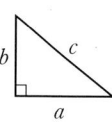

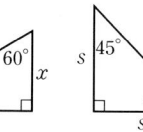

$A=\pi r^2$
$C=2\pi r$

$A=lw$

$A=\frac{1}{2}bh$

$c^2=a^2+b^2$

Special Right Triangles

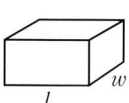

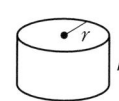

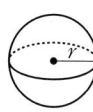

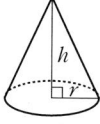

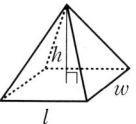

$V=lwh$

$V=\pi r^2h$

$V=\frac{4}{3}\pi r^3$

$V=\frac{1}{3}\pi r^2h$

$V=\frac{1}{3}lwh$

The number of degrees of arc in a circle is 360.

The number of radians of arc in a circle is 2π.

The sum of the measures in degrees of the angles of a triangle is 180.

CONTINUE ➤

1

A boat rental company charges an initial deposit in addition to an hourly rental fee. The equation $F = 21h + 100$ models the total fee F, in dollars, when a boat is rented for h hours. What does 21 represent in the equation?

A) The initial deposit, in dollars

B) The rental fee charged for renting boat each additional hour, in dollars

C) The total rental fee charged for renting boat 21 hours, in dollars

D) The total rental fee charged for renting boat 100 hours, in dollars

2

In Port Ridge High School, there are x male students and y female students, and 20% of all male students and 25% of all female students are sophomores. If there are 150 sophomores in this high school, which of the following represents the relationship between the number of male sophomores and the number of female sophomores?

A) $0.25x + 0.2y = 150$

B) $0.2x + 0.25y = 150$

C) $25x + 20y = 150$

D) $20x + 25y = 150$

3

$$p = 2 + 3i$$
$$q = 4 + 6i$$

If p and q are defined by the equations above, and $i = \sqrt{-1}$, which of the following is equivalent to $p+q$?

A) 15

B) $15i$

C) $6 + 9i$

D) $8 + 18i$

4

$$16x^2 - 25 = y$$

If the equation above can be factored into $(ax+b)(ax-b)$, which of the following is a possible value of b?

A) 4

B) 5

C) 16

D) 25

CONTINUE

5

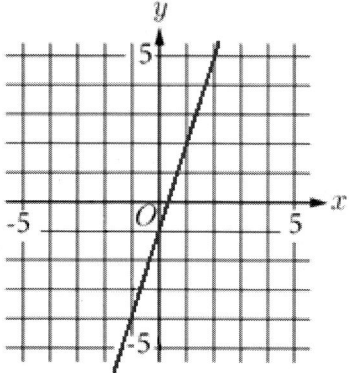

Which of the following is a possible equation of the line shown in the xy-plane above?

A) $y = 3x - 1$
B) $y = 3x + 1$
C) $y = -3x - 1$
D) $y = -3x + 1$

6

x	$f(x)$
-1	5
3	9
5	11

What is the value of $f(x) - 7$ if $x = 3$?

A) -4
B) -2
C) 2
D) 4

7

The total kinetic energy of an object is calculated by the formula $K = \frac{1}{2}mv^2$, where K is the kinetic energy of the object, m is its mass, and v is its velocity. If $v > 0$, what is v in terms of K and m?

A) $v = (\frac{2K}{m})^2$

B) $v = (\frac{K}{2m})^2$

C) $v = \sqrt{\frac{2K}{m}}$

D) $v = \sqrt{\frac{K}{2m}}$

8

x	$f(x)$	$g(x)$
-3	-10	-2
0	-1	1
1	3	6
2	6	8
5	14	14

The table above shows the value of $f(x)$ and $g(x)$ for five different x values. Which value of x satisfies the equation $f(x) + x = g(x)$?

A) -3
B) 0
C) 1
D) 2

Unauthorized copying or reuse of any part of this page is illegal.

CONTINUE

194 | Paul's SAT Math 800

9

If $x^{\frac{3}{2}} - 18 = \sqrt{81}$, what is the value of x ?

A)   1

B)   4

C)   9

D)   27

10

Jay scored 85, 90 and 89 on his first three physics tests. In order to receive an 'A' grade for the class, he must have an average test score of at least 90. Which inequality can be used to represent the minimum score that Jay has to score on the fourth test and final test in order to receive an 'A' grade?

A) $\dfrac{85 + 90 + 89}{3} + x \geq 90$

B) $85 + 90 + 89 \geq x(90)$

C) $\dfrac{85}{4} + \dfrac{90}{4} + \dfrac{89}{4} + x \geq 90$

D) $85 + 90 + 89 + x \geq 4(90)$

11

Which of the following best represents the graph of $y = -2(x-2)^2 + 3$?

A)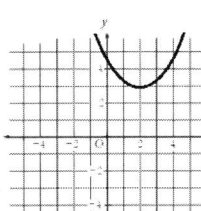

B)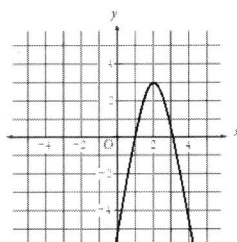

C)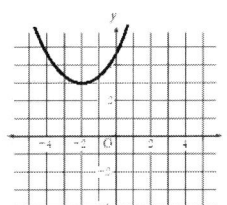

D)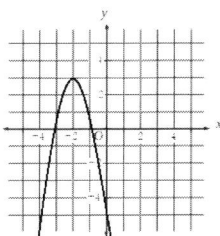

12

$$\frac{6y^2 + 5y}{3y + 1}$$

Which of the following is equivalent to the expression above?

A) $2y$

B) $2y + 4$

C) $2y - \dfrac{1}{3y + 1}$

D) $2y + 1 - \dfrac{1}{3y + 1}$

CONTINUE

13

How many real solutions are there to the equation $5x^2 = 4x + 1$?

A) 0

B) 1

C) 2

D) The answer cannot be determined from the information given.

14

A group of tourists are planning to visit an amusement park in Los Angeles. The entrance fee costs \$10 for each adult and \$5 for each child. If the group paid \$400 in total, and if each adult brought two children with them, what is the total number of tourists in this group?

A) 20

B) 40

C) 48

D) 60

15

$$9a^2 + 2ab + \frac{1}{9}b^2$$

Which of the following is equivalent to the expression above?

A) $3(a+b)^2$

B) $9(a+b)^2$

C) $(9a + \frac{1}{9}b)^2$

D) $(3a + \frac{1}{3}b)^2$

CONTINUE

DIRECTIONS

For questions 16-20, solve the problem and enter your answer in the grid, as described below, on the answer sheet.

1. Although not required, it is suggested that you write your answer in the boxes at the top of the columns to help you fill in the circles accurately. You will receive credit only if the circles are filled in correctly.

2. Mark no more than one circle in any column.

3. No question has a negative answer.

4. Some problems may have more than one correct answer. In such cases, grid only one answer.

5. **Mixed numbers** such as $3\frac{1}{2}$ must be gridded as 3.5 or 7/2. (If [3 1 / 2 grid] is entered into the grid, it will be interpreted as $\frac{31}{2}$, not $3\frac{1}{2}$.)

6. **Decimal answers**: If you obtain a decimal answer with more digits than the grid can accommodate, it may be either rounded or truncated, but it must fill the entire grid.

Answer: $\frac{7}{12}$ Answer: 2.5

Write answer in boxes. ← Fraction line

Grid in result. ← Decimal point

Acceptable ways to grid $\frac{2}{3}$ are:

Answer: 201 - either position is correct.

NOTE: You may start your answer in any column, space permitting. Columns you don't need to use should be left blank.

CONTINUE ▶

16

If $3^a = 9^b$, what is the value of $\dfrac{a}{b}$?

17

$$g(x) = \frac{3}{5}x$$

The function g(x) is defined as above. If $g(a) = \dfrac{3}{2}$, what is the value of a?

18

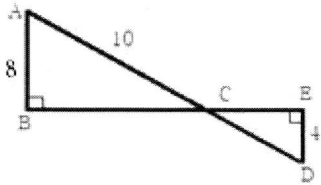

Note: Figure not drawn to scale.

In the figure above, if the length of $\overline{AB}$ is 8, what is the length of $\overline{AD}$?

CONTINUE

19

In Sun Valley High School, sophomores and freshmen share one gym. Currently, there are 60 sophomores in the gym, 40% of whom are playing basketball, and there are m freshmen, 15% of whom are also playing basketball. If 30% of all students in the gym are playing basketball, what is the value of m?

20

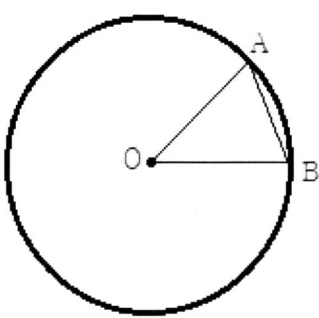

Note: Figure not drawn to scale.

A and B are points lying on the circle. If the length of $\overline{OB}$ is $\dfrac{3}{\pi}$, and the angle $\angle OAB$ is $75°$, what is the length of $\overparen{AB}$?

STOP

**If you finish before time is called, you may check your work on this section only.
Do not turn to any other section.**

Math Test (Calculator)

55 MINUTES, 38 QUESTIONS

Turn to Section 4 of your answer sheet to answer the questions in this section.

DIRECTIONS

For questions 1-30, solve each problem, choose the best answer from the choices provided, and fill in the corresponding circle on your answer sheet. **For questions 31-38,** solve the problem and enter your answer in the grid on the answer sheet. Please refer to the directions before question 31 on how to enter your answers in the grid. You may use any available space in your test booklet for scratch work.

NOTES

1. The use of a calculator **is permitted**.
2. All variables and expressions used represent real numbers unless otherwise indicated.
3. Figures provided in this test are drawn to scale unless otherwise indicated.
4. All figures lie in a plane unless otherwise indicated.
5. Unless otherwise indicated, the domain of a given function f is the set of all real numbers x for which $f(x)$ is a real number.

REFERENCE

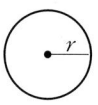 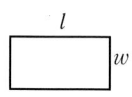 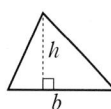 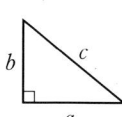 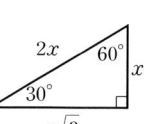

$A = \pi r^2$ $A = lw$ $A = \frac{1}{2}bh$ $c^2 = a^2 + b^2$ Special Right Triangles
$C = 2\pi r$

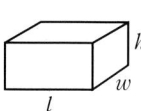 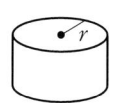 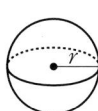 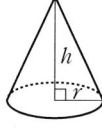 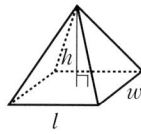

$V = lwh$ $V = \pi r^2 h$ $V = \frac{4}{3}\pi r^3$ $V = \frac{1}{3}\pi r^2 h$ $V = \frac{1}{3}lwh$

The number of degrees of arc in a circle is 360.
The number of radians of arc in a circle is 2π.
The sum of the measures in degrees of the angles of a triangle is 180.

CONTINUE ➤

1

Which of the following is equivalent to $(-3m+5p)-(4m-2n+3p)$?

A) $-7m+2n+2p$
B) $-7m-2n-2p$
C) $m-2n+8p$
D) $m+2n+8p$

2

Solar batteries charge at a constant rate under sunlight. The total amount of energy e, in watt-hours, contained in the battery can be modeled by the equation $e=17t+25$, where t is the time spent charging, in hours. What does 25 represent in the equation?

A)   The rate at which solar battery charges up energy under sunlight.
B)   The time it takes to fully charge solar battery.
C)   The initial amount of energy in the solar battery.
D)   The amount of energy charged in the solar battery after t hours.

Unauthorized copying or reuse of any part of this page is illegal.

CONTINUE

Practice Test 1 | 201

3

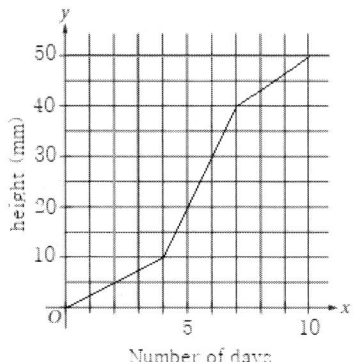

Number of days

Edward decided to grow a violet, so he started growing it inside his house. After 4 days, he thought it might grow faster outdoors, so he moved the violet to his garden. On day 7, however, the weather changed from a sunny weather to rainy weather. If the graph above shows the height of the violet, in millimeters, as a function of time, in days, during which time period did the violet grow at the fastest rate?

A) Day 0 to Day 4
B) Day 4 to Day 7
C) Day 7 to Day 10
D) The answer cannot be determined from the information given.

4

Sarah's family went on a barbecue party on the beach. She brought fish and pork ribs, but she had to rent a barbecue grill. The rental fee for barbecue grill was $80 for initial deposit and x dollars for each hour. If she paid $176 after 6 hours, what is the value of x?

A) 13
B) 14
C) 15
D) 16

5

If $14c + 7d = 21$, which of the following correctly expresses d in terms of c?

A) $d = 3 - c$
B) $d = 3 - 2c$
C) $d = \dfrac{3}{2} - c$
D) $d = \dfrac{3}{2} - \dfrac{1}{2}c$

CONTINUE

6

In Palazzo Hospital, 41% of the doctors are surgeons, 26% are psychiatrists, 17% are neurosurgeons and rest of the doctors are dentists. If there are a total of 200 doctors working in the hospital, how many more psychiatrists are there than dentists?

A)   2

B)   18

C)   20

D)   50

7

Distribution of Final Exam Scores

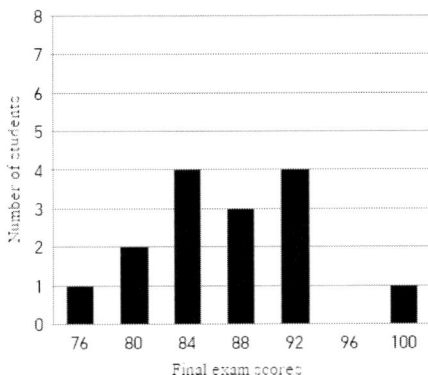

The graph above shows the distribution of 15 students' final exam scores. What is the median final exam scores of these 15 students?

A)   3

B)   4

C)   84

D)   88

CONTINUE

8

Practice session participation at different times of day

	Swimming	Baseball
Morning	25	11
Afternoon	19	22

The table above shows the number of students who participated in a swimming or basketball practice session. No student participated in more than one practice session. Of the students who participated in morning practice, what fraction participated in swimming?

A) $\dfrac{25}{77}$

B) $\dfrac{11}{36}$

C) $\dfrac{36}{77}$

D) $\dfrac{25}{36}$

9

The density, which is mass divided by volume, of pure gold is $19g/cm^3$. If a certain bar of gold has a volume of $125cm^3$, and exactly 80% of its volume is made of pure gold, what is the mass, in grams, of pure gold contained in the bar of gold?

A) $475g$

B) $1900g$

C) $2375g$

D) $2969g$

CONTINUE

10

Annie and Daniel went to a burger shop, and both of them ordered one cheese burger. In addition to that, Annie also ordered a can of sprite, which costs $5. If Annie and Daniel paid $29 in total, how much did Annie pay?

A) 12
B) 14
C) 17
D) 19

11

$$2a + 4b = 7$$
$$a - 8b = 1$$

If the solution to the system of equations above is (a,b), what is the value of $\dfrac{a}{b}$?

A) $\dfrac{1}{4}$

B) $\dfrac{3}{4}$

C) 3

D) 12

CONTINUE

— ▼ —

Questions 12-14 refer to the following information.

Patrick wanted to test his RC car's performance, so he ran his car on the track, and recorded the total distance it traveled every 5 seconds for 25 seconds on the table above.

Time(sec)	Distance(m)
0	0.0
5	2.9
10	6.9
15	12.4
20	17.9
25	23.4

12

Over which of the following time periods was the distance traveled by Patrick's RC car the greatest?

A) From 0 seconds to 10 seconds after it started running

B) From 10 seconds to 15 seconds after it started running

C) From 15 seconds to 20 seconds after it started running

D) From 20 seconds to 25 seconds after it started running

13

For a more detailed analysis, Patrick drew the line of best fit for the data shown in the table above. The equation of the line was $d(t) = 0.97t - 1.7$, where $d(t)$ is the total distance his RC car traveled after t seconds. What does 0.97 represent in the equation?

A) The total time, in seconds, elapsed during the race

B) The total distance, in meters, traveled in 1.7 seconds

C) The average speed, in meters per second, of Patrick's RC car

D) The time, in seconds, it takes for Patrick's RC car to travel one meter

14

Patrick wanted to calculate the difference between the average speed, in meters per second, of his RC car during the first 5 seconds and during the last 5 seconds. What would be the calculated difference according to the table?

A) $0.52m/s$

B) $0.936m/s$

C) $1.68m/s$

D) $2.6m/s$

— ▲ —

CONTINUE

15

The price of a phone decreases by a factor of $\frac{1}{2}$ every year after it is released. If one model of phone was released with initial price of \$200, which of the following equation best represents the price of phone p, in dollars, after t years?

A) $p = (200)^{\frac{1}{2}t}$

B) $p = (\frac{1}{2})^{200t}$

C) $p = \frac{1}{2}(200)^t$

D) $p = 200(\frac{1}{2})^t$

16

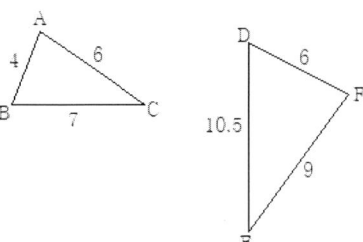

Note: Figure not drawn to scale.

If $\angle ABC$ is $58.8°$ and $\angle DEF$ is $34.8°$, what is the measure of $\angle DFE$ in degree?

A)   34.8

B)   58.8

C)   86.4

D)   93.6

CONTINUE

— ▼ —

Questions 17-19 refer to the following information.

Jacob is preparing for a Halloween party, so he is planning to buy chocolates and candies from a store. However, he has a limited budget of $37 to spend on chocolates and candy. The price of each bag of chocolate is $5, and the price of each bag of candy is $3, so the total cost can be modeled by the equation

$$p = 5h + 3c$$

where p is the total cost of the goods Jacob bought, h is the number of the bags of chocolate bought, and c is the number of the candy bags bought.

17

Which of the following expresses h, the number of bags of chocolate Jacob bought, in terms of c, the number of bags of candy bought and p, the total amount he had to pay?

A) $h = \dfrac{1}{5}(p + 3c)$

B) $h = \dfrac{1}{5}(p - 3c)$

C) $h = -\dfrac{1}{5}(p + 3c)$

D) $h = -\dfrac{1}{5}(p - 3c)$

18

If Jacob wants to buy at least 3 bags of candy for his Halloween party, what is the maximum number of bags of chocolate he can buy?

A) 5
B) 6
C) 7
D) 8

19

If Jacob wants to buy bags of chocolate and candy in such way that he spends his entire budget of $37, and if he wants to buy an odd number of bags of candy, then how many bags of chocolate should he buy?

A) 2
B) 3
C) 7
D) 9

— ▲ —

Unauthorized copying or reuse of any part of this page is illegal.

208 | Paul's SAT Math 800

CONTINUE

20

$$x^2 - 4 = 0$$

If a and b are two different solutions to the equation above, what is the value of $|a-b|$?

A) -2

B) 0

C) 2

D) 4

21

A study was done on different types of drink customers order in a cafe of an urban city. One day, there were 200 customers in this cafe, and 70% of the customers ordered coffee while the remaining 30% ordered fruit juice. Which of the following conclusions is best supported by this study?

A)   Approximately 70% of the people who live in this city prefer coffee.

B)   Approximately 30% of the people who live in this city prefer coffee.

C)   Approximately 70% of the customers who visit this cafe prefer coffee.

D)   Approximately 30% of the customers who visit this cafe prefer coffee.

22

The median of 17 students' quiz scores is m, the highest score is $m+2$, and the second highest score is m. If there were two late students who did not take the quiz on time, and if they both score higher than $m+2$ on the quiz, what would be the median quiz score of the 19 students?

A) m

B) $m+1$

C) $m+2$

D) $m+3$

CONTINUE

23

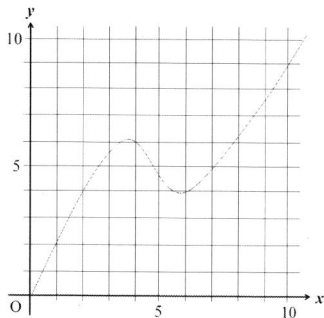

The graph above is the graph of helicopter's altitude, in meters, as a function of time after takeoff, in seconds. At about 4 seconds after takeoff, the driver saw a flock of birds flying toward the helicopter, so he had to temporarily drop the altitude, and then start rising again after the birds passed by. Between the time period of 0 to 10 seconds after takeoff, how many times was the helicopter's altitude exactly 5 meters above the ground?

A)   1
B)   2
C)   3
D)   4

24

Due to a severe drought, the market supply for agricultural products decreased, and the price of wheat increased from $5.20 per bushel to $5.79 per bushel. By what percent, to the nearest tenth of a percent, did the price of wheat increase?

A)   5.9%
B)   9.6%
C)   10.2%
D)   11.3%

25

$(2,3)$, $(-1,-6)$, and $(x,6)$ are three points on the graph of a linear function. What is the value of x?

A)   1
B)   2
C)   3
D)   4

Unauthorized copying or reuse of any part of this page is illegal.

CONTINUE

210 | Paul's SAT Math 800

26

Susan and Joanne are riding bicycle at the same speed covering the same distance. However, because the size of their wheels are different, Susan's wheels rotate at a rate of 50 revolutions per minute (rpm) while Joanne's wheels rotate at a rate of 60 rpm. If the radius of both of Susan's wheels is 30cm, what is the radius of both of Joanne's wheels?

A) $20cm$

B) $25cm$

C) $36cm$

D) $40cm$

27

What is the diameter of the circle in the xy-plane given by the equation $x^2 - 4x + y^2 + 6y = 3$?

A) 2

B) 3

C) 4

D) 8

28

What does $|x+2| = 5$ indicate?

A) x is 5 units away from -2

B) x is 5 units away from 2

C) x is 2 units away from -5

D) x is 2 units away from 5

CONTINUE

29

If the average speed v, in meters per second, of a jet over the first t seconds is given by the equation $v = 20$, which of the following correctly expresses the distance, in meters, the jet travels over the first t seconds?

A) $400t$

B) $20t$

C) 20

D) $\sqrt{20}$

30

Number of Cups of Hot Chocolates Sold at Different Temperatures

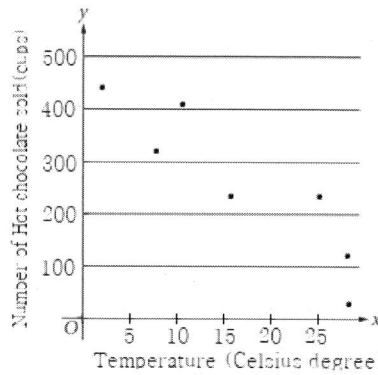

The scatterplot above shows the number of cups of hot chocolate sold on days of various outdoor temperatures. Which of the following equation best models the line of best fit for the scatter plot?

A) $y = 17x - 510$

B) $y = 17x + 510$

C) $y = -17x - 510$

D) $y = -17x + 510$

CONTINUE ▶

DIRECTIONS

For questions 31-38, solve the problem and enter your answer in the grid, as described below, on the answer sheet.

1. Although not required, it is suggested that you write your answer in the boxes at the top of the columns to help you fill in the circles accurately. You will receive credit only if the circles are filled in correctly.

2. Mark no more than one circle in any column.

3. No question has a negative answer.

4. Some problems may have more than one correct answer. In such cases, grid only one answer.

5. **Mixed numbers** such as $3\frac{1}{2}$ must be gridded as 3.5 or 7/2. (If $\boxed{3\ 1\ /\ 2}$ is entered into the grid, it will be interpreted as $\frac{31}{2}$, not $3\frac{1}{2}$.)

6. **Decimal answers**: If you obtain a decimal answer with more digits than the grid can accommodate, it may be either rounded or truncated, but it must fill the entire grid.

Answer: $\frac{7}{12}$ Answer: 2.5

Write answer in boxes.   ←Fraction line

Grid in result.   ←Decimal point

Acceptable ways to grid $\frac{2}{3}$ are:

Answer: 201 - either position is correct.

NOTE: You may start your answer in any column, space permitting. Columns you don't need to use should be left blank.

CONTINUE

31

A group of students won 70 oranges by participating in a school activity, and were planning on sharing the prize equally among themselves. However, two of the students were allergic to oranges, so the two distributed their share equally to all other group members. As a result, every other student in the group received 4 more oranges. How many students were in the group originally?

32

$$-3(2x - 10) + (5x + a) = 5$$

If the value of a is -14, what is the value of x?

Unauthorized copying or reuse of any part of this page is illegal.

CONTINUE

214 | Paul's SAT Math 800

33

George is ordering pint glasses for the restaurant that he is opening. He wants the glasses to be cylindrical, have a volume larger than 400 cubic inches but smaller than 450 cubic inches, and have a height of exactly 15 inches. If the glass manufacturer produced glasses in such way that he satisfied all of George's conditions and the radius, in inches, of each of the glasses is an integer, what is the radius, in inches, of each of the glasses produced?

34

$$y = x^2 - x$$
$$y = 2x - \frac{9}{4}$$

In the xy-plane, how many times do the graphs of the two equations above intersect?

CONTINUE

35

The equation $ax + 3y = 7$ is graphed in the xy-plane. If the x-intercept of the graph is $(2,0)$, what is the value of a?

36

	Time (sec)				
James	12.0	11.4	11.7	12.0	11.9

The table above gives time, in seconds, it took James to finish $100m$ sprints. The average time of the five tries shown above is 11.8 seconds. What should be the finish time, in seconds, on the sixth try if he wants to decrease his average time for $100m$ sprint by exactly 0.1 second?

CONTINUE

37

A type of radioactive isotope has a half life of 8 days. In other words, the mass of this radioactive isotope is halved every 8 days. In a lab, there were initially 80 grams of the radioactive isotope, but after x days, there were only 5 grams of it left. What is the value of x?

38

Number of Languages Spoken	Percentage of Participants
1	32%
2	44%
3	16%
4 or more	8%

A survey was conducted at a company about the number of different languages each employee could speak. If there are 42 more employees that speak two languages than employees that speak three languages, how many more employees are there that speak only one language than employees that speak three languages?

STOP
If you finish before time is called, you may check your work on this section only.
Do not turn to any other section.

Practice Test 1:
Answer Key and Explanations

Test 1 Answer Key

Math - No Calculator	
Question #	Answer
1	B
2	B
3	C
4	B
5	A
6	C
7	C
8	D
9	C
10	D
11	B
12	D
13	C
14	D
15	D
16	2
17	5/2 or 2.5
18	15
19	40
20	1/2 or 0.5

Math - Calculator	
Question #	Answer
1	A
2	C
3	B
4	D
5	B
6	C
7	D
8	D
9	B
10	C
11	D
12	A
13	C
14	A
15	D
16	C
17	B
18	A
19	A
20	D
21	C
22	A
23	C
24	D
25	C
26	B
27	D
28	A
29	B
30	D
31	7
32	11
33	3
34	1
35	7/2 or 3.5
36	11.2
37	32
38	24

*To get your estimated scaled SAT score, please turn to page 301.

Answer Explanations
Section 3 (No Calculator)

1.

$F = 21h + 100$

F: The total fee charged

100: The initial deposit $\rightarrow$ no matter how many hours the boat is rented, $100 is charged only once

21h: the hourly rental fee

$\therefore$ B)

2.

$20\% = 0.2 \qquad 25\% = 0.25$

$0.2x$ is the number of male sophomore students at Port Ridge High School, and $0.25y$ is the number of female sophomore students. The sum of the two numbers is 150.

$\therefore$ The total number of male and female sophomore students can be expressed as $0.2x + 0.25y = 150$

$\therefore$ B)

3.

$p = 2 + 3i$

$q = 4 + 6i$

$p + q = (2 + 3i) + (4 + 6i) = 6 + 9i$

$\therefore$ C)

4.

Memorize:

$a^2 - b^2 = (a+b)(a-b)$

$16x^2 - 25 = y$

$16x^2 - 25 = (4x)^2 - (5)^2$

$(4x+5)(4x-5)$

$b = 5$

$\therefore$ B)

5.

As seen on the graph, the slope is $\dfrac{\text{rise}}{\text{run}} = \dfrac{3}{1} = 3$

$y - \text{intercept} = -1$

$\therefore \ y = 3x - 1$

$\therefore$ A)

6.

Find $f(x) - 7$ when $x = 3$

$f(3) = 9$ according to the table.

$f(x) - 7 = 9 - 7 = 2$

$\therefore$ C)

7.

$K = \dfrac{1}{2} mv^2$

$(K)\dfrac{2}{m} = \left(\dfrac{1}{2} mv^2\right)\dfrac{2}{m}$

$\dfrac{2K}{m} = v^2$

$\sqrt{\dfrac{2K}{m}} = \sqrt{v^2}$

$\sqrt{\dfrac{2K}{m}} = v$

$\therefore$ C)

8.

According to the table,

x	$f(x)$	$g(x)$
-3	-10	-2
0	-1	1
1	3	6
2	6	8
5	14	14

When $x = 2$,

$f(x) + x = g(x) \Rightarrow 6 + 2 = 8$

$\therefore$ B)

9.

$x^{\frac{2}{3}} - 18 = \sqrt{81}$

$x^{\frac{2}{3}} - 18 = 9$

$x^{\frac{2}{3}} = 27$

$\sqrt[3]{x^{\frac{2}{3}}} = \sqrt[3]{27}$

$x^{\frac{1}{2}} = 3$

$\sqrt{x} = 3$

$\{\sqrt{x}\}^2 = (3)^2$

$x = 9$

$\therefore$ C)

10.

Let x be the fourth test. The average of 4 tests (85, 90, 89, and x) must be above 90.

$$\frac{85+90+89+x}{4} \geq 90$$

$$85+90+89+x \geq 4(90)$$

$\therefore$ D)

11.

Memorize:

vertex form: $a(x-h)^2+k$

The coordinates of vertex: (h, k)

When a$>$1: Concave up

When a$<$1: Concave down

From the given equation, $y=-2(x-2)^2+3$, we know the graph is a parabola that is concave down with the vertex at $(2, 3)$.

$\therefore$ B)

12.

Use long division

$$\begin{array}{r} 3y+1 \\ -2y+1\overline{)6y^2+5y+0} \\ \underline{(6y^2+2y)} \\ 3y \\ \underline{-(3y+1)} \\ -1 \end{array}$$

$\therefore\ 2y+1-\dfrac{1}{3y+1}$

$\therefore$ D)

13.

$5x^2=4x+1$

$5x^2-4x-1=0$

Memorize:

Discriminant: $b^2-4ac>0 \Rightarrow$ 2 solutions

Use the discriminant to know how many solutions are there.

$(-4)^2-4(5)(-1)=0$

$16+20=36>0$

$\therefore$ 2 solutions

$\therefore$ C)

14.

$a=$ # of adult tickets

$c=$ # of child tickets

$c=2a$

$10a+5c=400$

$10a+5(2a)=400$

$20a=400$

$a=20$

$c=40$

$a+c=60$

$\therefore$ D)

15.

Memorize: $a^2+2ab+b^2=(a+b)(a+b)$

$9a^2+2ab+\dfrac{1}{9}b^2$

$(3a)^2+2ab+(\dfrac{1}{3}b)^2$

$\left(3a+\dfrac{1}{3}b\right)\left(3a+\dfrac{1}{3}b\right)$

$\left(3a+\dfrac{1}{3}b\right)^2$

$\therefore$ D)

16.

$3^a=9^b$

$3^a=(3^2)^b$

$a=2b$

$\dfrac{a}{b}=2$

$\therefore$ 2

17.

Plug a into $g(x)=\dfrac{3}{5}x$

$g(a)=\dfrac{3}{5}a=\dfrac{3}{2}$

$\dfrac{3}{5}a\left(\dfrac{5}{3}\right)=\dfrac{3}{2}\left(\dfrac{5}{3}\right)$

$a=\dfrac{5}{2}=2.5$

$\therefore\ \dfrac{5}{2}$ or 2.5

18.

$\triangle ABC \approx \triangle DEC$

Thus, $\dfrac{AB}{AC} = \dfrac{ED}{CD}$

$\dfrac{8}{10} = \dfrac{4}{CD}$

$8CD = 40$

$CD = 5$

$AC + CD = 10 + 5 = 15$

$\therefore\ 15$

19.

60 sophomores$(40\%) = 60(0.40) = 24$ sophomores playing basketball

m freshmen$(15\%) = m(0.05)$ freshmen playing basketball

$(60 + m)(0.30) = 24 + m(0.15)$

$18 + 0.3m = 24 + 0.15m$

$18 - 18 + 0.3m - 0.15m = 24 - 18 + 0.15m - 0.15m$

$0.15m = 6$

$\therefore\ m = 40$

20.

Memorize: $\theta = \dfrac{\overset{\frown}{Arc}}{radius}$

Since $\angle OAB$ is $75°$ and $\triangle AOB$ is an isosceles triangle, $\angle AOB$ is $30°$.

Convert to radians: $30° \cdot 180° = \dfrac{\pi}{6}$

Use the foula $\theta = \dfrac{\overset{\frown}{Arc}}{radius}$ to find $\overset{\frown}{Arc}$

$\overline{OB} = radius = \dfrac{3}{\pi}$

$\dfrac{\pi}{6} = \dfrac{\overset{\frown}{AB}}{\frac{3}{\pi}}$

$\dfrac{\pi}{6}\left(\dfrac{3}{\pi}\right) = \dfrac{\overset{\frown}{AB}}{\frac{3}{\pi}}\left(\dfrac{3}{\pi}\right)$

$\dfrac{1}{2} = \overset{\frown}{AB}$

$\therefore\ \dfrac{1}{2}$ or 0.5

Section 4 (Calculator)

1.

$(-3m + 5p) - (4m - 2n + 3p)$

$-3m + 5p - 4m + 2n - 3p$

$-7m + 2p + 2n$

$\therefore$ A)

2.

The total amount of energy charged is

$e = 17t + 25$

The amount of energy increases by 17 every hour and 25 is a fixed amount of energy which does not depend on t number of hours.

$\therefore$ C) is the best interpretation of the number 25

3.

Fastest rate occurs at the steepest line on the graph. The steepest line happens from day 4 to day 7.

$\therefore$ B)

4.

$\$80 =$ fixed cost

hours=6

$\$x =$ variable cost

$80 + 6x = 176$

$80 - 80 + 6x = 176 - 80$

$6x = 96$

$6x\left(\dfrac{1}{6}\right) = 96\left(\dfrac{1}{6}\right)$

$x = 16$

$\therefore$ D)

5.

$14c + 7d = 21$

$14c - 14c + 7d = 21 - 14c$

$7d = 21 - 14c$

$d = 21 - 14c/7$

$d = 3 - 2c$

$\therefore$ B)

6.

The percentage of dentists is

$100\% - 41\% - 26\% - 17\% = 16\%$ of all doctors.

$\therefore\ 200(0.16) = 32$ dentists

$200(0.26) = 52$ psychiatrists.

$52 - 32 = 20$

$\therefore$ C)

7.

In the ascending-descending order, the middle person of the 15 students has received the final exam score of 88 according to the graph.

$\therefore$ D)

8.

The denominator should be the total number of students that participated in the morning practice session.

The numerator should be the number of students that participated in the morning swimming practice session.

Thus, $\dfrac{25}{25+11} = \dfrac{25}{36}$

$\therefore$ D)

9.

<u>Memorize</u>: $density = \dfrac{mass}{volume}$

$19\dfrac{g}{cm^3} = \dfrac{mass}{125cm^3(0.8)}$

$19\dfrac{g}{cm^3} = \dfrac{mass}{100cm^3}$

$19\dfrac{g}{cm^3}(100cm^3) = \dfrac{mass}{100cm^3}(100cm^3)$

$1900g = mass$

$\therefore$ B)

10.

C = price of cheese burger

A = $ Annie paid

D = $ Daniel paid

$D = C$

$A + D = 29$

$C + 5 + C = 29$

$2C + 5 = 29$

$2C + 5 - 5 = 29 - 5$

$2C = 24$

$2C\left(\dfrac{1}{2}\right) = 24\left(\dfrac{1}{2}\right)$

$C = 12$

$A = C + 5$

$A = 12 + 5 = 17$

$\therefore$ C)

11.

$\left(\begin{array}{c} 2a + 4b = 7 \\ a - 8b = 1 \end{array}\right)$

$\left(\begin{array}{c} 2a + 4b = 7 \\ 2(a - 8b = 1) \end{array}\right)$

$\left(\begin{array}{c} 2a + 4b = 7 \\ -(2a - 16b = 2) \end{array}\right)$

$20b = 5$

$b = \dfrac{1}{4}$

$a = 3$

$\dfrac{a}{b} = \dfrac{3}{\frac{1}{4}} = 12$

$\therefore$ D)

12.

From 0 to 10 seconds, Patrick traveled 6.9 meters, which is the greatest distance traveled. Out of the 4 answer choices, choice A) is correct

$\therefore$ A)

13.

average speed = average rate of change = slope

In the given equation, $d(t) = 0.97t - 1.7$

Note that the coefficient of t represents the slope

$\therefore$ C)

14.

1st five seconds: Average rate is $\dfrac{2.9m}{5\text{secs}} = 0.58$

Last five seconds: Average rate is $\dfrac{5.5m}{5\text{secs}} = 1.1$

Difference: 1.1 - 0.58 = 0.52

$\therefore$ A)

15.

future amount = initial amount $\cdot (1 + \text{rate})^{\text{time}}$

Intial amount: \$200

Rate: declining at a rate of 50% each year {0.5} or $\left(\dfrac{1}{2}\right)$

$\therefore \ p = 200\left(\dfrac{1}{2}\right)^t$

$\therefore$ D)

16.

Notice that the triangles are similar to each other since the side lengths $(4,6,7)$ become $(6,9,10.5)$ by multiplying by a factor of $\dfrac{3}{2}$ Thus, $\angle EDF = \angle ABC$

and $\angle DFE = 180 - 58.8 - 34.8 = 86.4$

$\therefore$ C)

17.

$p = 5h + 3c$

$p - 3c = 5h$

$(p - 3c)\left(\dfrac{1}{5}\right) = 5h\left(\dfrac{1}{5}\right)$

$\dfrac{p - 3c}{5} = h$

$\dfrac{p}{5} - \dfrac{3c}{5} = h$

$\dfrac{1}{5}(p - 3c) = h$

$\therefore$ B)

18.

Jacob's budget = \$37

Min possible # of bags of candy=3

Thus, using $p = 5h + 3c, \ 37 = 5h + 3(3)$

$37 = 5h + 9$

$28 = 5h$

$\dfrac{28}{5} = \dfrac{5h}{5}$

$\dfrac{28}{5} = h$

$h = 5.6$

the max # of bags of chocolate=5

$\therefore$ A)

19.

$p = 5h + 3c$

$h = $ # of bags of chocolate

$c = $ an odd number

$37 = 5h + 3(\text{odd \#})$

See the answer choices.

Only when $h = 2$,

Jacob can use \$37 completely

$37 = 5(2) + 3(c)$

$37 = 10 + 3c$

$27 = 3c$

An odd number $= 9 = c$

$\therefore$ A)

20.

$x^2 - 4 = 0$

$x^2 - 4 + 4 = +4$

$x^2 = 4$

$\sqrt{x^2} = \sqrt{4}$

$x = \pm 2$

$a = 2 b = -2$ or vice versa.

$|a - b| = |2 - (-2)| = 4$

$\therefore$ D)

21.

The sample of 200 customers was selected at a certain time at the cafe, and since 70% of them ordered coffee, it can be concluded that approximately 70% of all the customers at the cafe would prefer coffee over fruit juice.

$\therefore$ C)

22.

The score of the 9^{th}(median) person of 17 students is m.

The highest and 2nd highest scores are $m+2$ and m, respectively.

Since the scores of the 17 students are

$?, ?, ?, ?, ?, ?, ?, ?, m, ?, ?, ?, ?, ?, ?, m, m+2,$

all the scores between the median and 2nd highest score must be all same.

Thus, the scores are:

$?, ?, ?, ?, ?, ?, ?, ?, m, m, m, m, m, m, m, m, m+2.$

As 2 new studnets score higher than m+2, the new median which is the 10th person, must be m also.

For example,

$?,?,?,?,?,?,?,?, m(\text{old median}), m(\text{new median}), m, m,$ $m, m, m, m, m+2,$ new student 1, new student 2

$\therefore$ A)

23.

It is clearly shown on the graph that the helicopter was 5 meters above the ground 3 times approximately at $x=2.5,\ 4.8,\ 7.$

Check by drawing $y=5$ on the graph.

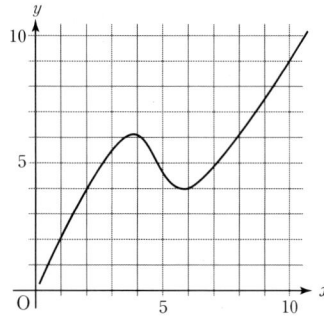

$\therefore$ C)

24.

$5.20x=5.79$

$x=1.11=111\%=100\%(\text{initial amount})+11\%$

Thus, 5.20 increased by 11%

$\therefore$ D)

25.

$(2,3),(-1,-6)$ and $(x,6)$ are colinear and share the same slope.

Thus, using the slope foula we get,

$$\frac{-6-3}{-1-2}=\frac{6-(-6)}{x-(-1)}$$

$$\frac{-9}{-3}=\frac{12}{x+1}$$

$$\frac{3}{1}=\frac{12}{x+1}$$

Cross multiply.

$3(x+1)=12$

$3x+3=12$

$3x+3-3=12-3$

$3x=9$

$$\frac{3x}{3}=\frac{9}{3}$$

$x=3$

$\therefore$ C)

26.

Despite the difference in radii of Susan's and Joanne's wheels, they travel the same distance.

Note that 1 revolution=the circumference of the wheel.

The circumference of Susan's

wheel$=2\pi r=2\pi(30)=60\pi$

Susan's total distance$=(50 \text{ revolutions})(60\pi)$

Joanne's total distance$=(60 \text{ revolutions})(2\pi r)$

Thus, $(50)(60\pi)=(60)(2\pi r)$

$3{,}000\pi=60\cdot 2\pi r$

$$\frac{3{,}000\pi}{\pi}=\frac{60\cdot 2\pi r}{\pi}$$

$3{,}000=120r$

$$\frac{3{,}000}{120}=\frac{120r}{120}$$

$25=r$

$\therefore$ B)

27.

$x^2-4x+y^2+6y=3$

complete the square using $\left(\dfrac{b}{2}\right)^2$

$x^2-4x+4+y^2+6y+9=3+4+9=16$

Memorize:

The center-radius fo of the circle equation:

$(x-h)^2+(y-k)^2=r^2$

The right side of the equation gives us that $r^2=16$

$\sqrt{16}=\sqrt{r^2}$

$\pm4=r$

radius$=4$ diameter$=8$

$\therefore$ D)

28.

$|x+2|=5$

① $x+2=5$ ② $-(x+2)=5$

                               $x+2=-5$

    $x=3$ or $x=-7$

This shows x is 5 units away from -2

Remember:

$|x-c|=d$ when

$$\begin{array}{ccc} \shortmid & \shortmid & \shortmid \\ x-c & x & x+d \end{array}$$

$\therefore$ A)

29.

Speed $\cdot$ Time $=$ Distance

Thus, $20\cdot t=D$

$20t=D$

$\therefore$ B)

30.

Draw the line of best fit on the graph.

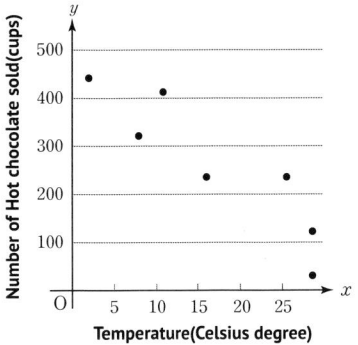

Notice the slope is negative and the y$-$intercept is very close to 500.

$\therefore$ D) is the best answer choice.

31.

# of students in the group $=x$

$\dfrac{70}{x-2}=\dfrac{70}{x+4}$

$\dfrac{70}{x-2}(x-2)(x)=\left(\dfrac{70}{x}+4\right)(x-2)(x)$

$70x=70(x-2)+4(x-2)(x)$

$70x-70x=70x-70x-140+(4x-8)(x)$

$0=-140+4x^2-8x$

$4x^2-8x-140=0$

Here, use calculator or solve algebraically.

$(4x^2-8x-140)\left(\dfrac{1}{4}\right)=0\left(\dfrac{1}{4}\right)$

$x^2-2x-35=0$

$(x-7)(x+5)$

$x=7$ or -5

x must be 7.

32.

$-3(2x-10)+(5x+a)=5$

$-6x+30+5x+a=5$

$-x+30+a=5$

$a=-14$

$-x+30-14=5$

$-x+16=5$

$x=11$

33.

$400 < $ volume of pint glass $ < 450$

Height $=15$

$400 < \pi r^2 15 < 450$

$$\frac{400}{15} < \frac{\pi r^2 15}{15} < \frac{450}{15}$$

$$\frac{262}{3} < \pi r^2 < 30$$

$$\frac{26\frac{2}{3}}{\pi} < \frac{\pi r^2}{\pi} < \frac{30}{\pi}$$

$2.91 < r < 3.09$

$r = 3$

34.

$y = x^2 - x$

$y = 2x - \dfrac{9}{4}$

Use calculator or solve algebraically.

Algebraic method: Set the equations equal to each other.

$x^2 - x = 2x - \dfrac{9}{4}$

$x^2 - 3x + \dfrac{9}{4} = 0$

Use the discriminant $b^2 - 4ac$

$9 - 4(1)\left(\dfrac{9}{4}\right)$

9-9=0

Since $b^2 - 4ac = 0$, there is 1 distinct root which means that there is 1 intersection point.

$\therefore$ 1

35.

$ax + 3y = 7$

Plug in $(2,0)$

$a(2) + 3(0) = 7$

$a2 = 7$

$a = \dfrac{7}{2}$ or 3.5

36.

$$\frac{\text{total time}}{5} = 11.8 \text{ seconds}$$

Total time = 59 seconds

$$\frac{\text{total time} + x}{6} = 11.7 \text{ seconds}$$

$59 + x = 70.2$

$x = 11.2$

$\therefore$ 11.2 seconds

37.

Method 1:

By half life,

$80 \xrightarrow{\text{8 days}} 40 \xrightarrow{\text{8 days}} 20 \xrightarrow{\text{8 days}} 10 \xrightarrow{\text{8 days}} 5$

Total 32 days

Method 2:

$80\left(\dfrac{1}{2}\right)^{\frac{x}{8}} = 5$

$\left(\dfrac{1}{2}\right)^{\frac{x}{8}} = \dfrac{5}{80}$

$\ln\left(\dfrac{1}{2}\right)^{\frac{x}{8}} = \ln\dfrac{5}{80}$

$\dfrac{x}{8}\ln\left(\dfrac{1}{2}\right) = \ln\dfrac{5}{80}$

$x = \dfrac{\ln\dfrac{5}{80}}{\ln\left(\dfrac{1}{2}\right)}(8)$

$x = 32$ days

38.

B=Bilingual employees=44%

T=Trilingual employees=16%

B=T+42

B-T=42

44%-16%=28%=42

42/28% · 16%=24 trilingual employees

42/28% · 32%=48 unilingual employees

48-24=24 more unilingual employees

SAT Math Practice Test 2

Math Test (No Calculator)

25 MINUTES, 20 QUESTIONS

Turn to Section 3 of your answer sheet to answer the questions in this section.

DIRECTIONS

For questions 1-15, solve each problem, choose the best answer from the choices provided, and fill in the corresponding circle on your answer sheet. **For questions 16-20,** solve the problem and enter your answer in the grid on the answer sheet. Please refer to the directions before question 16 on how to enter your answers in the grid. You may use any available space in your test booklet for scratch work.

NOTES

1. The use of a calculator **is not permitted.**
2. All variables and expressions used represent real numbers unless otherwise indicated.
3. Figures provided in this test are drawn to scale unless otherwise indicated.
4. All figures lie in a plane unless otherwise indicated.
5. Unless otherwise indicated, the domain of a given function f is the set of all real numbers x for which $f(x)$ is a real number.

REFERENCE

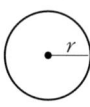 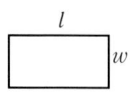 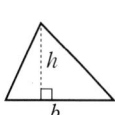 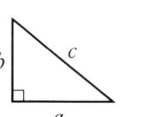 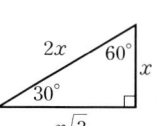 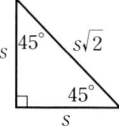

$A = \pi r^2$ $A = lw$ $A = \frac{1}{2}bh$ $c^2 = a^2 + b^2$ Special Right Triangles
$C = 2\pi r$

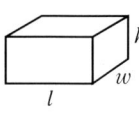 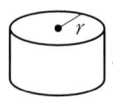 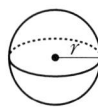 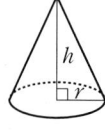 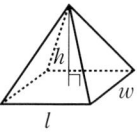

$V = lwh$ $V = \pi r^2 h$ $V = \frac{4}{3}\pi r^3$ $V = \frac{1}{3}\pi r^2 h$ $V = \frac{1}{3}lwh$

The number of degrees of arc in a circle is 360.

The number of radians of arc in a circle is 2π.

The sum of the measures in degrees of the angles of a triangle is 180.

CONTINUE

1

$$\frac{7x+3}{-2}+5=-7y$$

In the equation above, what is the value of $x-2y$?

A) No solution
B) -1
C) 0
D) 1

2

Which of the following complex numbers is equal to $(2i+13)+(-2i^2+6i)$ for $i=\sqrt{-1}$?

A) 15+8i
B) 13+10i
C) -13-10i
D) -15-8i

3

The range of shipping weights of 4 packs of lip balm is 2.0 ounces to 2.4 ounces. If s represents the shipping weight, in ounces, of one of the packs, which of the following must be true?

A) $|s| \le 0.4$
B) $|s-0.2| \le 2.3$
C) $|s-0.55| \le 0.05$
D) $|s-2.1| \le 0.2$

4

$$P=50+20n$$

The cost P, in dollars, of buying a propolis spray at a membership warehouse store is modeled by the function above, where n is the number of sprays purchased. Based on this model, which of the following must be true?

A) The membership fee costs $50 and the spray can be bought for no extra cost.
B) The membership fee costs $50 and $20 each time the spray is purchased.
C) The membership fee costs $20 and $50 each time the spray is purchased.
D) The spray costs $20 each time it is purchased, but there is also an extra fee of $50 per purchase.

CONTINUE

5

$$j(x) = 2x^2 + 5x + 2y$$
$$k(x) = -5x^2 + 2xy + 5$$

Which of the following expressions is equivalent to $j(x) - k(x)$?

A) $7x^2 + 5x - 5$

B) $-3x^2 + 5x + 2y - 2xy - 5$

C) $7x^2 + 5x + 2y - 2xy - 5$

D) $-3x^2 + 5x + 2y + 2xy + 5$

6

A supercomputer can be rented at home with a fixed initial cost of \$130 and a variable cost of \$2.5 for each month used. Based on this information, what is the estimated total cost, in dollars, to rent a supercomputer for 1 year?

A) 30

B) 132.5

C) 155

D) 160

7

$$C_p = \frac{(D_G)(k_a)}{(V_d)(k_a - k_e)}$$

The concentration of a drug in the body C_p can be modeled by the equation above, where D_G is the dosage, in milligrams, administered, V_d is the volume, in liters, of distribution, k_a is the absorption rate constant (h^{-1}), and k_e is the elimination rate constant (h^{-1}). Which of the following gives k_e in terms of C_p, D_G, V_d, and k_a?

A) $k_e = \dfrac{(D_G)(k_a)}{(V_d)(C_p)} - k_a$

B) $k_e = -\dfrac{(D_G)(k_a)}{(V_d)(C_p)} + k_a$

C) $k_e = -\dfrac{(V_d)(C_p)}{(D_G)} + 1$

D) $k_e = -\dfrac{(V_d)(C_p)}{D_g}$

CONTINUE

8

If $\dfrac{g}{3d} = 6$, $\dfrac{g}{c} = 4$, and $9d + 9c = 22$, what is the value of c?

A) 0

B) 1

C) 2

D) $\dfrac{9}{2}$

9

$$2x - 6y = 5$$
$$1 + x = 2y$$

Which of the following best describes the system of equations above?

A) A system with infinitely many solutions

B) A system with one solution formed by lines that are <u>not</u> perpendicular to each other

C) A system with one solution formed by lines that are perpendicular to each other

D) A system with no solutions

10

Function f is defined by the equation $f(x) = dx^2 + 4dx$. If $f(2) - f(1) = 24$, what is a possible value of d?

A) $\dfrac{1}{2}$

B) 3

C) $\dfrac{24}{7}$

D) 4

11

If 21 is three fourths as much as the sum of x and 5, then $x + 5$ exceeds 21 by what amount?

A) $-10\dfrac{1}{4}$

B) 7

C) $10\dfrac{1}{4}$

D) 33

12

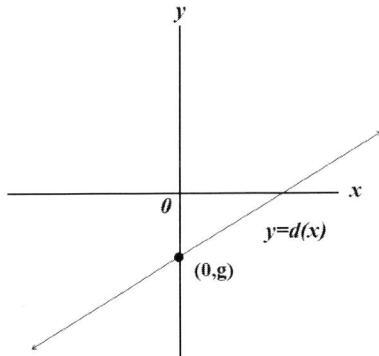

The figure above shows the graph of the linear function $y = d(x)$. If the slope of the line is $\dfrac{4}{5}$ and $d(10) = -19$, what is the value of g?

A) -27

B) -9

C) -5

D) -1

13

$$x^2 = 4gx + 2d$$

In the quadratic equation above, d and g are constants. What are the solutions for x ?

A) $2g \pm \dfrac{1}{4}\sqrt{16g + 8d}$

B) $2g \pm \sqrt{4g^2 + 2d}$

C) $-2g \pm \dfrac{1}{2}\sqrt{16g + 8d}$

D) $-2g \pm \sqrt{2g^2 + d}$

14

If $2 = 24^k$, what is the value of $\dfrac{24^{3k}}{4}$?

A) $\dfrac{\sqrt[3]{2}}{4}$

B) 1

C) 2

D) 6^3

15

$$42x^2 + dx + (c+3) = (gx+2)(cx-2)$$

If the equation above is true for all values of x where c, d, and g are non-zero constants, what is the value of d?

A) -28

B) -26

C) -2

D) 83

CONTINUE

DIRECTIONS

For questions 16-20, solve the problem and enter your answer in the grid, as described below, on the answer sheet.

1. Although not required, it is suggested that you write your answer in the boxes at the top of the columns to help you fill in the circles accurately. You will receive credit only if the circles are filled in correctly.

2. Mark no more than one circle in any column.

3. No question has a negative answer.

4. Some problems may have more than one correct answer. In such cases, grid only one answer.

5. **Mixed numbers** such as $3\frac{1}{2}$ must be gridded as 3.5 or 7/2. (If [3 1 / 2 grid] is entered into the grid, it will be interpreted as $\frac{31}{2}$, not $3\frac{1}{2}$.)

6. **Decimal answers**: If you obtain a decimal answer with more digits than the grid can accommodate, it may be either rounded or truncated, but it must fill the entire grid.

Answer: $\frac{7}{12}$

Write answer in boxes.

←Fraction line

Grid in result.

Answer: 2.5

←Decimal point

Acceptable ways to grid $\frac{2}{3}$ are:

Answer: 201 - either position is correct.

NOTE: You may start your answer in any column, space permitting. Columns you don't need to use should be left blank.

CONTINUE

16

If $25 \leq \dfrac{5}{t} - 1$ and $t > 0$, what is the greatest possible value for t?

17

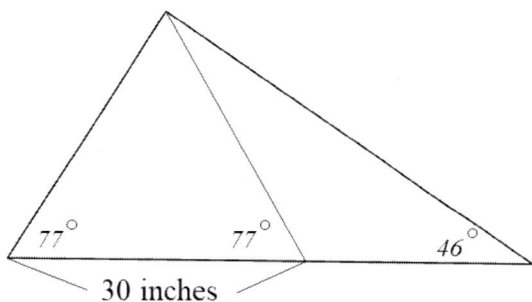

30 inches

Note: Figure not drawn to scale.

Gables roofs are made by placing two right triangles together. The building structure above is a modification of the Gable roof using two non-right triangles. The measurements are partially shown above. Based on these measurements, what is the sum of the area of the two triangles in <u>feet</u>? (1 foot = 12 inches) Round your answer to the nearest integer.
Use the values: tan(77°)=4, tan(46°)=0.8

18

$$2x - 5y = 10$$
$$10x + 2y = 68$$

If (x,y) is the solution to the system of equations above, what is the value of y?

19

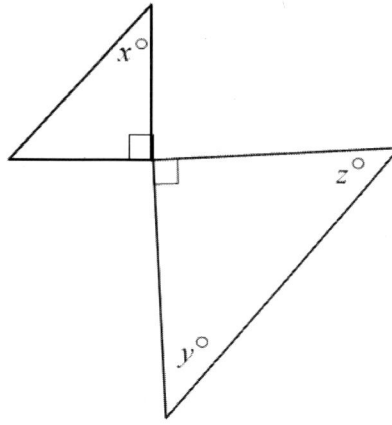

Note: Figure not drawn to scale.

In the triangle above, $x°$ and $z°$ are complementary angles. The $\cos x° = \dfrac{10}{26}$ and $\sin y° = \dfrac{a}{b}$, what is the value of a if a and b are relatively prime? (That is, a and b have no common factor.)

20

If $g \neq 0$, what is the value of $\dfrac{3(10\sqrt{\dfrac{1}{g}})^2}{(\sqrt[3]{2g})^{-3}}$?

STOP
If you finish before time is called, you may check your work on this section only.
Do not turn to any other section.

No Test Material On This Page

Math Test (Calculator)

55 MINUTES, 38 QUESTIONS

Turn to Section 4 of your answer sheet to answer the questions in this section.

DIRECTIONS

For questions 1-30, solve each problem, choose the best answer from the choices provided, and fill in the corresponding circle on your answer sheet. **For questions 31-38,** solve the problem and enter your answer in the grid on the answer sheet. Please refer to the directions before question 31 on how to enter your answers in the grid. You may use any available space in your test booklet for scratch work.

NOTES

1. The use of a calculator **is permitted**.
2. All variables and expressions used represent real numbers unless otherwise indicated.
3. Figures provided in this test are drawn to scale unless otherwise indicated.
4. All figures lie in a plane unless otherwise indicated.
5. Unless otherwise indicated, the domain of a given function f is the set of all real numbers x for which $f(x)$ is a real number.

REFERENCE

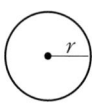 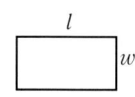 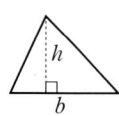 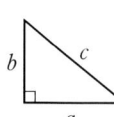 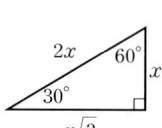 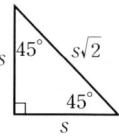

$A = \pi r^2$ $A = lw$ $A = \frac{1}{2}bh$ $c^2 = a^2 + b^2$ Special Right Triangles
$C = 2\pi r$

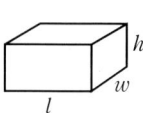 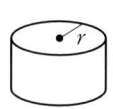 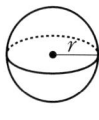 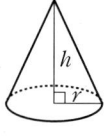 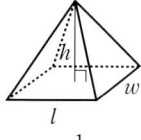

$V = lwh$ $V = \pi r^2 h$ $V = \frac{4}{3}\pi r^3$ $V = \frac{1}{3}\pi r^2 h$ $V = \frac{1}{3}lwh$

The number of degrees of arc in a circle is 360.

The number of radians of arc in a circle is 2π.

The sum of the measures in degrees of the angles of a triangle is 180.

CONTINUE ➡

1

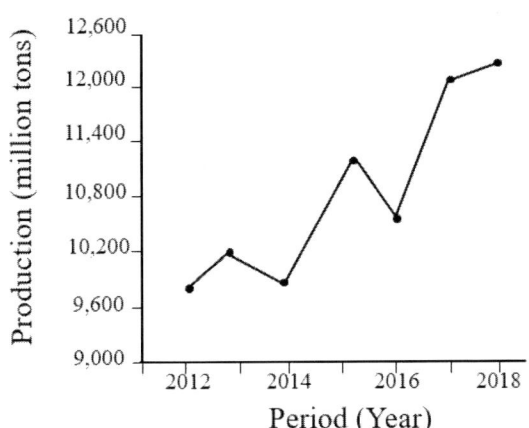

The graph above shows the yearly production of mangoes in Southeast Asia from year 2012 to 2018. According to the graph, what was the smallest change (in millions of tons) in yearly production between two consecutive years?

A)   0
B)   200
C)   400
D)   600

2

An internet cafe is offering 3 hours of use for $2.50 and then charges $2.50 per each additional hour. If one customer spent $37.50 for x number of hours, then what is the value x?

A)   7.5
B)   14
C)   15
D)   17

3

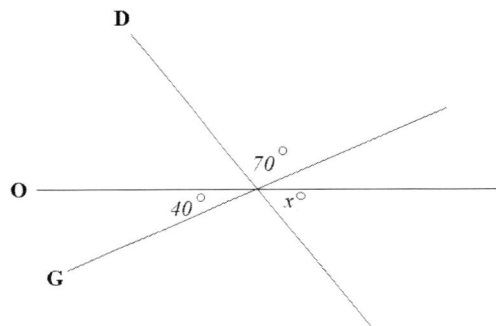

Note: Figure not drawn to scale.

In the figure above, lines D, O, and G all intersect at one point. What is the value of $x°$?

A)   40°
B)   50°
C)   70°
D)   90°

4

If $\frac{5}{3}$ exceeds $\frac{3}{5}n$ by $\frac{2}{3}$, what is the value of n ?

A) $\frac{1}{3}$

B) $\frac{5}{8}$

C) $\frac{5}{3}$

D) $\frac{25}{9}$

5

In North America, there is a strong positive association between the husband's age and the wife's age. Which of the following scatterplots best shows this relationship?

A)

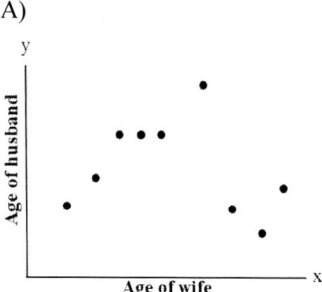

B)

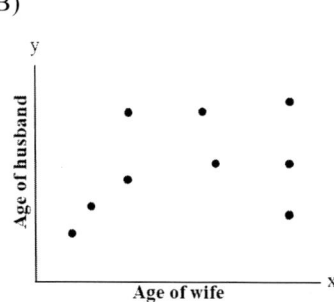

C)

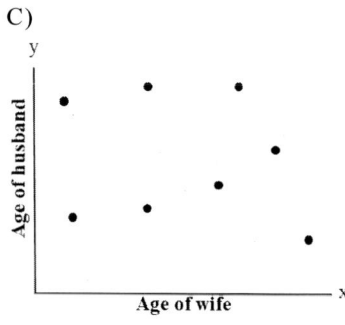

D)

6

Coconut oil contains 82 grams of saturated fat per 100 grams. Approximately how many grams of saturated fat are there in 3 pounds of coconut oil? (28.35 grams = 1 ounces, 16 ounces = 1 pound) Round your answer to the nearest integer.

A)   7

B)   39

C)   378

D) 1,116

Unauthorized copying or reuse of any part of this page is illegal.

CONTINUE

240 | Paul's SAT Math 800

7

Weekly Exercise Habits by Age

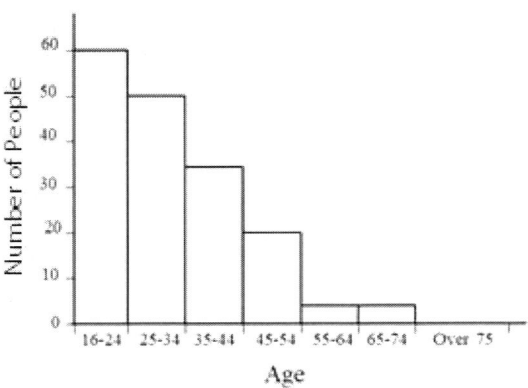

The histogram above shows the number of people that spend at least one hour per week exercising, by age. If the total number of people sampled is 175, what is the probability that a person selected at random is between 25 and 34 years old?

A) $\dfrac{1}{4}$

B) $\dfrac{1}{2}$

C) $\dfrac{2}{7}$

D) $\dfrac{5}{17}$

8

For what values of x is $|6x+2|=7$?

A) $x=\dfrac{3}{2},\ x=-\dfrac{5}{6}$

B) $\dfrac{3}{2}>x>-\dfrac{5}{6}$

C) $-\dfrac{3}{2}<x<\dfrac{5}{6}$

D) $x=-\dfrac{3}{2},\ x=\dfrac{5}{6}$

— ▼ —

Questions 9 and 10 refer to the following information.

$$y - 270 = -9x$$

A professional gamer spends long hours practicing on a keyboard and mouse. The gamer sets monthly goals for practice hours. The equation above can be used for a professional gamer to model the number of practice hours, y, that need to be played in order to meet the monthly goal, x days after the first day of the month.

9

(30, 0) is a solution set to this equation. Which of the following is the correct interpretation of this solution set?
A) It takes 30 days of practice for the monthly goal to be met.
B) There are 30 days in each month.
C) It takes 30 days during a month to play 1052 games.
D) Every month, the gamer spends 30 days practicing.

10

After how many number of days will y be closest to 234 hours?
A) 3 days
B) 4 days
C) 5 days
D) 6 days

— ▲ —

11

If $\dfrac{2x-3}{4} \le 5 + 3x$, what is the value of x ?
A) $x \ge -2.3$
B) $x \ge 2.3$
C) $x \le 2.3$
D) $x \le -2.3$

12

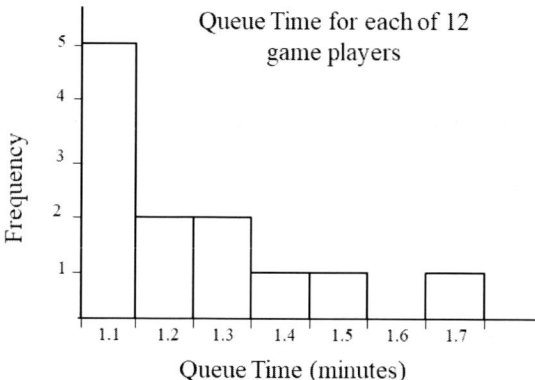

Queue Time for each of 12 game players

The histogram above shows the distribution of the queue time, in minutes, of 12 gamers in Antarctica. Which of the following is the mode queue time in minutes?
A) 0.6
B) 1.0
C) 1.1
D) 1.258

CONTINUE ▶

13

Year	Production (in tons)				Total production
	Coal	Petroleum	Natural gas	Other	
2000	30	40	40	6	116
2010	28	35	46	8	117
2020	32	28	44	13	117

The chart above is data from a study on energy production. If the category "Other" is excluded from the total for each year, what proportion, to the nearest hundredth, of the total production of energy from 2000 to 2020 was generated in 2010?

A) 0.1
B) 0.34
C) 0.78
D) 0.91

14

Student Scores			
92	84	70	89
100	82	74	95
80	66	60	75
65	75	90	50

The table above shows the average scores obtained by 16 students in Biology. If a new student transfers to this class and receives a score of 100, which statement is true?

A) The range will change by a certain amount.
B) The median test score will not change.
C) The mean test score will change by a certain amount.
D) The new student's score will be an outlier to the data set given by the table.

CONTINUE

— ▼ —

Questions 15 and 16 refer to the following information.

A country's employed population was 86 million in 2018, and it is expected to fall 1.5% each year. Starting from 2018, the government uses the equation $E = E_0(r)^n$ to estimate the employed population, E, after n years.

15

What value should be used for the value of r?
A) -0.5
B) 0.85
C) 0.985
D) 1.5

16

Which of the following represents r in term of other variables for the year 2021?

A) $r = \dfrac{E}{3E_0}$

B) $r = \sqrt[2]{\dfrac{E}{E_0}}$

C) $r = \sqrt[3]{\dfrac{E}{E_0}}$

D) $r = \sqrt[2021]{\dfrac{E}{E_0}}$

— ▲ —

17

If function f is defined by $f(x) = 5x + 2$ and $2f(g) = 6$, what is the value of $f(2g)$?

A) $\dfrac{16}{5}$

B) 4

C) 5

D) 6

CONTINUE

18

In the xy-plane, if the relationship between g and d is that $g > d$ where g and d are positive integers, which of the following solutions satisfy the equations $y > x + d$ and $y < x + g$?

A) (6,2)
B) (2,6)
C) (2,1)
D) (1,2)

19

A Japanese toy-maker has opened up pre-orders for two action figures. One figure costs \$70 and the other costs \$175. A toy collector spent a total of \$1680 for these action figures. If the collector purchased two \$175 action figures for each \$70 action figure purchased, what is the total number of action figures purchased?

A) 4
B) 8
C) 12
D) 15

CONTINUE

20

A multinational electronics company produced 2 million tablets and 3.2 million mobile phones in 2018. In 2019, the company decided to increase the production of tablets by 110 percent, and the production of mobile phones by 50 percent. Approximately, by what percentage did the total production increase?

A)   7 percent
B)   35 percent
C)   58 percent
D)   73 percent

21

Land Degradation in 2017, millions of hectares

Region	Over-grazing	Over-cultivation	Deforestation	Total Land Degraded
Asia	1.2	2.0	2.8	6
North America	2.2	3.4	4.4	10
Africa	0.5	4.0	0.5	5

The data in the table above presents the total land degraded, in millions of hectares, by various causes in three continents. What proportion of the total degraded land is deforested land that is not located in Asia?

A) $\dfrac{7}{30}$

B) $\dfrac{49}{150}$

C) $\dfrac{7}{11}$

D)   4.9

Unauthorized copying or reuse of any part of this page is illegal.

CONTINUE

246 | Paul's SAT Math 800

— ▼ —

Questions 22 and 23 refer to the following information.

Top 6 cities with the most Global 500 companies

City	Number of Companies	Revenues	Average Revenue
Tokyo	51	$2,165,350	$42,458
Paris	27	$1,488,150	$55,117
Beijing	26	$1,315,050	$50,578
New York	18	$846,810	$47,045
London	15	$994,510	$66,300
Seoul	11	$542,950	$49,359

The table above shows the data set consists of the list of top 6 cities with the highest number of Fortune 500 companies and their combined revenue figures.

22

If a company is selected from the cities where companies reported average revenues of $50,000 or more, what is the best estimate of the probability that the company is located in Beijing?

A) 0.38
B) 0.52
C) 0.59
D) 0.64

23

Which of the following lists the ratio of two cities' revenues in descending order?
(Tokyo = T, Paris = P, Beijing = B, New York = N, London = L, Seoul = S)

A) $\dfrac{P}{T}, \dfrac{B}{P}, \dfrac{L}{N}, \dfrac{S}{L}$

B) $\dfrac{L}{N}, \dfrac{B}{P}, \dfrac{P}{T}, \dfrac{S}{L}$

C) $\dfrac{L}{N}, \dfrac{B}{P}, \dfrac{N}{B}, \dfrac{P}{T}$

D) $\dfrac{P}{T}, \dfrac{N}{B}, \dfrac{S}{L}, \dfrac{B}{P}$

— ▲ —

CONTINUE

24

If an equation of a circle is
$x^2 + 2x + y^2 + 4y = 44$, which of the statements below are true?

A) The coordinates of the center are (-1,-2)

B) The coordinates of the center are (1,2)

C) The length of the radius is 49

D) The length of the radius is $\sqrt{7}$

25

An arch has the shape of a parabola with the equation $h = -4w^2 + 20w$ where $h \geq 0$. What is the difference between the maximum height of the arch and the maximum width of the arch?

A) 0

B) 5

C) 20

D) 25

26

Dickson and Jane each posted a video of themselves via a social media website. They received a total of 2369 likes. If Jane received 30% more likes than Dickson, how many likes did Jane receive?

A) 1030

B) 1170

C) 1199

D) 1339

27

In a survey of a random sample of 760 students aged 14 years or older from a particular school, 360 students had Instagram accounts. If the entire city in which the school is located had 840,000 students, which of the following conclusions can be made about the number of students in the city that have Instagram accounts?

A) There are more students with Instagram accounts in the city than there are students without Instagram accounts.

B) It is expected that approximately 397,895 students in the city have Instagram accounts.

C) No conclusion can be drawn because there is no evidence that the students surveyed at a particular school represent all students in the city.

D) No conclusion can be drawn because there is no information about the total population of the city.

CONTINUE

28

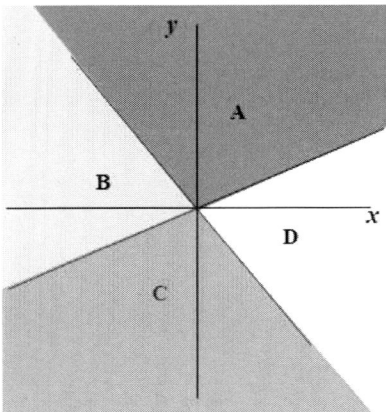

A system of inequalities and a graph are shown above. Which section or sections of the graph could represent the solutions to the system of equations below?

$$y \le \frac{1}{5}x$$

$$y \le \frac{-13}{6}x$$

A) Section C
B) Section C and D
C) Section A and B
D) Section B and C

29

If f(x) is a polynomial function and f(-41)=1, which of the following statements must be true?
A) $x-1$ is a factor of $f(x)$.
B) $x+41$ is a factor of $f(x)$.
C) The remainder when $f(x)$ is divided by $x-41$ is 1.
D) The remainder when $f(x)$ is divided by $x+41$ is 1.

30

The equation of a parabola in the xy-plane is $y = 7x^2 + 14x + 3$. What is the distance between the vertex of the parabola and the point (12,-4)?
A) 0
B) $\sqrt{905}$
C) 11
D) 13

Unauthorized copying or reuse of any part of this page is illegal.

CONTINUE

Practice Test 2 | 249

DIRECTIONS

For questions 31-38, solve the problem and enter your answer in the grid, as described below, on the answer sheet.

1. Although not required, it is suggested that you write your answer in the boxes at the top of the columns to help you fill in the circles accurately. You will receive credit only if the circles are filled in correctly.

2. Mark no more than one circle in any column.

3. No question has a negative answer.

4. Some problems may have more than one correct answer. In such cases, grid only one answer.

5. **Mixed numbers** such as $3\frac{1}{2}$ must be gridded as

   3.5 or 7/2. (If [3 1 / 2] is entered into the grid, it

   will be interpreted as $\frac{31}{2}$, not $3\frac{1}{2}$.)

6. **Decimal answers**: If you obtain a decimal answer with more digits than the grid can accommodate, it may be either rounded or truncated, but it must fill the entire grid.

Answer: $\frac{7}{12}$ Answer: 2.5

Write answer in boxes. →   ← Fraction line

← Decimal point

Grid in result.

Acceptable ways to grid $\frac{2}{3}$ are:

Answer: 201 - either position is correct.

NOTE: You may start your answer in any column, space permitting. Columns you don't need to use should be left blank.

Unauthorized copying or reuse of any part of this page is illegal.

CONTINUE ▶

250 | Paul's SAT Math 800

31

$$\frac{3}{4}g = x$$
$$5g + x = y$$

In the system of equations above, g is a constant such that $\frac{1}{2} < g < \frac{3}{2}$. If $(x,\ y)$ is a solution to the system of equations, what is one possible value of y?

32

Jenny, a junior chemist, wants to make a 250mL of 4% solution by mixing a 3% solution with a 8% solution. What amount of the 3% solution does she have to use?

33

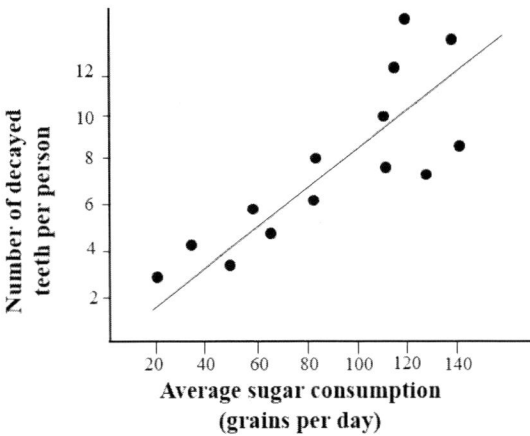

The scatterplot above shows the number of decayed teeth of 14 people with different levels of sugar consumption. What fraction of the 14 people have a greater number of cavities than what is estimated by the best fit line?

34

A certain music critic can listen to 8 songs per hour. The critic is rushed for time and decides to listen to music for 8 consecutive days without any break except for eating and sleeping. He spends 11.5 hours eating and sleeping each day. How many hours does he have to listen to music during these 8 days?

CONTINUE

35

Nicolas wants to customize a cylindrical thermos. If he wants a thermos with a radius between 3.5 and 3.7 inches, and a height of 12 inches, what is one possible volume, rounded to the nearest hundredth cubic foot, of a thermos Nicolas could select?
(1 foot = 12 inches)

36

$$\frac{x^2 - 4x - 77}{x - 11}$$

If the expression above is equivalent to an expression of the from $x + c$, what is the value of c?

Questions 37 and 38 refer to the following information.

The number of marriages held in South Korea in 2018 is 19,000. The government believes that the number of marriages will decrease by 1.8 percent every 6 months for the next 7 years. The government uses the equation $M = 19(r)^t$ to estimate the number of marriages, in thousands, in the future, where r is the rate of decrease, and t is the number of years passed after the year of the initial value.

37

What value should the government use for r to the nearest hundredth decimal place?

38

To the nearest integer, how many thousands of marriages does the government expect will take place 7 years later?

STOP
If you finish before time is called, you may check your work on this section only.
Do not turn to any other section.

Practice Test 2:
Answer Key and Explanations

Test 2 Answer Key

Math - No Calculator	
Question #	Answer
1	D
2	A
3	C
4	B
5	C
6	D
7	B
8	C
9	B
10	C
11	B
12	A
13	B
14	C
15	C
16	5/26
17	19
18	2/3 OR .666 OR .667
19	12
20	600

Math - Calculator	
Question #	Answer
1	B
2	D
3	C
4	C
5	D
6	D
7	C
8	D
9	A
10	B
11	A
12	C
13	B
14	C
15	C
16	C
17	B
18	B
19	C
20	D
21	A
22	A
23	B
24	A
25	C
26	D
27	C
28	A
29	D
30	D
31	$23/8 < y < 69/8$
32	200
33	4/7
34	100
35	$0.27 < x < 0.30$
36	7
37	0.98
38	15

*To get your estimated scaled SAT score, please turn to page 301.

Answer Explanations
No Calculator Section

1.

$$\frac{7x+3}{-2+5}=-7y$$

$$\frac{7x+3}{-2}(-2)+5(-2)=-7y(-2)$$

$$7x+3-10=14y$$

$$7x-7=14y$$

$$7x-14y=7$$

$$x-2y=1$$

$$\therefore D)$$

2.

Memorize: $i=\sqrt{-1}$ $i^2=-1$ $i^3=-i$ $i^4=1$

This repeats every 4 exponents.

$$(2i+13)+(-2i^2+6i)$$

$$2i+13-2i^2+6i$$

$$2i+13+2+6i$$

$$8i+15$$

$$\therefore A)$$

3.

$s=$ the shipping weight of one pack of lip balm.

The weight is between 0.5oz and 0.6oz

Note that 0.55 is exactly between 0.5 and 0.6, and

$-0.05 \le s-0.55 < 0.05$ or $|s-0.55| \le 0.05$

$$\therefore C)$$

4.

$$P=50+20n$$

P: The cost of buying a propolis spray at Costco

50: The fixed cost.

20: The variable cost that depends on the n sprays.

Choice B is the best interpretation of the equation

$$\therefore B)$$

5.

$$j(x)=2x^2+5x+2y$$

$$k(x)=-5x^2+2xy+5$$

$$j(x)-k(x)$$

$$\Rightarrow 2x^2+5x+2y-(-5x^2+2xy+5)$$

$$2x^2+5x+2y+5x^2-2xy-5$$

$$7x^2+5x+2y-2xy-5$$

$$\therefore C)$$

6.

Fixed cost: $130

Variable cost: $.25 for each month

1 year $=12$ months

Thus, $130+2.5(12)$

$$130+30=160$$

$$\therefore D)$$

7.

$$C_p=\frac{(D_G)(k_a)}{(V_d)(k_a-k_e)}$$

$$C_p(k_a-k_e)=\frac{(D_G)(k_a)}{(V_d)(k_a-k_e)}(k_a-k_e)$$

$$\frac{C_p(k_a-k_e)}{C_p}=\frac{(D_G)(k_a)}{(V_d)(C_p)}$$

$$k_a-k_e=\frac{(D_G)(k_a)}{(V_d)(C_p)}$$

$$k_a-k_e+k_e=\frac{(D_G)(k_a)}{(V_d)(C_p)}+k_e$$

$$k_a=\frac{(D_G)(k_a)}{(V_d)(C_p)}+k_e$$

$$k_a-\frac{(D_G)(k_a)}{(V_d)(C_p)}=\frac{(D_G)(k_a)}{(V_d)(C_p)}-\frac{(D_G)(k_a)}{(V_d)(C_p)}+k_e$$

$$k_e=-\frac{(D_G)(k_a)}{(V_d)(C_p)}+k_a$$

$$\therefore B)$$

8.

$\frac{g}{3d}=6,\ \frac{g}{c}=4,$ and $9d+9c=22$

$\frac{g}{3d}(3d)=6(3d)\qquad \frac{g}{c}(c)=4(c)$

$\qquad 9=18d\qquad\qquad 9=4c$

$18d=4c$

$d=\frac{4}{18}c=\frac{2}{9}c$

Plug $\frac{2}{9}c$ into $9d+9c=22$

$9\left(\frac{2}{9}c\right)+9c=22$

$2c+9c=22$

$11c=22$

$\frac{11c}{11}=\frac{22}{11}$

$c=2$

$\therefore$ C)

9.

$\begin{cases} 2x-6y=5 \\ 1+x=2y \end{cases} \Rightarrow \begin{cases} 2x-6y=5 \\ x-2y=-1 \end{cases}$

$\Rightarrow \begin{cases} 2x-6y=5 \\ 2(x-2y=-1) \end{cases} \Rightarrow \begin{cases} 2x-6y=5 \\ -(2x-4y=-2) \end{cases}$

$-2y=7\quad y=-\frac{7}{2}$

Plug in $-\frac{7}{2}$ to find $x \Rightarrow x=-8$.

The equations intersect at $\left(-8,-\frac{7}{2}\right)$

Also, Check the slopes of the both equations and see that they are not negative reciprocals.

$\therefore$ B)

10.

$f(x)=dx^2+4dx$

$f(2)=d(2)^2+4d(2)$

$f(2)=4d+8d=12d$

$f(1)=d(1)^2+4d(1)$

$f(1)=d+4d=5d$

$f(2)-f(1)=12d-5d=7d$

Since, $f(2)-f(1)=24$

Thus, $7d=24$

$d=\frac{24}{7}$

$\therefore$ C)

11.

$21=\frac{3}{4}(x+5)$

$21\left(\frac{4}{3}\right)=\left(\frac{3}{4}(x+5)\right)\frac{4}{3}$

$28=x+5$

$23=x$

Thus, $x+5=23+5=28$

28 exceeds 21 by 7

$\therefore$ B)

12.

The slope $=\frac{4}{5}$ and $(10,-19)$ lies on the line.

Thus, $y=\frac{4}{5}x+g$

Plug in $(10,-19)$

$-19=\frac{4}{5}(10)+g$

$-19=8+g$

$-27=g$

$\therefore$ A)

13.

$x^2=4gx+2d$

$x^2-4gx-2d=0$

Memorize:

$\frac{-b\pm\sqrt{b^2-4ac}}{2a} \Rightarrow \frac{4g\pm\sqrt{16g^2-4(1)(-2d)}}{2}$

$2g\pm\frac{1}{2}\sqrt{16g^2+8d}$

$2g\pm\frac{1}{2}\sqrt{4(4g^2+2d)}$

$2g\pm\sqrt{4g^2+2d}$

$\therefore$ B)

14.

$$\frac{24^{3k}}{4}=\frac{(24^k)^3}{4}$$

Since, $2=24^k$

$$\frac{(24^k)^3}{4}=\frac{(2)^3}{4}=\frac{8}{4}=2$$

$\therefore$ C)

15.

$42x^2+dx+(c+3)=(gx+2)(cx-2)$

$42x^2+dx+(c+3)=gcx^2-2gx+2cx-4$

First know that, $c+3=-4$

$c=-7$

And, $42x^2=gcx^2$

$\qquad 42=gc$

$\qquad 42=g(-7)$

$\qquad -6=g$

Lastly, $dx=-2gx+2cx$

$\qquad dx=-2(-6)x+2(-7)x$

$\qquad dx=12x-14x$

$\qquad dx=-2x$

$\qquad d=-2$

$\therefore$ C)

16.

$25\leq 5/t-1$

$\Downarrow$

$25+1\leq\frac{5}{t}-1+1$

$26(t)\leq\frac{5}{t}(t)$

$\frac{26t}{26}\leq\frac{5}{26}$

$t\leq\frac{5}{26}$

$\therefore\ \frac{5}{26}$

17.

Since $\tan(77°)=4$, the ratio $4:1$ applies as shown below

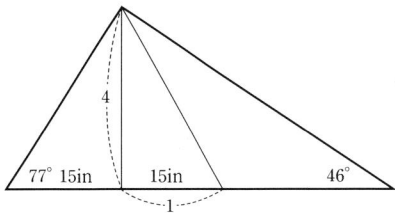

Thus, the height of the triangle is $\frac{4}{1}=\frac{h}{15}\ \Rightarrow\ h=60$.

Since, $\tan(46°)=0.8$ or $\frac{8}{10}$ or $\frac{4}{5}$

The ratio 4:5 applies as below.

Thus, $\frac{4}{5}=\frac{60}{x}$ and $x=75$ which indicates that the base of the $\triangle$ is $75+15=90$ inches wide.

Area$=\frac{90in\cdot60in}{2}=2700in^2$

In feet, $\frac{2,700in^2}{1}\cdot\frac{1ft^2}{12in^2}=\frac{2,700ft^2}{12\cdot12}$

$\approx 19ft^2$

$\therefore\ 19$

18.

$\begin{cases} 2x-5y=10 \\ 10x+2y=68 \end{cases} \Rightarrow \begin{cases} 5(2x-5y=10) \\ 10x+2y=68 \end{cases}$

$\Rightarrow \begin{cases} 10x-25y=50 \\ -(10x+2y=68) \end{cases}$

$\Rightarrow\ -27y=-18$

$\frac{-27}{-27y}=\frac{-18}{-27}$

$\therefore\ y=\frac{2}{3}$

19.

$x° + z° = 90°$

$z° = 90 - X°$

Memorize: $\cos(x) = \sin(90 - x)$

Since $\cos x° = \dfrac{10}{26}$

Thus, $\sin z° = \dfrac{10}{26}$

Any multiple of $5 - 12 - 13$ are pythagorean triples and $10 - 24 - 26$ is a pythagorean triple.

Thus, $\sin y° = \dfrac{a}{b} = \dfrac{24}{26} = \dfrac{12}{13}$

$\therefore a = 12$

20.

$$\frac{3\left(10\sqrt{\dfrac{1}{g}}\right)^2}{\left(\sqrt[3]{2g}\right)^{-3}} \Rightarrow \frac{3\left(10^2\left(\sqrt{\dfrac{1}{g}}\right)^2\right)}{\left(\sqrt[3]{2g}\right)^{-3}} \Rightarrow \frac{3\left(\dfrac{100}{g}\right)}{\left(\sqrt[3]{2g}\right)^{-3}}$$

$$\Rightarrow \frac{300}{g} \cdot \left(\sqrt[3]{2g}\right)^3 \Rightarrow \frac{300}{g} \cdot 2g$$

$$\Rightarrow 300 \cdot 2 = 600$$

Calculator Section

1.

Look for the segment with the smallest slope in absolute terms (positive or negative). The period from 2017 to 2018 indicates the smallest change in the yearly production. From 2017 to 2018, there were approximately 200 million tons of production.

$\therefore$ B)

2.

$37.50 = 2.50 + 2.50(x - 3)$

$37.50 - 2.50 = 2.50 - 2.50 + 2.50(x - 3)$

$\dfrac{35}{2.5} = \dfrac{2.5(x - 3)}{2.5}$

$14 = (x - 3)$

$17 = x$

$\therefore$ D)

3.

Find the vertical angles as shown below.

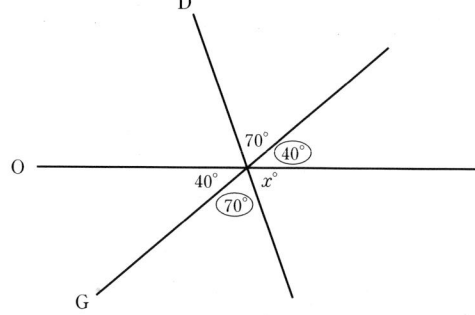

Then, $180° - 70° - 40° =$ to get the answer, $70°$

$\therefore$ C)

4.

$\dfrac{5}{3} = \dfrac{3n}{5} + \dfrac{2}{3}$

$1 = \dfrac{3n}{5}$

$\left(\dfrac{5}{3}\right) = \dfrac{3n}{5}\left(\dfrac{5}{3}\right)$

$\dfrac{5}{3} = n$

$\therefore$ C)

5.

Of the four graphs, the points on graph D are most aligned with a line with a positive slope.

$\therefore$ D)

6.

$$\frac{82\%}{100grams} = \frac{x\%?}{3pounds}$$

Convert 100 grams to pounds

$$100grams \cdot \frac{1ounce}{28.35grams} \cdot \frac{1pound}{16ounces}$$

$$= \frac{100pounds}{28.35 \cdot 16} \approx 0.2205pounds$$

$$\frac{82\%}{0.2205pounds} = \frac{x\%?}{3pounds}$$

$$1,116\% \approx x$$

$\therefore$ D)

7.

The number of people in the age range of $25-34$ is 50.
We want to find 50/Total number of people

$$\frac{50}{60+50+35+20+5+5} \approx 0.29 \rightarrow \text{fraction using calcu-}$$

lator

$$= \frac{2}{7}$$

$\therefore$ C)

8.

$$|6x+2| = 7$$

$$6x+2=7 \qquad -(6x+2)=7$$

$$6x=5$$

$$x = \frac{5}{6} \rightarrow \text{enough to find the answer}$$

$\therefore$ D)

9.

$$y-270=-9x \Rightarrow y=270-9x$$

y: game practice hours

x: number of days after the first day of a month.

When $x=30$, y becomes 0 meaning that after 30 days there will be no game practice hours left to play

$\therefore$ A)

10.

$$y-270=-9x$$

$$y=234 \text{ hours}$$

$$234-270=-9x$$

$$-36=-9x$$

$$4=x$$

$\therefore$ B)

11.

$$\frac{2x-3}{4} \le 5+3x$$

$$\frac{2x-3}{4}(4) \le (5+3x)(4)$$

$$2x-2x-3 \le 20+12x-2x$$

$$-3-20 \le 20-20+10x$$

$$\frac{-23}{10} \le \frac{10x}{10}$$

$$\frac{-23}{10} \le x$$

$$-2.3 \le x$$

$\therefore$ A)

12.

Memorize:
Mode: The number which appears most often in a set of numbers.
At 1.1, the frequency is the highest.

$\therefore$ C)

13.

The production except "other" in 2010
The production that is not other

$$\frac{28+35+46}{104+109+110} = 0.34$$

$\therefore$ B)

14.

A) False. With the new score 100, the range is still the same because there was already a number 100 in the table.

B) False. The median changes by a certain amount.

C) True. The mean changes to a little higher number since we have another maximum score.

D) False. 100 is not an outlier since there are numbers that are close enough to 100.

$\therefore$ C)

15.

The rate is falling 1.5% yearly
thus, $r = (100\% - 1.5\%) \Rightarrow 98.5\% = 0.985$

$\therefore$ C)

16.

For the year 2021, $n = 3$

$E = E_0(r)^3$

$E/E_0 = E_0(r)^3/E_0$

$\sqrt[3]{\dfrac{E}{E_0}} = \sqrt[3]{r^3}$

$\sqrt[3]{\dfrac{E}{E_0}} = r$

$\therefore$ C)

17.

$f(x) = 5x + 2$

$f(g) = 5(g) + 2$

$2f(g) = 2(5g + 2) = 6$

$\Rightarrow 10g + 4 = 6$

$\Rightarrow 10g = 2$

$\Rightarrow g = \dfrac{1}{5}$

$f(2g) = f\left(2\left(\dfrac{1}{5}\right)\right) = f\left(\dfrac{2}{5}\right)$

$\Rightarrow f\left(\dfrac{2}{5}\right) = 5\left(\dfrac{2}{5}\right) + 2 = 2 + 2 = 4$

$\therefore$ B)

18.

Solve backwards by trying out every answer choice.

Note that g and d are positive integers.

A) $2 > 6 + d$ and $2 < b + g$

$\quad -4 > d$ and $-4 < g$

$\quad g > d$ but g and d can be both negative

$\quad \therefore$ No.

B) $6 > 2 + d$ and $6 < 2 + g$

$\quad 4 > d$ and $4 < g$

$\quad g > d$ and both can be positive

$\quad \therefore$ Yes.

C) $2 > 1 + d$ and $2 < 1 + g$

$\quad 1 > d$ and $1 < g$

$\quad g > d$ but d can be 0 as an integer

$\quad \therefore$ No.

D) $1 > 2 + d$ and $1 < 2 + g$

$\quad -1 > d$ and $-1 < g$

$\quad$ both are negative.

$\quad \therefore$ No.

$\therefore$ B)

19.

Figure #1: $70

Figure #2: $175

x: number of figures #1

y: number of figures #2

The ratio of x to y: 1 to $2 \Rightarrow 2x = y$.

Thus, $70x + 175y = 1680$

$70x + 175(2x) = 1680$

$420x = 1680$

$x = 4$

Total number of figures: $x + 2x = 4 + 8 = 12$

$\therefore$ C)

20.

2 million of tables increased by 110 percent
$=2(100\%+110\%)=2(1+1.1)=2(2.1)$
3.2 million of mobile phones increased by 50 percent
$=3.2(100\%+50\%)=3.2(1.5)$
Thus, the total production$=2(2.1)+3.2(1.5)=9$
The total increase: 5.2 rarrow 9
$5.2x=9$
$x=1.73=100\%+73\%$
Increased by 73%
$\therefore$ D)

21.

The percent of deforestation in NA & Africa Total
Land degraded
$$\frac{4.4+0.5}{6+10+5}=\frac{4.9}{21}=\frac{49}{210}=\frac{7}{30}$$
$\therefore$ A)

22.

The cities that reported average revenue $50,000 or
more are Paris, Beijing, and London.
Thus, $\dfrac{\text{Beijing}}{\text{Paris}+\text{Beijing}+\text{London}}=\dfrac{26}{27+26+15}=0.38$
$\therefore$ A)

23.

First, calculate the ratios between all the cities.
B} is the answer as the ratios are in descending order.
$$\frac{L}{N}=\frac{994,510}{846,810}\approx1.17$$
$$\frac{B}{P}=\frac{1,315,050}{1,488,150}\approx0.88$$
$$\frac{P}{T}=\frac{1,488,150}{2,165,350}\approx0.69$$
$$\frac{S}{L}=\frac{542,950}{994,510}\approx0.55$$
$\therefore$ B)

24.

First, convert the given equation, $x^2+2x+y^2+4y=44$
into the center-radius form, $(x-h)^2+(y-k)^2=r^2$ by
completing the square.
For x^2+2y, $\left(\dfrac{b}{2}\right)^2=\left(\dfrac{2}{2}\right)^2=1$
For y^2+4y, $\left(\dfrac{b}{2}\right)^2=\left(\dfrac{4}{2}\right)^2=4$
Thus, $x^2+2x+1+y^2+4y+4=44+1+4$
$(x+1)^2+(y+2)^2=49$
The center of the circle: $(-1,-2)$ and the radius
$r^2=49 \Rightarrow r=7$
$\therefore$ A)

25.

Visualize $h=-4w^2+20w$ in the $xy-$plane

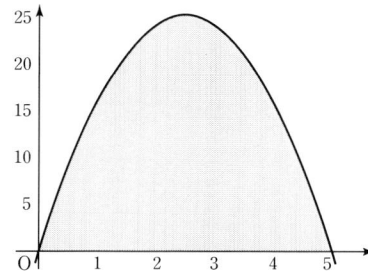

The roots of $h=-4w^2+20w$ indicate the width of the
arch and the $y-$coordinate of the vertex indicate the
height of the arch.
$-4w^2+20w \Rightarrow w(-4w+20)$
$w=0$ or $-4w+20=0$
$\therefore w=0$ or 5
The width: 5-0=5
The $x-$coordinate of the vertex is midway of the
width. $x=2.5$
Plug in 2.5 to find the $y-$coordinate.
$h(2.5)=25$
Finally, find the difference of the height and the width.
25-5=20
$\therefore$ C)

26.

D = # of likes Dickson receives

J = # of likes Jane receives

J = D(100% + 30%) = D(1.3)

Thus, D(1.3) + D = 2,369

2.3D = 2,369

D = 1030

J = 1339

∴ D)

27.

Population: The entire students in the city

Sample: 760 students aged 14 years or older from a particular school.

The sample cannot represent the population because it has not been selected randomly from various schools and from various regions. Also, the selected students are 14 years older whereas the population would represent students regardless of their age.

∴ C)

28.

$y \leq \dfrac{1}{5}x$

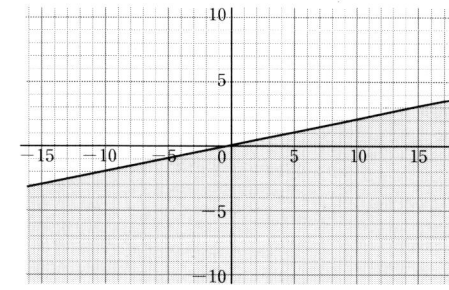

$y \leq \dfrac{-13}{6}x$

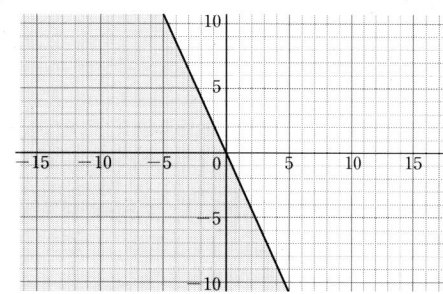

$y \leq \dfrac{1}{5}x \quad + \quad y \leq \dfrac{-13}{6}x$

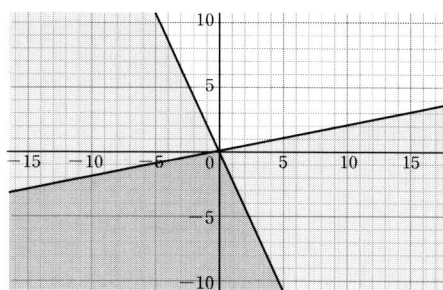

The overlapped region is the section C

∴ A)

29.

If $f(x)$ is a polynomial function and $f(-41)=1$, then when $f(x)$ is divided by $x-(-41)$ or, equivalently, $x+41$, the remainder is 1.

∴ D)

30.

$y = 7x^2 + 14x + 3$

First, find the coordinates of the vertex using $\dfrac{-b}{2a}$

$\dfrac{-b}{2a} = x-$ coordinate of the vertex.

$\dfrac{-b}{2a} = \dfrac{-14}{7(2)} = -1$

Plug in -1.

$7(-1)^2 + 14(-1) + 3$

$= 7 - 14 + 3 = -4$

∴ the vertex $= (-1, -4)$ and is located as shown below:

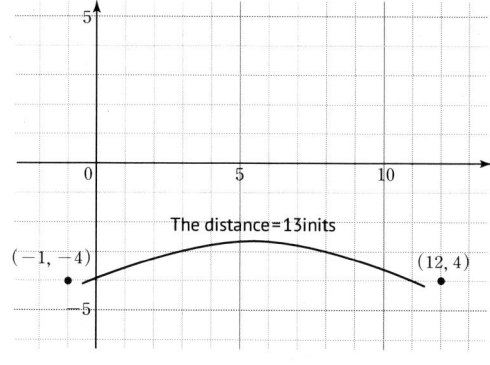

The distance = 13 inits

$(-1, -4)$ $(12, 4)$

Notice that the distance between $(-1, -4)$ and $(12, -4)$ is 13

$\therefore$ D)

31.

$\frac{3}{4}g = x$

$5g + x = y$

Since $\frac{1}{2} < g < \frac{3}{2}$, let $g = 1$.

Then, $\frac{3}{4}(1) = x$ and $5(1) + x = y$

$5(1) + x = y \Rightarrow 5 + \left(\frac{3}{4}\right) = y \Rightarrow y = 5\frac{3}{4} = \frac{23}{4}$

In fact, y can be any number between $23/8$ and $69/8$

$\therefore \frac{23}{8} < y < \frac{69}{8}$

32.

$x = $ mL of 3% solution

$y = $ mL of 8% solution

$(3\%)x + (8\%)(250 - x) = 250(4\%)$

$(0.03)x + (0.08)(250 - x) = 250(0.04)$

$0.03x + 20 - 0.08x = 10$

$-0.05x = -10$

$x = 200$

33.

Another name for the regression line is the line of best fit.

We make predictions using the line of best fit.

There are 8 dots above the line of the best fit which are underestimated by the straight line.

$\therefore \frac{8}{\text{total number of dots}} = \frac{8}{14} = \frac{4}{7}$

34.

A music critic listens to $\frac{8 songs}{1 hour}$

Work hours (listening hours) each day
= 24hours - 11.5hours = 12.5hours

For 8 consecutive days = $8 \cdot (12.5) = 100$ hours

$\therefore$ 100 hours

35.

Choose a radius between $3.5in$ & $3.7in$

e.g. $3.6in$

height $= 12in$

Volume of cylinder $= \pi r^2 h$

$\therefore \pi(3.6in)^2 \cdot 12in \approx 488.6in^3$

Convert to the nearest foot.

$488.6in^3 \cdot \frac{1ft^3}{12in \cdot 12in \cdot 12in} \approx 0.28$ is one possible

answer. Any radius between 3.5 and 3.7 can be plugged in. Make sure to round your answer to the nearest hundredth.

$\therefore 0.27 < x < 0.30$

36.

$\frac{x^2 - 4x - 77}{x - 11} \Rightarrow \frac{(x - 11)(x + 7)}{(x - 11)} \Rightarrow x + 7$

$\therefore c = 7$

37.

of marriages decreases by 1.8 percent

= 100% - 1.8% = 98.2% = $0.982 \approx 0.98\%$

38.

Using the foula $M = I(r)^t$, we know that the number of marriages, in thousands, after 7 years is

$M = 19(0.982)^t$.

$t = $ # of years but there is a decrease in # of marriages every 6 months or half a year.

$\therefore M = 19(0.982)^{\frac{t}{0.5}} = 19(0.982)^{2t}$

Let $t = 7$

Then, $M = 19(0.982)^{14} \approx 15$ to the nearest integer.

$\therefore$ 200

SAT Math Practice Test 3

Math Test (No Calculator)

25 MINUTES, 20 QUESTIONS

Turn to Section 3 of your answer sheet to answer the questions in this section.

DIRECTIONS

For questions 1-15, solve each problem, choose the best answer from the choices provided, and fill in the corresponding circle on your answer sheet. **For questions 16-20,** solve the problem and enter your answer in the grid on the answer sheet. Please refer to the directions before question 16 on how to enter your answers in the grid. You may use any available space in your test booklet for scratch work.

NOTES

1. The use of a calculator **is not permitted.**
2. All variables and expressions used represent real numbers unless otherwise indicated.
3. Figures provided in this test are drawn to scale unless otherwise indicated.
4. All figures lie in a plane unless otherwise indicated.
5. Unless otherwise indicated, the domain of a given function f is the set of all real numbers x for which $f(x)$ is a real number.

REFERENCE

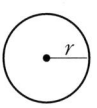

$A = \pi r^2$
$C - 2\pi r$

$A = lw$

$A = \frac{1}{2}bh$

$c^2 = a^2 + b^2$

Special Right Triangles

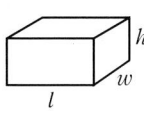

$V = lwh$

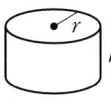

$V = \pi r^2 h$

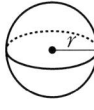

$V = \frac{4}{3}\pi r^3$

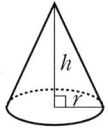

$V = \frac{1}{3}\pi r^2 h$

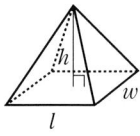

$V = \frac{1}{3}lwh$

The number of degrees of arc in a circle is 360.

The number of radians of arc in a circle is 2π.

The sum of the measures in degrees of the angles of a triangle is 180.

CONTINUE ⮕

1

$$4x + y - 2xy = x + y + xy$$

In the equation above, if $x \neq 0$, what is the value of y ?

A) No solution

B) 0

C) $\dfrac{1}{3}$

D) 1

2

$$2x - y = 4$$
$$13x + 5y = 3$$

What are the solutions of the system of equations above?

A) $\left(-\dfrac{17}{3}, -15\dfrac{1}{3}\right)$

B) $(1, -2)$

C) $(-2, 1)$

D) $(-1, -2)$

3

Nate wants to hire a house cleaner for one day. The house cleaner charges a one-time travel expense and an hourly fee. The equation $C = 0.5h + 4$ represents the total amount C, in dollars, that Nate will pay the house cleaner. h is the total number of hours the cleaner worked. What does 0.5 represent in the equation?

A) The amount the house cleaner charges per hour

B) The minimum of number of hours the house cleaner needs to work

C) The average cost of a house-cleaning visit

D) The minimum amount the house cleaner charges per visit

4

Which of the following is equivalent to the expression $16x^2 - 24xy + 9y^2$?

A) $(4x - 3y)^2$

B) $(4x + 3y)^2$

C) $(4x - 3y)(4x + 3y)$

D) $(16x - 9y)^2$

5

$$-4 + x = \sqrt{x - 5} + 1$$

What is the solution set of the equation above?

A) (5,6)

B) (9)

C) (6,9)

D) (0,6,9)

CONTINUE

6

Which of the following is the graph of the equation $-\dfrac{3}{10}x - \dfrac{y}{10} = 1$ in the xy-plane?

A)

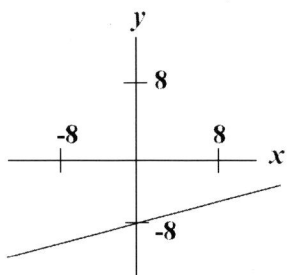

B)

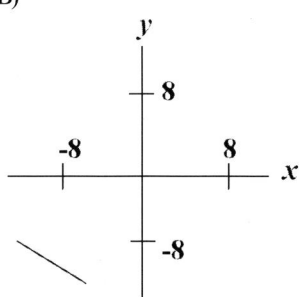

C)

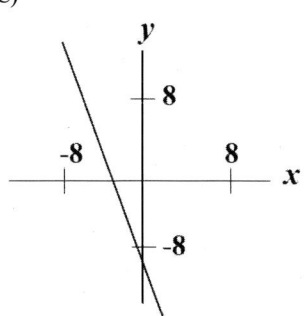

D)

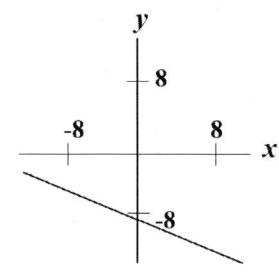

7

If $6x - 4y = \dfrac{1}{2}$, what is the value of $\dfrac{64^x}{16^y}$?

A) $\dfrac{1}{4}$

B) $\sqrt{\dfrac{1}{2}}$

C) $\sqrt{2}$

D) 4

8

The sum of the measure of interior angles of a regular polygon is $180(n-2)$, where n is the number of sides of the polygon. If the sum of the measure of interior angles of a certain polygon is 720, how many sides does the polygon have?

A) 4
B) 5
C) 6
D) 7

CONTINUE

9

The graph of a line in the xy-plane passes through the points (3, -8) and (1, 4). The graph of a second line has a slope of 3 and passes through the point (3, 1). If the two lines intersect at (c, d), what is the value of $c+d$?

A) -4

B) 0

C) 20

D) $\dfrac{188}{9}$

11

$$\frac{5i^{99} - 16i^{22}}{3 - i}$$

If the expression above is written in the form a+bi, where a and b are real numbers, what is the value of a? (Note: $i=\sqrt{-1}$)

A) $\dfrac{16}{3} - 5i$

B) $\dfrac{16}{3} + 5i$

C) $\dfrac{53}{10} + \dfrac{i}{10}$

D) $\dfrac{53}{10} - \dfrac{i}{10}$

10

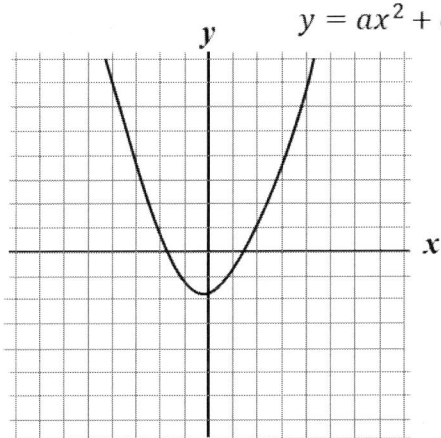

$$y = ax^2 + c$$

In the xy-plane graph above, c is a negative constant and the vertex of the parabola is $(0,c)$. Which of the following is true about the parabola with the equation $y=-a(x+j)^2-k$?

A) The vertex is (j,k) and the graph is concave downward.

B) The vertex is (j,k) and the graph is concave upward.

C) The vertex is $(-j,-k)$ and the graph is concave downward.

D) The vertex is $(-j,-k)$ and the graph is concave upward.

12

Scientists use the equation $p = (s + \dfrac{d}{t})^2$ to estimate the probability, p, of an asteroid with a diameter of d feet, a mass of t tons hitting the earth at a speed of s kilometers per second. Which of the following correctly expresses t in terms of d, s, and p?

A) $t = \dfrac{d}{s - \sqrt{p}}$

B) $t = \dfrac{d}{\sqrt{p} - s}$

C) $t = \dfrac{\sqrt{p} - s}{d}$

D) $t = \dfrac{s - \sqrt{p}}{d}$

13

What is the sum of all values of g that satisfy the equation $4g^2 - 8g + 16 = 0$?

A) -2

B) $-\dfrac{1}{4}$

C) $\dfrac{1}{4}$

D) 2

14

The European honey bee population is declining rapidly at a rate of 11% per year. If there were 60,000 bees in the beginning of 2018, which of the following functions, B, models the number of bees (in thousands) remaining t years after 2018?

A) $B(t) = 60(0.89)^t$

B) $B(t) = 60(0.11)^t$

C) $B(t) = 0.89(60)^t$

D) $B(t) = 60{,}000(0.89)^t$

15

$$\frac{15x - 3}{x + 1}$$

Which of the following functions is equivalent for $x \neq -1$?

A) $1 + \dfrac{18}{x + 1}$

B) $1 - \dfrac{12}{x + 1}$

C) $15 + \dfrac{12}{x + 1}$

D) $15 - \dfrac{18}{x + 1}$

CONTINUE

DIRECTIONS

For questions 16-20, solve the problem and enter your answer in the grid, as described below, on the answer sheet.

1. Although not required, it is suggested that you write your answer in the boxes at the top of the columns to help you fill in the circles accurately. You will receive credit only if the circles are filled in correctly.

2. Mark no more than one circle in any column.

3. No question has a negative answer.

4. Some problems may have more than one correct answer. In such cases, grid only one answer.

5. **Mixed numbers** such as $3\frac{1}{2}$ must be gridded as 3.5 or 7/2. (If $\boxed{3\ 1\ /\ 2}$ is entered into the grid, it will be interpreted as $\frac{31}{2}$, not $3\frac{1}{2}$.)

6. **Decimal answers**: If you obtain a decimal answer with more digits than the grid can accommodate, it may be either rounded or truncated, but it must fill the entire grid.

Answer: $\frac{7}{12}$ Answer: 2.5

Write answer in boxes. → ← Fraction line

Grid in result. ← Decimal point

Acceptable ways to grid $\frac{2}{3}$ are:

Answer: 201 - either position is correct.

NOTE: You may start your answer in any column, space permitting. Columns you don't need to use should be left blank.

CONTINUE ▶

16

In order to build a house, Sue plans to buy 6000 board feet of lumber from vendor A and vendor B. Vendor A sells in bundles of 300 board feet of lumber and vendor B sells in bundles of 1500 board feet of lumber. If at most two bundles are purchased from vendor B, what is one possible number of bundle(s) that can be purchased from the vendor A?

17

The equation of a circle in the xy-plane is $x^2 + y^2 + 6x - 6y = 7$. If the line $x = c$, where c is a constant, intersects the circle at exactly one point, what is one possible positive value of c?

18

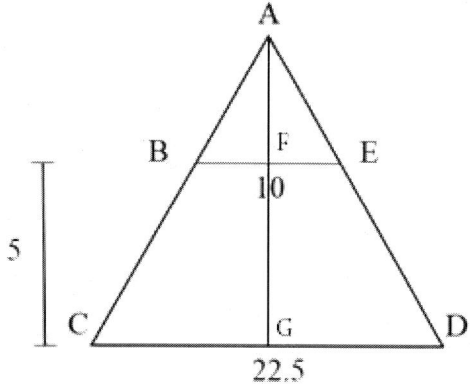

In the figure above, $\overline{BE}$ is parallel to $\overline{CD}$. What is the length of $\overline{AF}$?

CONTINUE

19

A regular hexagon is made up of 6 equilateral triangles. The sum of the measure of the central angles can be written as $\dfrac{\pi}{x}$, where x is a rational number. What is the value of x?

20

$$x^2 - y + 2 = 6x - 2$$
$$5x^2 + 8 = -2 + y$$

How many real solutions are there to the system of equations above?

STOP

If you finish before time is called, you may check your work on this section only.
Do not turn to any other section.

Math Test (Calculator)

55 MINUTES, 38 QUESTIONS

Turn to Section 4 of your answer sheet to answer the questions in this section.

DIRECTIONS

For questions 1-30, solve each problem, choose the best answer from the choices provided, and fill in the corresponding circle on your answer sheet. **For questions 31-38,** solve the problem and enter your answer in the grid on the answer sheet. Please refer to the directions before question 31 on how to enter your answers in the grid. You may use any available space in your test booklet for scratch work.

NOTES

1. The use of a calculator **is permitted**.
2. All variables and expressions used represent real numbers unless otherwise indicated.
3. Figures provided in this test are drawn to scale unless otherwise indicated.
4. All figures lie in a plane unless otherwise indicated.
5. Unless otherwise indicated, the domain of a given function f is the set of all real numbers x for which $f(x)$ is a real number.

REFERENCE

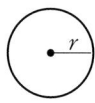 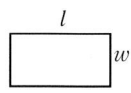 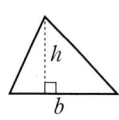 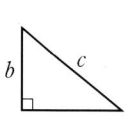 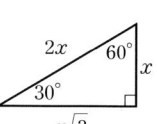 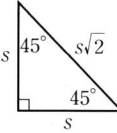

$A = \pi r^2$ $A = lw$ $A = \frac{1}{2}bh$ $c^2 = a^2 + b^2$ Special Right Triangles

$C = 2\pi r$

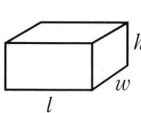 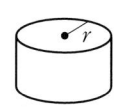 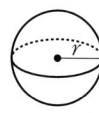 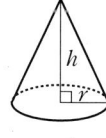 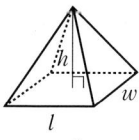

$V = lwh$ $V = \pi r^2 h$ $V = \frac{4}{3}\pi r^3$ $V = \frac{1}{3}\pi r^2 h$ $V = \frac{1}{3}lwh$

The number of degrees of arc in a circle is 360.

The number of radians of arc in a circle is 2π.

The sum of the measures in degrees of the angles of a triangle is 180.

CONTINUE ➡

1

If $\frac{4}{7}y = \frac{5}{4}$, what is the value of y?

A) $\frac{16}{35}$

B) $\frac{5}{7}$

C) $\frac{7}{5}$

D) $\frac{35}{16}$

2

In a random survey of 730 people of a certain country, 5 replied that they do not have a religion. At this rate, if 7,200 people of the same country were asked the same question, how many will reply that they have a religion? Round your answer to the nearest integer.

A) 49

B) 62

C) 7151

D) 7250

3

A car rental company has been offering "cheap-as-chips" rentals since 2018. For just $2, motorists can rent a car or van for 8 hours and thereafter pay $1 for every 2 additional hours. Which of the following expressions best represents the total cost, C, of x hours of the rental assuming every customer rents an automobile for at least 8 hours?

A) $C = \frac{1}{2}x - 2$

B) $C = 2 + 2x$

C) $C = 2 + x$

D) $C = 1 + \frac{1}{8}x$

CONTINUE

— ▼ —

Questions 4 and 5 refer to the following information.

Yeast is an important ingredient in the baking industry, and global demand for baked goods is increasing rapidly. The yeast market's growth and the growth rate of consumption of baked goods are directly proportional. A 7.5% growth rate in yeast market's growth is associated with a 5% growth rate in consumption of baked goods.

4

If consumption for baked goods rose by 24% last year, what would be the increase in size of the global yeast market last year?
A) 16%
B) 36%
C) 160%
D) 360%

5

This year, the relationship between the yeast market and the consumption for baked goods changed. A 5% increase in consumption of baked goods is now associated with a 6.25% increase in the yeast market's size. What is this the yeast market's growth rate this year if consumption of baked goods increases by 16%?
A) 0.2%
B) 2%
C) 20%
D) 24%

— ▲ —

6

If $f(x) = \dfrac{3x^2 + 2x - 4}{2x + 3}$, what is $f(-2)$?
A) -22
B) -4
C) 4
D) 22

7

$$x^2 - 4x + 14 = 0$$

Which of the following is equivalent to the expression above?
A) $(x+2)^2 - 18 = 0$
B) $(x+2)^2 + 10 = 0$
C) $(x-2)^2 - 18 = 0$
D) $(x-2)^2 + 10 = 0$

CONTINUE

8

The liberal United Progressive Party (UPP) won z of the 300 seats in the legislature this year. It has ambitions to become the largest party in later legislative elections by gaining y seats every year. Which of the following equations best represents the total number of seats that the UPP plans to gain x years from 2018?

A) $z + yx > 300$

B) $xz - y < 300$

C) $y + xz < 300$

D) $z + yx < 300$

9

A soccer player's salary is $33,000 a week during the season and $10,500 a week during the off season. He plans to save his entire salary for 1 year to buy a house which is worth $1,600,000. Although his savings went according to plan, the total amount of money he saved was not enough to buy the house he wanted. Which of the following systems of inequalities describes x, the number weeks he was paid $33,000 and y, the number of weeks he was paid $10,500 over the year? (1 year = 52 weeks)

A) $\begin{cases} 33,000x + 10,500y < 1,600,000 \\ x + y = 52 \end{cases}$

B) $\begin{cases} 33,000x + 10,500y > 1,600,000 \\ x + y = 52 \end{cases}$

C) $\begin{cases} 33,000x + 10,500y < 1,600,000 \\ x + y = 1 \end{cases}$

D) $\begin{cases} 33,000x + 10,500y > 1,600,000 \\ x + y = 1 \end{cases}$

10

If an equation of a parabola in the xy-plane is $f(x) = -3(x-5)^2 + 2$, what are the coordinates of the vertex of the parabola defined by $g(x) = f(x+6)$?

A) (5, 8)

B) (-1, 2)

C) (11, 2)

D) (1, 2)

11

Number of training sessions per month	8
Number of miles to run in each training session	25
Number of miles Elisa runs per hour	8
Number of laps to run during each training session	36
Number of steps Elisa takes per mile	132,652

The table above summarizes information about a MMA boxer named Elisa: her average training time each day and her running speed. If training only consists of running, and Elisa runs at the rates given in the table, which of the following is closest to the number of hours it would take Elisa to complete her training per month?

A)   5.6

B)   10.9

C)   25

D)   900

CONTINUE

12

Cynthia has an idea for an app and wants to start a company together with w co-workers. She found an office at $1,200 per month and the utility bill is $12.5 per person (including Cynthia). She will split up the cost among the workers including herself while she will be responsible for all other extra expenses. If her goal is to keep the average cost per person between $172.5 and $200, how many workers, w, does she need to hire?

A) 3
B) 4
C) 5
D) 6

13

A researcher conducted a survey to determine whether people in a large city prefer drinking coffee or tea. The researcher asked 180 people who visited a local cafe on a Sunday, and 11 people refused to respond. Which of the following factors makes it least likely that a reliable conclusion can be drawn about the beverage-drinking preferences of all people in the city?

A)   Sample Size
B)   The day of the week the survey was given
C)   The number of people who refused to respond
D)   Where the survey was given

14

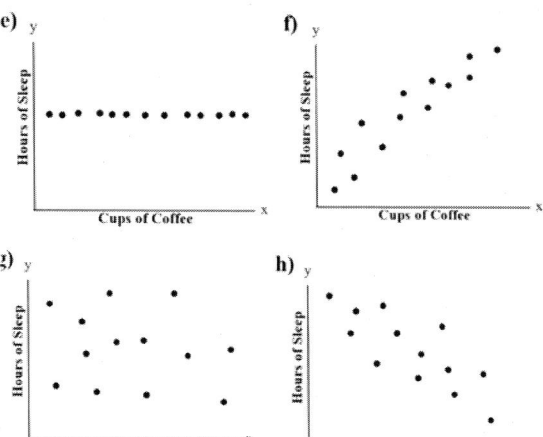

Which of the four graphs above best represents a strong negative relationship between the number of cups of coffee college students drink on one day and the number of hours of sleep each student gets on the same day?

A)   Graph e
B)   Graph f
C)   Graph g
D)   Graph h

Unauthorized copying or reuse of any part of this page is illegal.

278 | Paul's SAT Math 800

CONTINUE

15

If 15 grams of sugar contains 60 calories, which of the following is closest to the amount of calories in 25 <u>ounces</u> of sugar? Use the fact that 20 ounces is approximately 577 grams.

A) 144.25
B) 180
C) 2,308
D) 2,885

16

Survey of Suburban Residents in 2018

	Good	Neither Good Nor Bad	Bad	Total
Shops	78	15	13	106
Healthcare	83	11	12	106
Accomodation	66	18	22	106
Education	85	12	9	106
Environment	69	24	13	106
Transportation System	67	19	20	106
Total	448	99	89	636

The table above show results of a survey of 636 residents' opinions related to various aspects of life in 2018. Each person was asked exactly 1 question, and no person was surveyed more than once. Furthermore, the participants that responded "Neither Good Nor Bad" were excluded from the sample. If a participant from the sample is selected at random, what is the best estimate of the probability that the participant was asked on accommodation and replied that it was good?

A) 0.1
B) 0.12
C) 0.17
D) 0.18

17

A farmer is harvesting two types of perfectly spherical tangerines. The diameter of one type is 2 inches, and the diameter of the other type is 4 inches. What is the difference, in cubic inches, between the volumes of these two tangerines?

A) 3π

B) $\dfrac{28\pi}{3}$

C) 12π

D) $\dfrac{224\pi}{3}$

18

The arithmetic mean of $e, f, g, h,$ and j is one-fifth times the median. If $2 < e < f < g < h < j$, what is e in terms of all other variables?

A) $f+g+h+j$
B) $f+h+j$
C) $-f-h-j$
D) $-f-h-j-2$

CONTINUE

— ▼ —
Questions 19 and 20 refer to the following information.

A veterinarian examined 200 dogs from each of three animal shelters to determine number of health problems each dog has. The results are shown in the table below.

Number of Health Problems	Animal Shelter A	Animal Shelter B	Animal Shelter C
0	105	80	135
1	45	60	25
2	30	40	30
3	20	20	10

There are a total of 1,200 dogs at Animal Shelter A, 800 dogs at Animal Shelter B, and 1,300 dogs at Animal Shelter C.

19

What is the mean number of health problems for all the dogs examined? (Round your answer to the nearest integer.)
A) 0
B) 1
C) 2
D) 3

20

Based on the survey data of only Animal Shelter A and Animal Shelter B, which of the following most accurately compares the expected total number of dogs with 3 health problems?
A) The total number of dogs with 3 health problems is expected to be equal at the two animal shelters.
B) The total number of dogs with 3 health problems at Animal Shelter B is expected to be 40 more than at Animal Shelter A.
C) The total number of dogs with 3 health problems at Animal Shelter A is expected to be 40 more than at Animal Shelter B.
D) The total number of dogs with 3 health problems at Animal Shelter A is expected to be 100 more than at Animal Shelter B.

— ▲ —

21

A movie director estimates a budget of d dollars to produce a new movie. The movie director's goal is for the estimate to be within $3 million of the actual cost of production. If the director meets this goal and it costs c dollars to produce the movie, which of the following inequalities represents the relationship between the estimated cost and the actual cost?
A) $c+d < 3$
B) $c \geq d+3$
C) $c \leq d-3$
D) $-3 \leq c-d \leq 3$

Unauthorized copying or reuse of any part of this page is illegal.

CONTINUE

280 | Paul's SAT Math 800

—▼—
Questions 22 and 23 refer to the following information.

$$\triangle d = vt + \frac{1}{2}at^2$$

The equation above defines the change in position of a particle that has initial velocity v, the acceleration of the particle a, and time t.

22

Which of the following expresses the acceleration of the particle in terms of the time, the initial velocity and the change in position of the particle?

A) $a = 2\triangle dt^2 - 2vt$

B) $a = \dfrac{2\triangle d}{t^2} - \dfrac{2v}{t}$

C) $a = \dfrac{2\triangle d - vt}{t^2}$

D) $a = \dfrac{t^2}{2\triangle d} - \dfrac{t}{2v}$

23

For constant acceleration, the equation $v = v_0 + at$ can be used, where v_0 is the initial velocity, v is the final velocity, a is the acceleration and t is the time. If a driver traveling 30 m/s towards an intersection brakes as he sees a pedestrian and decelerates at a rate of 50 m/s^2, how many seconds does it take the car to come to a complete stop?

A) 0.6

B) $\dfrac{5}{3}$

C) 36

D) 360

—▲—

24

$$x^2 + y^2 + 14x - 3y = -6$$

The equation above defines a circle in the xy-plane. What are the coordinates of the center of the circle?

A) (-7, $\frac{3}{2}$)

B) (14, -3)

C) (-14, 3)

D) (7, 2)

CONTINUE ▶

25

In the xy-plane, line l passes through the y-axis at g and contains points $(g,4g)$ or (g,z^2). Which of the following could be the value of z?

A) $2\sqrt{g}$
B) $2g$
C) $6\sqrt{g}$
D) $6g$

26

x	$z(x)$
1	2
15	9
19	11
65	34

Some of the values of the linear function z are shown in the table above. What is the y-intercept of the function z?

A) 0
B) 0.5
C) 1
D) 1.5

27

The stock price, y, for Company A can be modeled by using the equation $y = ax^b$, where a is positive and b is negative. The stock price, z, for Company B can be modeled using the equation $z = \dfrac{x^d}{c}$, where c is positive and d is negative. Variable x is the time in years for both equations. Which of the following answer choices accurately describe the stock price trends for Company A and B?

A) The stock price for Company A constantly increases and stock price for Company B constantly decreases.

B) The stock price for Company A increases rapidly at first and later increases at a slower rate; the stock price for Company B decreases rapidly at first and later decreases at a slower rate.

C) Both the stock prices for Company A and Company B decrease rapidly at first and later decrease at a slower rate, before they eventually become 0.

D) Both the stock prices for Company A and Company B decrease rapidly at first and later decrease at a slower rate, but will never reach 0.

CONTINUE

28

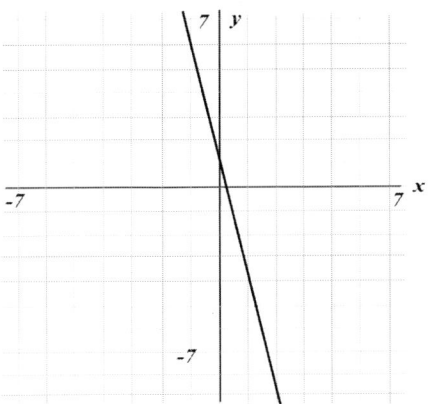

The graph of the linear function g is shown in the xy-plane above. The function f is perpendicular to g and the slope of the function h is the negative reciprocal of the slope of the function g. If the function h passes through the point $(3, -14)$, what is the value of $h(2)$?

A) -9

B) $-12\dfrac{2}{5}$

C) -13

D) $-\dfrac{71}{5}$

29

$$5c + 10 - x = 6c$$
$$3d + 2 - y = 2d$$

In the equation above, x and y are constants. If x is $3y - 1$, which of the following is true?

A) $c = 5 + 3d$

B) $c = 5 - 3d$

C) $c = 3 - 3d$

D) $c = 3 + 3d$

30

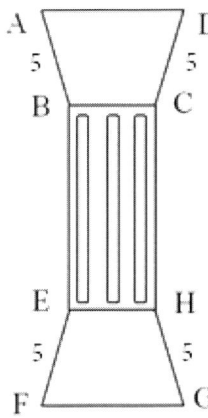

Note: Figure not drawn to scale.

A pillar is a structure that transmits the weight of the structure above to the structural elements below. A pillar is being designed so that it has the shape of two identical trapezoids $ABCD$ and $EFGH$ at the top and bottom and a rectangle in the center. The measures of $\angle B, \angle C, \angle E, \angle H$ inside the trapezoids are 120 degrees, and the sides AB, BC, CD, EF, EH, HG are all 5 inches in length. What is the area, in square inches, of $EFGH$ to the nearest tenth decimal place?

A) 2.2

B) 10.8

C) 32.5

D) 37.5

DIRECTIONS

For questions 31-38, solve the problem and enter your answer in the grid, as described below, on the answer sheet.

1. Although not required, it is suggested that you write your answer in the boxes at the top of the columns to help you fill in the circles accurately. You will receive credit only if the circles are filled in correctly.

2. Mark no more than one circle in any column.

3. No question has a negative answer.

4. Some problems may have more than one correct answer. In such cases, grid only one answer.

5. **Mixed numbers** such as $3\frac{1}{2}$ must be gridded as

3.5 or 7/2. (If [3 1 / 2] is entered into the grid, it

will be interpreted as $\frac{31}{2}$, not $3\frac{1}{2}$.)

6. **Decimal answers**: If you obtain a decimal answer with more digits than the grid can accommodate, it may be either rounded or truncated, but it must fill the entire grid.

Answer: $\frac{7}{12}$ Answer: 2.5

Write answer in boxes. ← ← Fraction line   ← Decimal point

Grid in result.

Acceptable ways to grid $\frac{2}{3}$ are:

Answer: 201 - either position is correct.

NOTE: You may start your answer in any column, space permitting. Columns you don't need to use should be left blank.

Unauthorized copying or reuse of any part of this page is illegal.

CONTINUE ➤

284 | Paul's SAT Math 800

31

One dollar is equivalent to 1,075 South Korean won. When compared to the Japanese yen, 1 dollar has the same value as 109.79 yen. Based on these relationships, 15,000 won is equivalent to how many yen? Round your answer to the nearest integer.

32

Tony Davis is a point guard on a professional basketball team. Tony's height is f feet and 9 inches. If Tony is 78 inches tall, what is the value of f? (1 foot = 12 inches)

33

$$10x - 6 + 3(x - 2) = 4x$$

What value of x satisfies the equation above?

34

Jeff and Liz together collected 257 rare cards in a game over many months. If Jeff collected 35 more cards in the game than Liz did, how many rare cards did Liz collect in the game?

CONTINUE

35

1 year ago, Bethany brought a puppy to her home. She wants to measure how fast the puppy grew in weight. $W(t) = 3 + 0.25t$ models the weight of the puppy in kilograms, t years since Bethany brought it home. According to the model, what is the puppy's weight when Bethany first decides to measure it?

36

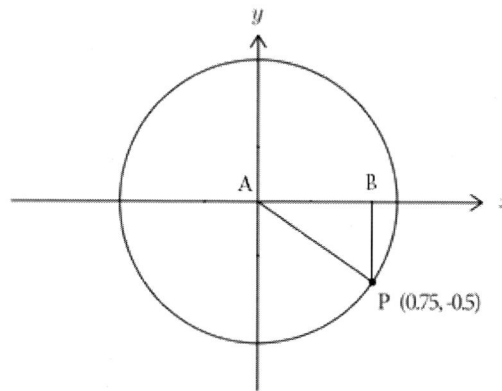

If $P(0.75, -0.5)$ is a point on a circle with radius 1 in the figure above, what is the value of the area of the triangle ABP?

CONTINUE

—▼—

Questions 37 and 38 refer to the following information.

A projectile is launched from sea level at a speed of 134.2 meters per second from a naval ship. The equation for the object's height h at time t seconds after launch can be defined by

$$h(t) = -6.1t^2 + 134.2t$$

37

According to the formula given above, how many seconds after the projectile is launched will it hit the ground?

38

What will be the object's maximum height? Grid your answer to the nearest meter.

—▲—

STOP
If you finish before time is called, you may check your work on this section only.
Do not turn to any other section.

Practice Test 3:
Answer Key and Explanations

Test 3 Answer Key

Math - No Calculator	
Question #	Answer
1	D
2	A
3	C
4	B
5	C
6	D
7	B
8	C
9	B
10	C
11	B
12	A
13	B
14	C
15	C
16	5/26
17	19
18	2/3 OR .666 OR .667
19	12
20	600

Math - Calculator	
Question #	Answer
1	B
2	D
3	C
4	C
5	D
6	D
7	C
8	D
9	A
10	B
11	A
12	C
13	B
14	C
15	C
16	C
17	B
18	B
19	C
20	D
21	A
22	A
23	B
24	A
25	C
26	D
27	C
28	A
29	D
30	D
31	$23/8 < y < 69/8$
32	200
33	4/7 OR .571
34	100
35	$0.27 < x < 0.30$
36	7
37	0.98
38	15

*To get your estimated scaled SAT score, please turn to page 301.

Answer Explanations
No Calculator Section

1.

$4x+y-2xy=x+y+xy$

$3x-2xy=xy$

$3x=3xy \qquad x \neq 0$

$y=1$

$\therefore$ D)

2.

$\begin{pmatrix} 2x-y=4 \\ 13x+5y=3 \end{pmatrix}$

$\Rightarrow \begin{pmatrix} (2x-y)=4 \\ (13x+5y=3) \end{pmatrix}$

$\Rightarrow \quad (10x-5y=20)$

$\underline{+(13x+5y=3)}$

$\qquad\qquad 23x=23$

$x=\dfrac{23}{23}$

$x=1$

then, $y=-2$

$\therefore (1,-2)$

$\therefore$ B)

3.

The price of the job is

$C=0.5w+4$

4 is the fixed cost and 0.5 is a variable cost where w must be the number of hours of hiring the house cleaner. The cost increases by 0.5 dollars, or 50 cents, every hour.

A} is the best interpretation of the number 0.5

$\therefore$ A)

4.

Memorize: $a^2-2ab+b^2=(a-b)(a-b)$

$16x^2-24xy+9y^2$

$=(4x)^2-2(4x)(3y)+(3y)^2$

$=(4x-3y)(4x-3y)$

$=(4x-3y)^2$

$\therefore$ A)

5.

$-4+x=\sqrt{x-5}+1$

$x-5=\sqrt{x-5}$

$(x-5)^2=(\sqrt{x-5})^2$

$(x-5)^2=x-5$

$x^2-10x+25=x-5$

$x^2-11x+30$

$(x-5)(x-6)$

$x=5$ or 6

$\therefore$ A)

6.

Find the x-intercept and y-intercept.

x-int: Let $y=0$

$$-\frac{3}{10}x-\frac{(0)}{10}=1$$

$$-\frac{3}{10}x=1$$

$$x=-\frac{10}{3}$$

y-int: Let $x=0$

$$-\frac{3}{10}(0)-\frac{y}{10}=1$$

$$-\frac{y}{10}(-10)=1(-10)$$

$$y=-10$$

C) has x-int$=-\dfrac{10}{3}$

and y-int$=-10$

$\therefore$ C)

7.

$$\frac{64^x}{16^y} \Rightarrow \frac{4^{3x}}{4^{2y}} \Rightarrow 4^{3x} \cdot 4^{-2y}$$
$$\Rightarrow (2^2)^{3x} \cdot (2^2)^{-2y}$$
$$\Rightarrow 2^{6x} \cdot 2^{-4y} \Rightarrow 2^{6x-4y}$$

Since, $6x - 4y = \frac{1}{2}$

$$2^{(6x-4y)} \Rightarrow 2^{\frac{1}{2}} \Rightarrow \sqrt{2}$$

$\therefore$ C)

8.

Let A = the sum of the measure of the interior angles

$A = 180(n-2)$

$720 = 180(n-2)$

$$\frac{720}{180} = (n-2)$$

$4 = n - 2$

$n = 6$

$\therefore$ C)

9.

The 1st line contains points $(3, -8)$ and $(1, 4)$

Slope of the 1st line: $\left(\dfrac{4-(-8)}{1-(3)}\right) = \dfrac{12}{-2} = -6$

$\therefore \ y = -6x + b$

Use {1,4} to find b.

$(4) = -6(1) + b$

$4 + 10 = b$

$\therefore b = 10$

$\therefore \ y = -6x + 10$

The 2nd line has a slope of 3 and passes through $(3,1)$.
The 2nd line is $y = 3x + b$. Use $(3,1)$ to find b.

$(1) = 3(3) + b$

$1 = 9 + b$

$-8 = b$

Thus, $y = 3x - 8$

Find the intersection of the 2 lines:

Let $3x - 8 = -6x + 10$

$9x = 18$

$x = 2$

then, $y = -2$

$c + d \Rightarrow 2 - 2 \Rightarrow 0$

$\therefore$ B)

10.

The parabola on the graph is for a reference.
Focus on the given function, $y = -a(x+j)^2 - k$.
The vertex is $(-j, -k)$.
Since $-a$ is negative, the graph is concave downward.
$\therefore$ C)

11.

Memorize: $i = \sqrt{-1}$ $i^2 = -1$ $i^3 = -i$ $i^4 = 1$

This repeats every 4 exponents.

$$\begin{array}{r} 24 \\ 4\overline{)99} \\ \underline{8} \\ 19 \\ \underline{16} \\ 3 \end{array}$$
$\therefore i^{99} = -i$

$$\begin{array}{r} 5 \\ 4\overline{)22} \\ \underline{20} \\ 2 \end{array}$$

$\therefore i^{22} = -1$

Simplify the expression: $\dfrac{5i^{99} - 16i^{22}}{3-i} = \dfrac{-5i + 16}{3-i}$

Multiply the top and bottom by the conjugate of the denominator.

$$\frac{-5i+16}{3-i} \cdot \frac{(3+i)}{(3+i)} \Rightarrow \frac{-15i - 5i^2 + 48 + 16i}{9 - i^2}$$

$$\Rightarrow \frac{-15i + 5 + 48 + 16i}{10} = \frac{i + 53}{10} \Rightarrow \frac{53}{10} + \frac{i}{10}$$

$\therefore$ C)

12.

$$p=\left(s+\frac{d}{t}\right)^2$$

$$\sqrt{p}=\sqrt{\left(s+\frac{d}{t}\right)^2}$$

$$\sqrt{p}=s+\frac{d}{t}$$

$$\sqrt{p}-s=\frac{d}{t}$$

$$t(\sqrt{p}-s)=\left(\frac{d}{t}\right)t$$

$$\frac{t(\sqrt{p}-s)}{(\sqrt{p}-s)}=\frac{d}{(\sqrt{p}-s)}$$

$$\therefore\ t=\frac{d}{\sqrt{p}-s}$$

$\therefore$ B)

13.

Memorize: When x_1 & x_2 are the solutions of a quadratic equation, $ax^2+bx+c=0$

Then, $x_1+x_2=-\dfrac{b}{a}$.

$$\therefore\ \frac{-(-8)}{4}=2$$

$\therefore$ D)

14.

future amount$=$initial amount $\cdot(1+$rate$)^{\text{time}}$

Intial amount: 60,000 in thousands$=$60

Rate: declining at a rate of 11% each year$=$89% of the previous year's amount remains$=\{0.89\}$

$\therefore\ B(t)=60(0.89)^t$

$\therefore$ A)

15.

Use long division.

$$
\begin{array}{r}
15 \\
x+1\overline{)15x-3} \\
\underline{15x+15} \\
-18
\end{array}
$$

$\therefore$ D)

16.

x: a number of bundles sold from vendor A

y: a number of bundles sold from vendor B

$300x+1500y=6000$

y is at most 2 bundles

$300x+1500(2)=6000$

$300x+3000=6000$

$300x=3000$

$x=10$

If y is 1 then, $x=15$

If y is 2 then, $x=10$

$\therefore$ The possible answers are 10 or 15

17.

Convert $x^2+y^2+6x-6y=7$ into the center$-$radius fo, $(x-h)^2+(y-k)^2=r^2$ by completing the square.

Rearrange: $x^2+6x+y^2-6y=7$ where $\left(\dfrac{b}{2}\right)^2=9$ for x & y.

$\therefore\ x^2+6x+9+y^2-6y+9=7+9+9$

$\Rightarrow (x+3)^2+(y-3)^2=25$, where the radius$=5$ and the center of the circle$=(-3,3)$.

Visualize by graphing $(x+3)^2+(y-3)^2=25$.

Notice $x=2$ intersects the circle exactly once.

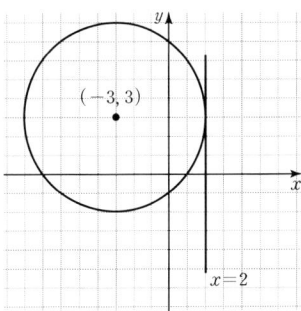

2 is a positive value

$\therefore\ c=2$

18.

$\triangle ABE \approx \triangle ACD$

Let x be the height of the $\triangle ABE$

Then, $\dfrac{x}{10} = \dfrac{5+x}{22.5}$

$22.5x = 50 + 10x$

$12.5x = 50$

$x = 4$

$\therefore \ 4$

19

Any sum of central angles of polygons is $360°$

To express in radians, $360 \cdot \dfrac{\pi}{180} = 2\pi$

The question says $2\pi = \dfrac{\pi}{x}$

$\therefore \ 2 = \dfrac{1}{x} \Rightarrow x = \dfrac{1}{2}$

$\therefore \ x = 0.5$ or $\dfrac{1}{2}$

20.

$\begin{cases} x^2 - y + 2 = 6x - 2 \\ 5x^2 + 8 = -2 + y \end{cases}$

$\Rightarrow \begin{pmatrix} -y + 2 = -x^2 + 6x - 2 \\ -1(-2+y) = -1(5x^2 + 8) \end{pmatrix}$

$\Rightarrow \begin{pmatrix} -y + 2 = -x^2 + 6x - 2 \\ -y + 2 = -5x^2 - 8 \end{pmatrix}$

$\Rightarrow -5x^2 - 8 = -x^2 + 6x - 2$

$\Rightarrow 4x^2 + 6x + 6 = 0$

<u>Memorize</u>: discriminant: $b^2 - 4ac < 0 \Rightarrow$ no solutions

$36 - 4(4)(6)$

$\Rightarrow 36 - 96 < 0$

$\therefore$ no solutions

$\therefore$ number of solutions $= 0$

*** You could also make a sketch of $4x^2 + 6x + 6$ and see that there is no $x-$int. Which means there is no solution.

$\therefore \ 0$

Calculator Section

1.

$\dfrac{4y}{7} = \dfrac{5}{4}$

$35 = 16y$

$y = \dfrac{35}{16}$

$\therefore$ D)

2.

Out of 730, 5 do not have a religion, and 725 have a religion.

$\therefore \ \dfrac{725}{730} = \dfrac{x}{7200}$

$x = 7151$

$\therefore$ C)

3.

$1 for every 2 hours $= \$\dfrac{1}{2}$ for every 1 hour

Fixed cost: $2

$\therefore \ 2 + \dfrac{1}{2}(x-8)$

$\Rightarrow 2 + \dfrac{1}{2}x - 4$

$\Rightarrow \dfrac{1}{2}x - 2$

$\therefore$ A)

4.

Directly proportional means $y = kx$ or $\dfrac{y}{x} = k$

$\therefore \ \dfrac{7.5}{5} = \dfrac{x}{24}$

$x = 36$

$\therefore$ B)

5.

$$\frac{6.25}{5} = \frac{\text{the yeast market's growth rate}}{\text{increase in consumption of baked goods}}$$

$$= \frac{x}{16}$$

By cross multiplying,

$x = 20$

$\therefore$ C)

6.

$$f(x) = \frac{3x^2 + 2x - 4}{2x + 3}$$

Plug in -2 for x in the equation

$$\frac{3(-2)^2 + 2(-2) - 4}{2(-2) + 3}$$

$$= \frac{12 - 4 - 4}{-4 + 3} = \frac{4}{-1} = -4$$

$\therefore$ B)

7.

$x^2 - 4x + 14 = 0$

Complete the square

Find $\left(\frac{b}{2}\right)^2 = \left(\frac{-4}{2}\right)^2 = 4$

Add 4 on both sides of the equation.

$x^2 - 4x + 4 + 14 = 4$

$(x-2)^2 = 4 - 14$

$(x-2)^2 = -10$

$(x-2)^2 + 10 = 0$

$\therefore$ D)

8.

In 2018, UPP has z number of seats out of 300 seats. Starting 2018, every year UPP wants to gain y seats for x number of years.

$\therefore$ $z + yz < 300$

$\therefore$ D)

9.

$30,000x$: the money the soccer player makes for x number of weeks.

$10,500y$: the money the soccer player makes for y number of weeks.

$x + y$: The total number of weeks over the year.

Since the soccer player did not have enough money to buy the house($1,000,000$), the inequality that represents this is $33,000x + 10,500y < 1,600,000$. Since the athlete saved his salary for 1 year, that is, 52 weeks, the equation that represents this is $x + y = 52$.

Thus, $\begin{cases} 33,000x + 10,500y < 1,600,000 \\ x + y = 52 \end{cases}$

$\therefore$ A)

10.

$f(x) = -3(x-5)^2 + 2$

$g(x) = f(x+6)$

$f(x+6)$ signifies that the function f has shifted 6 units to the .

Memorize: vertex form: $a(x-h)^2 + k$

Thus, the vertex of $f(z)$ is $(5, 2)$.

Since, $f(x) \rightarrow f(x+6)$, $(5, 2) \rightarrow (-1, 2)$

$\therefore$ B)

11.

The training that Elisa does only consists of running. Therefore, we only need to know

Number of times of training where she only runs per month	8
Number of miles to run in the Elisa's personal sports field.	25
Number of miles Elisa runs per hour	8

to solve the question.

$\dfrac{\text{Number of times of training} \cdot \text{number of miles to run}}{\text{Number of miles Elisa runs per hour}}$

$\dfrac{8 \cdot 5}{8} = 25$

$\therefore$ C)

12.

$x = w(\text{\# of workers}) + \text{Cynthia}$

Solve, $172.5 < \dfrac{1200}{x} + 12.5 < 200$

$172.5 - 12.5 < \dfrac{1200}{x} + 12.5 - 12.5 < 200 - 12.5$

$160 < \dfrac{1200}{x} < 187.5$

$6.4 < x < 7.5$

7, the only possible choice.

Exclude Cynthia: $x - 1 = 7 - 1 = 6$

$\therefore\ 5.4 < w < 6.5$

$\therefore\ D)$

13.

In order to reliably generalize the result of survey research to a larger population, the participants should be randomly selected from all people in that population. The sample, however, was not randomly selected since the visitors at a local cafe are not reliably representative of all people in the city. Therefore, of the given choices, where the survey was given makes it least likely that a reliable conclusion can be drawn.

$\therefore\ D)$

14.

Here, we make an assumption that the more people drink coffee, the less they sleep.

Of the choices given, the graph $h)$ best describes the situation.

$\therefore\ D)$

15.

$\dfrac{15grams}{60calories} = \dfrac{25ounces}{xcalories}$

$25ounces \rightarrow ?grams$

$25oz \cdot \dfrac{577grams}{20oz} = 721.25grams$

$\dfrac{15grams}{60calories} = \dfrac{721.25grams}{xcaolories}$

Cross multiply,

$x = 2{,}885$

$\therefore\ D)$

16.

the number of residents who believe accommodation is good

the number of participants who selected good or bad

$\dfrac{66}{448 + 89} = 0.12$

$\therefore\ B)$

17.

Diameter of type 1 tangerine: 2

Diameter of type 2 tangerine: 100% greater than $2 \Rightarrow$ 4.

Compare their volumes.

Volume: $\dfrac{4}{3}\pi r^3$

$\dfrac{4}{3}\pi(1)^3 vs \dfrac{4}{3}\pi(2)^3$

$\dfrac{4\pi}{3} vs \dfrac{32\pi}{3}$

Their difference is $\dfrac{32\pi}{3} - \dfrac{4\pi}{3} = \dfrac{28\pi}{3}$

$\therefore\ B)$

18.

g is the median, and

$$\frac{1}{2}e+f+g+h+j/5=\frac{1}{5}g$$

$$\left(\frac{e+f+g+h+j}{5}\right)5=\left(\frac{g}{5}\right)5$$

$$e+f+g+h+j=g$$

$$e+f+g+h+j-g=g-g$$

$$e+f+h+j=0$$

$$e=-f-h-j$$

∴ C)

19.

Find the weighted average.

$$\frac{[0\times(105+80+135)]+[1\times(45+60+25)]}{+[2\times(30+40+30)]+[3\times(20+20+10)]}{\text{Total \# of dogs examined}=600}$$

$$\frac{130+200+150}{600}=0.8\approx1$$

∴ B)

20.

From the survey, the ratio of number of dogs with 3 health problems to the number of dogs surveyed at Shelter A and B respectively are:

Shelter A: $\frac{20}{200}=\frac{1}{10}$ Shelter B: $\frac{20}{200}=\frac{1}{10}$

The expected

of dogs with 3 health problems in total:

A: $1200\left(\frac{1}{10}\right)$ B: $800\left(\frac{1}{10}\right)$

⇒120 vs. 80

Difference of A & B=40

∴ C)

21.

If the movie director's goal is met, the difference between the actual cost and the estimate is less than $3 million, which can be represented by

$$|c-d|<3 \text{ or } -3\leq c-d\leq3$$

∴ D)

22.

$$\triangle d=vt+\frac{1}{2}at^2$$

$$\triangle d-vt=\frac{1}{2}at^2$$

$$\frac{2}{t^2}(\triangle d-vt)=\left(\frac{1}{2}at^2\right)\frac{2}{t^2}$$

$$\frac{2\triangle d-2vt}{t^2}=a$$

$$a=\frac{2\triangle d}{t^2}-\frac{2v}{t}$$

∴ B)

23.

$$v=v_0+at$$

⇒ complete stop=initial velocity+(acceleration or deceleration)·time

$$0=30+(-50t)$$

$$-30=-50t$$

$$0.6 \text{ or } \frac{3}{5}=t$$

∴ A)

24.

$$x^2+y^2+14x-3y=-6$$

Rearrange and complete the squares

$$x^2+14x+y^2-3y=-6$$

$$x:\left(\frac{b}{2}\right)^2=49 \quad y:\left(\frac{b}{2}\right)^2=\frac{9}{4}$$

$$\underline{x^2+14x+49+y^2-3y+\frac{9}{4}}=\underline{-6+49+\frac{9}{4}}$$

$$\Downarrow \qquad \text{*This side is not important}$$

$$(x+7)^2+\left(y-\frac{3}{2}\right)^2$$

Center: $\left(-7,\frac{3}{2}\right)$

$\therefore$ A)

25.

Line l contains points $(g,\ 4g)$ or $(g,\ z^2)$. However, for a line, there is only 1 $y-$value for 1 $x-$value.

$\therefore$ $4g$ must be z^2

$$4g=z^2$$

$$\sqrt{4g}=z$$

$$2\sqrt{g}=z$$

$\therefore$ A)

26.

Note that the function is linear.

Pick any 2 points.

ex: $(1,2)$ & $(15,9)$

Find Slope. $\dfrac{9-2}{15-1}=\dfrac{7}{14}=\dfrac{1}{2}$

$\therefore$ $y=\dfrac{1}{2}x+b$

Plug in $(1,2)$

$$2=\frac{1}{2}+b$$

$$\frac{3}{2}=b$$

$\therefore$ D)

27.

Company A: b is negative

$$\therefore\ y=ax^b \Rightarrow y=\frac{a}{x^b}$$

Company B: d is negative

$$\therefore\ z=\frac{x^d}{c}\Rightarrow z=\frac{1}{cx^d}$$

Both equations decrease quadratically.

$\therefore$ D)

28.

Since h is perpendicular to g and f is perpendicular to g, both of their slopes are negative reciprocals of g. Find 2 points of g and find its slope.

ex: $\{-1,6\}$ and $\{2,-9\}$

$$\frac{-9-6}{2-(-1)}=\frac{-15}{3}=-5$$

$$\therefore\ h(x)=\frac{1}{5}x+b$$

Plug in $\{3,-14\}$

$$-14=\frac{(3)}{5}+b$$

$$\frac{-70}{5}=\frac{3}{5}+b$$

$$\frac{-70}{5}-\frac{3}{5}=\frac{3}{5}-\frac{3}{5}+b$$

$$-\frac{73}{5}=b$$

$$h(2)=\frac{1}{5}(2)-\frac{73}{5}=\frac{-71}{5}$$

$\therefore$ D)

29.

$$5c+10-x=6c$$

$$3d+2-y=2d$$

$$x=3y-1$$

Plug $3y-1$ into x.

$$5c+10-(3y-1)=6c$$

$$5c+10-3y+1=6c$$

$$11-3y=c$$

Simplify $3d+2-y=2d$

$d+2=y$

Plug $d+2$ into y

$11-3(d+2)=c$

$11-3d-6=c$

$5-3d=c$

$\therefore$ B)

30.

The top base of EFGH is 5 as it is given in the question.

Since EF$=$EH, EF$=5$.

$\angle$F is 60 degrees, since $\angle$F$+\angle$E$=180°$.

Use 30-60-90$\triangle$ rule to figure out the dimension of the $30-60-90\triangle$.

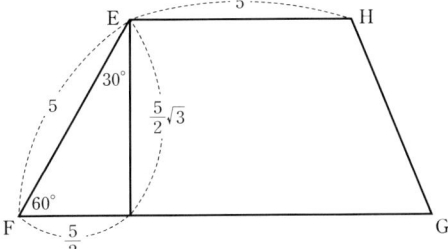

$B_1=5 B_2=\dfrac{5}{2}+\dfrac{5}{2}+5=10$

$Area=\dfrac{1}{2}(B_1+B_2)\cdot h$

$=\dfrac{1}{2}(5+10)\dfrac{5}{2}\sqrt{3}$

$=32.5$

$\therefore$ C)

31.

$\dfrac{1,075won}{1dollar}=\dfrac{15,000won}{xdollars}x\approx13.953dollars$

$\dfrac{xyen}{13.953dollars}=\dfrac{109.79yen}{1dollar}x\approx1531.95yen$

$\therefore$ 1,532yen

32.

Memorize:

1 feet=12 inches

f feet+9 inches=78 inches

f feet=78-9 inches=69 inches

$\dfrac{69in}{12in}$=5.75ft

$\therefore$ 5.75feet

33.

$10x-6+3(x-2)=4x$

$10x-6+3x-6=4x$

$9x=12$

$x=\dfrac{12}{9}=\dfrac{4}{3}$

34.

Liz$=$L   Jeff$=$J

J=35+L.

L+35+L=257

2L=222

$\therefore$ L=111

35.

Bethany first decided to measure her puppy's weight at the end of the first year.

Plug 1 into $W(t)=3+0.25(t)=$

$W(1)=3+0.25(1)=3.25$

$\therefore$ 3.25

36.

The coordinates for P are $(0.75, -0.5)$. In fractions, the lengths of the sides of the triangle are as follows

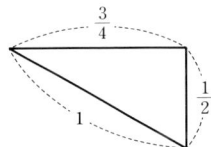

The area of the triangle is $\dfrac{3}{4}\left(\dfrac{1}{2}\right)\left(\dfrac{1}{2}\right)=\dfrac{3}{16}$

$\therefore$ $\dfrac{3}{16}$ OR. 187 OR. 188

37.

The object will hit the ground when $h(t)=0$

$\therefore \quad 0=-6.1t^2+134.2t$

Use calculator or solve for t seconds algebraically

$0=t(-6.1t+134.2)$

$t=0$ or 22

0 is not a possible answer.

$\therefore \quad 22$

38.

$y-$coordinate of the vertex gives the maximum height.

Memorize:

$\dfrac{-b}{2a}=x-$coordinate of the vertex

$h(t)=-6.1t^2+134.2t$

$\dfrac{-b}{2a}=\dfrac{-134.2}{2(-6.1)}=11$

Plug in 11 to get the $y-$coordinnate.

$-6.1(11)^2+134.2(11)$

$=738.1\approx738$

$\therefore \quad 738$

Raw Score Conversion Table

Raw Score (# of correct answers)	Math Section Score	Raw Score (# of correct answers)	Math Section Score
0	200	30	550
1	210	31	560
2	220	32	570
3	240	33	580
4	250	34	580
5	270	35	590
6	290	36	600
7	300	37	610
8	320	38	620
9	340	39	630
10	350	40	640
11	360	41	650
12	380	42	660
13	390	43	670
14	400	44	680
15	420	45	680
16	430	46	690
17	440	47	700
18	450	48	710
19	460	49	730
20	470	50	740
21	480	51	750
22	490	52	770
23	500	53	780
24	510	54	790
25	520	55	790
26	520	56	800
27	530	57	800
28	540	58	800
29	540		

*Please note that these scores are best approximations and that actual scores on the SAT may slightly vary, depending on individual adaptations made by the College Board.

Contributors

Written and edited by the talented test prep professionals at
 **Paul**Academy

PaulAcademy is a publishing arm of one of the industry-leading test prep organizations in Asia. PaulAcademy is a dedicated test prep organization that has helped thousands of students to realize their potentials and achieve their dreams. As a leader in test prep & strategy development specializing in SAT, ACT and AP preparation, PaulAcademy teaches pragmatic problem-solving skills that will ultimately help students obtain successful academic results. PaulAcademy aims to spread its expert knowledge to students worldwide.

Editor-in-Chief
Paul Kim

Head of Publishing
Niles Bliss

Material Development & Editing
Joe Kim
James Yang

PaulAcademy

Email: books@paulacademy.net   Website: http://www.paulacademy.net

ISBN : 979-11-86461-18-1